DIVERGENT WORLDS

DIVERGENT WORLDS

What the Ancient Mediterranean
and Indian Ocean Can Tell Us about
the Future of International Order

AMITAV ACHARYA AND
MANJEET S. PARDESI

Yale

UNIVERSITY

PRESS

New Haven and London

Published with assistance from the foundation established
in memory of Philip Hamilton McMillan of the
Class of 1894, Yale College.

Yale University Press books may be purchased in quantity for
educational, business, or promotional use. For information,
please e-mail sales.press@yale.edu (U.S. office) or
sales@yaleup.co.uk (U.K. office).

Set in Janson type by IDS Infotech, Ltd.
Printed in the United States of America.

Library of Congress Control Number: 2024934521
ISBN 978-0-300-21498-7 (hardcover : alk. paper)

A catalogue record for this book is available from
the British Library.

This paper meets the requirements of ANSI/NISO z39.48-1992
(Permanence of Paper).

10 9 8 7 6 5 4 3 2 1

Contents

Abbreviations

A2/AD	anti-access and area denial (strategies or capabilities)
ADMM-Plus	ASEAN Defence Ministers' Meeting-Plus
AOIP	ASEAN Outlook on the Indo-Pacific
APEC	Asia-Pacific Economic Cooperation
ARF	ASEAN Regional Forum
ASEAN	Association of Southeast Asian Nations
B.C.E.	Before the Common Era
BRI	Belt and Road Initiative
C.E.	Common Era
EAS	East Asia Summit
ECRL	East Coast Rail Link
EU	European Union
FPDA	Five Power Defence Arrangements
GATT	General Agreement on Tariffs and Trade
Global IR	Global International Relations
HADR	humanitarian and disaster relief
HST	Hegemonic Stability Theory
IMF	International Monetary Fund
IPE	International Political Economy
IR	International Relations
IRT	International Relations Theory
LHO	Liberal Hegemonic Order
LIO	Liberal International Order

LMC	Lancang-Mekong Cooperation mechanism
MSP	Malacca Straits Patrol
MSR	Maritime Silk Road
NATO	North Atlantic Treaty Organization
NHIO	Nonhegemonic International Order (Multiplex Order)
RCEP	Regional Comprehensive Economic Partnership
SKRL	Singapore–Kunming Rail Link
SSSP	Sulu-Sulawesi Seas Patrols
TAC	Treaty of Amity and Cooperation (in Southeast Asia)
UN	United Nations

DIVERGENT WORLDS

Introduction
Contrasting Hegemonic and Multiplex Orders

Our Argument

Soon after Donald J. Trump's election as U.S. president in November 2016, *Foreign Affairs*, one of America's most influential policy magazines, published a special issue under the title "Out of Order? The Future of the International System." It then released a book under the title *What Was the Liberal Order? The World We May Be Losing.*[1] The "liberal order" it was referring to is better known as the Liberal International Order (LIO), or, to use a variety of other terms coined especially by G. John Ikenberry, one of the most influential analysts of that concept, American-led Liberal International Order or "American-led liberal hegemonic order."[2] By this, what is usually meant is the end of the order that has existed since at least 1945, when World War II ended. This order had been established under U.S. hegemony, or the huge U.S. dominance of the world at large in economic and military terms.

But a longer underlying dynamic behind that order is rooted in the brilliance of the Greco-Roman civilization and then the rise of "the West," starting with the European "voyages of discovery," leading to Europe's colonization of much of the world, and then to the rise of the United States since the late nineteenth century, and its final emergence as the world's strongest military and economic power after the Second World War. The LIO also directs attention to the rules and institutions with which the Europeans and the Americans have organized the world, such as sovereignty, the nation-state, capitalist economy and its globalization; multilateral groups including the UN, NATO, and the EU; and Western values such as human rights, democracy, freedom of the seas, humanitarianism, and international cooperation. Furthermore, the LIO's proponents claimed that its dominance and success were due not to the coercive power of the United States and its allies, but to consent of the followers or their voluntary acceptance of the order that offered them major economic and security benefits.

We discuss the merits and limits of these arguments and claims about the benefits of the U.S.-led LIO in Chapter 1. What is important to note here is that these concerns about the fate of the LIO, which would reverberate around the West, reflected the dark and deep fears in the West about its fading dominance over the Rest, a dominance in ideas, institutions, and innovations. Above all, these fears reflected challenges to the West's claim to be a superior civilization, and the creator of the most advanced and inclusive international order in history.

Related to the above, underlying the concern about the fading LIO is a fear about what comes next. A variety of warnings under different labels have been issued: the end of the nation-state and the rise of the "civilization state," "the return of anarchy," or simply "the end of world order."[3] For Ikenberry, the alternative to the U.S.-led hegemonic order would be "less desirable alternatives," such as "great-power-balancing orders, regional blocs, or bipolar rivalries."[4] Putting it more specifically, columnist Charles Krauthammer, who coined the term "unipolar moment" after the Cold War, contended that decline of U.S. leadership would mean "[i]nsecure sea lanes, impoverished trading partners, exorbitant oil prices, explosive regional instability"[5] In a similar vein, Richard Haass, the former president of the Council on Foreign Relations who was also the head of the Policy Planning Bureau of the U.S. State Department in George W. Bush's first presidential term, flatly asserts: "With US hegemony waning, the likeliest future is a disorderly one."[6]

Part of the reason for such dark views of the post-LIO world is that it is discussed with little attention to history, especially the history of non-Western civilizations. Such claims marginalize the history of other polities and civilizations, including those of India, China, and Islam, and their efforts to build international orders in the past. Or more accurately, when these "other histories" are invoked, it is done with dismay and even dread. This is because the dominant history of world order casts the Western civilizations as the inventors or standard-bearers of progress, while the political ideas and organizations of others are seen as dark and forbidding. If the West's world is gone, then those of others might return, and that outcome would mean a triumph of chaos over stability and progress: a perennial struggle in the history of civilization.

A related reason for the misgivings about a post-LIO world is the close association between hegemony and international order. To varying degrees, as will be discussed in Chapter 1, Western scholars of international relations have traditionally privileged preponderant power in the making of international (including regional) orders.[7] In this book, we seek to move the study of international order away from an overriding concern with hegemony. We argue that international order is not simply a function of the power and preferences of hegemonic actors (or powerful states). Instead, we posit the possibility of an alternative conception of international order—a multiplex order—which may be defined as a relatively stable pattern of interactions among a group of states without the individual or collective hegemony of the great powers. Unlike hegemon-centered orders, multiplex orders are "decentered" orders without permanent or fixed power, political, and ideational centers across time and space. Furthermore, while hegemon-centered orders tend to be bounded and closed to rival and recalcitrant states, multiplex orders are "open" patchworks of partially and unevenly overlapping layers of governance in deeply interconnected systems.

One such multiplex international order existed in the eastern Indian Ocean before the arrival of European powers in the sixteenth century C.E. This was a nonhegemonic international order, in the sense that it was decentered and pluralistic. No single power or culture dominated the eastern Indian Ocean in which states and societies remained deeply interconnected so as to generate political stability and economic openness, including commerce and cultural diffusion.

Yet, as we will show below, the international order of the Indian Ocean has received far less attention than the hierarchic and anarchic orders such as those in the classical Mediterranean and in early modern and modern Europe. In this book, to bring out the contours of the Indian Ocean as an international system and order, we compare it to and contrast it with the international system/order of the classical Mediterranean, especially during the heydays of the Greco-Roman civilization. These two cases—the classical Mediterranean and the pre-European Indian Ocean—offer contrasting examples of the interplay between power and ideas in the making and functioning of international orders. To elaborate, approaching international systems and orders as material and ideational constructs, we compare the ideational influence of Greece and geopolitical control of Rome in the Mediterranean (~sixth century B.C.E.–third century C.E.) with the ideational influence of India and geopolitical role of China in the eastern Indian Ocean centering on modern Southeast Asia (~first–fifteenth centuries C.E.). Despite apparent similarities, there are striking differences.

First, these systems/orders displayed different approaches to the provision of collective goods by the leading power. Rome built a powerful empire and promoted trade by directly controlling the trade routes, with itself as the major beneficiary. The trading system in the eastern Indian Ocean was less coercive and more open, with more equitable benefits. Second, the two regions displayed different ideational dynamics. While the "Indianization" of Southeast Asia and the "Hellenization" of the Mediterranean show some similarities, the former was substantially more peaceful, and a two-way process. We explain these differences and conclude that the two regions offer powerfully contrasting images of international systems/orders. The Mediterranean conforms to the dominant theories of hegemony which stress how hegemons create/shape international orders, while the Indian Ocean suggests how "local initiative" can be a central basis of international systems/orders. Simply put, it is the Indian Ocean that offers a powerful classical precedent for open, nonhegemonic multiplex international orders compared to the closed and hegemonic Greco-Roman Mediterranean.

We believe that a comparative study of the two international orders provides important clues to the future of international order in the emerging Indo-Pacific. To be sure, we do not believe that history repeats itself. But this does not make history irrelevant to the understanding of the present and the future. We engage in this comparative historical exercise because this is a research approach that aims "to understand real-world transformations" after providing contextualized theoretical generalizations that emerge from such a macrohistorical analysis.[8] We show that based on the Mediterranean precedent, scholars associate order with hegemony. However, our research exercise that analyzes the Mediterranean in comparison with the classical Indian Ocean "may force us to change our views in important ways" because these two systems were configured differently.[9]

Comparative macrohistory provides us with new insights that may be extrapolated to the present. First, history allows us to challenge the supposedly universal claims of Mediterranean and European international orders. According to Wang Gungwu, history contextualizes, qualifies, and challenges the universal.[10] We do not think that Mediterranean history offers universal models for understanding the interplay of power and ideas in making international orders, neither the model of hegemony derived from the Roman Empire nor that of politico-cultural transformation from the ideational influence of Hellenization. Similarly, the modern European Westphalian model of international anarchy and order is also not a universal model. While these concepts are important, they should not blind us to other forms of statecraft and order building through history, such as empires, different forms of hierarchy, or indeed pluralist and decentered orders of the type that existed in the classical Indian Ocean. Without history, we remain stuck in the prison of Eurocentrism, taking the Eurocentric present as eternal and universal.

Second, the study of the past can be useful for understanding the present and anticipating the future. "There is no history that does not relate to the present."[11] History allows us to identify a wider range of possibilities in politics and world affairs, including norms, institutions, and types of international orders, and anarchic systems and empires. As Iver Neumann puts it, "memories of previous [international] systems are by necessity relevant for any entry into a new one. Former experience and present actions are tied together."[12] In a similar vein, Raymond Cohen and Raymond Westbrook argue that:

> True, ancient history lacks "immediate relevance," narrowly defined. But this remoteness from contemporary concerns is educative about such fundamental features of the contemporary international system as states, national identities, borders, sovereignty, government, international law, the balance of power, diplomacy, and so on. Are these permanent or transitory features of international life? How have these concepts been understood in times past? Have functional equivalents to them existed?[13]

Studying classical civilizations does not mean accepting a cyclical view of history. Rather, it teaches us a wider range of possibilities of cultural and political formations and practices that more accurately reflects how we got to the present stage of world order. Such an exercise, as Kurt Raaflaub notes, helps to "throw light not only on common patterns and marked differences but also illustrate the remarkable variety of responses humankind developed to meet common challenges."[14] And to quote Wang Gungwu again, while "[h]istory never really repeats itself and every event when closely examined is different," "history can teach us about [an] important kind of reality. . . . When enough of the historical is knowable, that might go some way in preparing ourselves for what individuals and societies might do in the future."[15]

We hold that the future world order will be a decentered or pluralistic one, more akin to the Indian Ocean pattern than to the Mediterranean one under Roman hegemony.

In particular, the eastern Indian Ocean provides a classical model of nonhegemonic multiplex international system in which the initiative of local actors helps make and shape the international order. Our aim is not to replace the "universalism" of the West (Greco-Roman/Euro-American) with that of the Rest (the East/ Asia). Instead, we argue that different interactionist dynamics, both material and ideational, point toward different configurations of power and ideas. Consequently, we challenge the theorization

that aims for universalization after studying only Western historical experiences.

Why Compare the Mediterranean and the Indian Ocean?

International relations scholars in search of the origins of their
theories and concepts often begin their journey with the Mediterranean worlds of Greece and Rome. As Daniel Deudney writes in
his *Bounding Power:* "The origin and early development of Western
political theory and republicanism in particular are intimately connected with the city-states that flourished around the Mediterranean prior to the Roman Imperial ascendancy."[16] Moreover, many
later philosophers whose work is regarded as foundational for
modern political theory, including IR theory, have themselves
drawn from Greek and Roman writers. To quote Deudney further:

> Action and words from classical Greece and republican
> Rome stand enshrined as foundational in the modern con-
> ception of the West as a distinct civilization, and ancient
> writers and events have exercised a startlingly powerful
> presence in all aspects of Western thought, particularly
> about politics.... For two millennia Western thinking
> about politics and history has been a long dialogue with the
> ancient figures of Herodotus, Hippocrates, Socrates, Plato,
> Thucydides, Aristotle, Livy, Polybius, Cicero, Tacitus, and
> others. The works of major modern political theorists such
> as Machiavelli, Montesquieu, and Rousseau, are as much
> about ancient writers and experiences as modern ones.[17]

The overall Mediterranean influence on politics, including international politics and its theory, has taken both indirect and direct forms.
Scholars have developed theories from ideas and processes found in
the Greco-Roman worlds and extended them all the way to the modern period. In this category one might start with Thucydides' *Peloponnesian War*, almost universally acknowledged as the foundational text
of realism. Aside from the Roman Republic, imperial Rome has
emerged as the paradigmatic case of empires in IR literature and policy discourse. In theoretical debates or policy discourses, Rome has

been "seen as . . . the archetypal empire, the epitome and supreme expression of imperial power. . . . As well as providing the template for how an empire ought to present itself, Rome was central to modern debates about the nature, dynamics and morality of imperialism."[18] And both as a republic and as an empire, Rome figures prominently as the source of modern international law, and dominates debates over the rise and fall of great powers.[19]

The Greek city-states and Rome figure prominently in the formulation of theories of hegemony, balance of power, and literature about the causes of war.[20] The politics of Greek city-states is also an important starting point of the liberal theory, especially as it pertains to democracy. Constructivists have looked to the Greek ideas of honor and hegemony and Roman ideas of law and justice to develop cultural and normative theories of international relations. Examples include Richard Ned Lebow's reinterpretations of Thucydides and his cultural theory of IR, and Christian Reus-Smit's analysis of fundamental institutions.[21] Even attempts to go beyond existing paradigms of IR, such as the realist–liberal divide, take off from the Mediterranean world, a key example being Daniel Deudney's republican security theory, which focuses on the republican restraints on power to avoid the extremes of anarchy and hierarchy and claims to subsume both realism and liberalism.[22] In the policy realm, analysts have compared the recent foreign policy behavior of the United States with that of the Roman Empire.[23]

The Mediterranean has also influenced contemporary international relations theory indirectly, via some of the European contributions to international relations and politics. One might include here Hobbes, who translated Thucydides' *Peloponnesian War,* and Machiavelli, who borrowed heavily from the Roman historian Livy's *Discourses* to generate his own ideas about power and hegemony. As Barry Buzan and Richard Little argue, "Since Græco-Roman civilization and feudalism were the antecedents of what became all-conquering European power, they easily slip into the position of seeming also to be the antecedents of the modern international system."[24]

In fact, the influence of the classical Mediterranean is particularly strong when it comes to maritime international systems. Decades ago, George Modelski and William Thompson observed that our modern international system is "characteristically and importantly, an oceanic system."[25] In spite of this, the discipline of international relations "has been a pathologically 'landlubber discipline.' "[26] When occasionally analyzed, international relations analyses of maritime systems look toward the Greco-Roman past. According to Modelski and Thompson, the "modern understanding of seapower is in part a process of practical learning handed down from the Greeks."[27] For Carla Norrlof, *Pax Romana* was "the first Pax," and *Pax Britannica* and *Pax Americana* "secured sea passages to promote long-distance trade" analogous to *Pax Romana*.[28]

More recently, Ali Parchami has shown that *Pax Britannica* has been understood "both [as] a modern incarnation of the 'Roman Peace' as well as its natural successor."[29] Furthermore, this *Pax* regime, with its "mastery of the seas" that envisaged the dominant navy securing the global maritime commons for the world economy, "form[s] the basis of a theoretical paradigm called hegemonic stability."[30] In fact, the importance of a hegemonic navy to secure maritime trading systems has also entered the textbook-level understanding of international relations. After invoking *Pax Romana* as "one of the earliest examples" of "hegemonic stability," Joseph Grieco, G. John Ikenberry, and Michael Mastanduno claimed in a recent textbook that hegemonic peace in the nineteenth and twentieth centuries was maintained by Britain and the United States.[31] When dominant states are unable to provide protection against piracy, and when the great powers struggle, "or if their presence disappears from regions with active commercial maritime traffic, the 'rule of the sea' declines or disappears."[32] In fact, they also asserted that "[h]egemonic peace here was not derived through direct imperial control but through leadership. States within British and American hegemonic orders became willing partners, as these leading states used their economic, political, and military capabilities to establish and maintain order—and ensure the peace."[33]

However, such an understanding of maritime international systems is deeply problematic. According to Andrew Lambert, Rome "wiped out every other navy in the Mediterranean, by conquering the countries that owned them. . . . This was the ultimate negative form of sea control."[34] Similarly, the denial of "imperial control," especially in the case of nineteenth-century Britain with its large formal empire, is also troubling. Likewise, as shown in Chapter 4, American naval dominance was also associated with rivalries, wars, and coercion. But perhaps the most serious issue here is the universalization of the Roman precedent—that a hegemonic navy is required to create and maintain a maritime trading system—as a timeless axiom of international relations after removing the historical context within which the Roman (or British/American) navy emerged.

What if our understanding of IR theory in general, and of maritime international systems in particular, was developed out of regions other than the Mediterranean and by extension, Europe (the latter as an offshoot of the former, and claiming much heritage from the former)? Sadly, we do not know the answer to this question, because other regions of the world have not fared as well as a springboard for IR theory. The answer might have come from comparing classical international systems. But this enterprise remains seriously underdeveloped. Raaflaub points out that "the application of the comparative approach to the ancient world at large has been rare."[35] Comparative work on classical international systems is rarer still. Contemporary textbooks on IR may include a section or two on the Chinese Warring States Period or the Mauryan-Indian empire in the chapters on the "history" of international systems. But with few exceptions, these efforts scarcely amount to a systematic and conscious effort at theory building.[36] Moreover, even in these efforts, the focus has been on land empires and continental systems created by the usual sets of great powers: Sumeria, Persia, Egypt, Greece, Rome, India, and China. They have left out other possible international systems and regional worlds, like the maritime world of the Indian Ocean, or its segments like Southeast Asia, where local states (or the nongreat powers) exercised their agency in nonimperial and nonhegemonic international orders.

This neglect of classical, especially maritime, international systems has unfortunate consequences. Among other things, it reinforces the dominant assumption among IR theorists that the very idea of an international system represents an extension of the European state system (or "Westphalia writ large"). As Buzan and Little put it, "such conceptions of international system as we do have are overwhelmingly biased by the structural characteristics of the European experience."[37] The result, they argue elsewhere, is that "Westphalia-based IR theory is not only incapable of understanding premodern international systems, but also . . . its lack of historical perspective makes it unable to answer, in many instances address, the most important questions about the modern international system."[38]

Recent scholarship has offered a broader conception of "international system" than the narrow Westphalian view that has dominated the traditional IR literature. There are several aspects of this broader conception which are especially relevant to the analytic framework of this book (and are discussed in detail in Chapter 1). First, the label "international system" should be applied not just to "anarchic" systems, but also to hierarchic ones that were more commonplace in ancient periods. Hence, empires and other types of hegemonic/hierarchic systems are also to be regarded as international systems.[39] Second, international systems are not to be seen exclusively in military-political terms, but also by their economic and socio-cultural characteristics. In fact, through history, economic systems have been more "extensive" than international political systems.[40] Third, the creation and operation of international systems depends not just on material forces, but also on ideational ones.[41]

In other words, international systems are constituted as much by the flow and distribution of ideas as by the distribution of military and economic power.[42] Even in empires and hegemonic international systems, ideas can be central to their legitimation.[43] Finally, international systems can be "less than global in extent."[44] This bridges the artificial intellectual gulf between the study of international systems (favored by discipline-based IR scholars) and those of regional systems (favored by area specialists), and allows IR scholars to draw upon the insights of regional specialists who tend to have a much greater historical perspective and a multidisciplinary approach. Hence the study of regional orders becomes an important complement to the study of international systems. Consequently, with a growing awareness and demand in the field that IRT should broaden itself by taking note of non-Western experiences, the question arises, if the history of international systems and IRT more generally were written from the backdrop of other regions and international systems, what might it look like? Would it be all that different?

In this book we address this question by comparing two classical international/maritime systems located within the Mediterranean and the Indian Ocean (especially the eastern part roughly comprising today's Southeast Asia), respectively. The time frame of the comparison is roughly the Mediterranean between the sixth century B.C.E. and the third century C.E., and the Southeast Asia/Indian Ocean between the first and fifteenth centuries C.E.[45] We will discuss the comparability of the two systems shortly. But the point of departure has to do with the fact that both were essentially maritime international systems, which, despite some obvious similarities, also constituted two different paradigms of international order. Just as the Mediterranean provided the stage for the exercise of the power and influence of its two greatest classical powers, Greece and Rome, Southeast Asia was one of the crucial stages for the "international" role of classical Asia's greatest powers, India and China.[46] It has been said that while the Greek role in the Mediterranean, coming first, was "essentially mental and spiritual," the Roman role that followed was "structural and practical, its essence was empire itself."[47] In a similar vein, in the eastern Indian Ocean, India and China both played major roles in shaping Southeast Asia's cultural, political, and strategic environment. But while the Indian influence was mainly economic, cultural, and ideational (including ideas about politics), China's was mainly a geopolitical, if not outright imperial, influence (although it also contained important economic, cultural, and ideational elements).

There is now a considerable body of evidence that makes the eastern Indian Ocean a natural candidate for a classical international system, and paves the way for a meaningful comparison between the Mediterranean and the eastern Indian Ocean. Inspired by the work of Fernand Braudel, scholars studying Southeast Asia have already found that the Mediterranean offers a useful point of reference for organizing their own thinking and analysis.[48] While we make the case for approaching the Mediterranean and the eastern Indian Ocean (centered on modern Southeast Asia) as international systems in Chapters 2 and 3, the "Mediterranean analogy" discourse

has been used to debate whether physical coherence or social construction, and external influence or indigenous initiative, has been
more crucial for the making of these worlds.[49] International relations scholars, including those paying attention to classical international systems, have not been as creative, but they can learn much
from the lead provided by Southeast Asian historiography. Nevertheless, it is noteworthy that Philip Steinberg's pioneering study of
the social construction of oceans used the classical Indian Ocean as
a typology of an oceanic space on a par with the Mediterranean.[50]

Although deep maritime interactions across vast spaces by dynamic and culturally pluralist polities make the Mediterranean and
eastern Indian Ocean systems comparable, the two international systems also differed markedly in material and ideational terms. In this
context, Theda Skocpol and Margaret Somers's distinction between
"contrast oriented comparative history" and "parallel comparative
history" assumes importance. In highlighting the differences between the two approaches, they argue:

> The Parallel comparativists seek above all to demonstrate
> that a theory similarly holds good from case to case; for
> them differences among the cases are primarily contextual
> particularities against which to highlight the generality of
> the processes with which their theories are basically con-
> cerned. But scholars such as Clifford Geertz in *Islam Ob-
> served*, James Lang in *Conquest and Commerce*, and Reinhard
> Bendix in *Nation-Building and Citizenship* and *Kings or Peo-
> ple* make use of comparative history to bring out the unique
> features of each particular case included in their discus-
> sions, and to show how these unique features affect the
> working-out of putatively general social processes.[51]

Instead of negating the uniqueness of each case, contrast-
oriented comparative history acknowledges it, and might even
enhance it. According to Kenneth Pomeranz, a leading global
historian, avoiding such comparison "makes it impossible even to
approach many of the most important questions in history (and in
contemporary life)."[52] The aim of research then is not "the same as
seeking general laws independent of historical context. ... [T]he

test of the worth of a work of comparative history is whether it identifies and illuminates relationships heretofore unrecognized or misunderstood in particular sequences of historical events that have occurred."[53] Doing so allows for "less ethnocentric appreciations of the manifold achievements of more peoples, communities, and cultures over long spans of human history."[54] The context-specific generalizations that emerge through this contrast-oriented historical approach may then be extrapolated to other cases instead of treating such generalizations as timeless, universal truths. In other words, such findings are sensitive to the nature of interactions between the different political groups.

We show that the classical Mediterranean and the eastern Indian Ocean present two entirely different images of the role of power and ideas in international orders—a central issue for international relations theory. First, they displayed very different approaches to provision of collective goods by the leading powers, Rome and China. The Roman Empire promoted trade by conquering all littoral states and directly controlling the trade routes, with Rome as the major beneficiary in a core–periphery international order. By contrast, the Chinese tributary system operating in Southeast Asia was just one part of a larger interconnected network of polities where the commercial benefits were more equitable. While Rome exercised sea control, maritime Asia lacked such a hegemonic actor as it was a system where the multitudes of large and small polities controlled only local waters at best. Second, the two regions displayed very different modalities when it came to the flow of ideas. Despite some similarities between the politico-cultural processes entailed in the "Indianization" of Southeast Asia and the "Hellenization" of the Mediterranean, the former was substantially a more peaceful and self-legitimizing phenomenon than the latter. Moreover, while both flows had transformative consequences for the local societies, the flow of ideas from India to Southeast Asia was marked by a substantial degree of local initiative and localization at the receiving end, whereas the ideational process of Hellenization was a substantially outside-in project that left relatively little agency for the local actors.

Hence, in the Mediterranean international system, order depended mainly on superior material power and ultimately on the coercive capacity of the hegemon. Here, order is a top-down construct, a one-way street. The Indian Ocean example suggests a more ideational and interactionist understanding of power and its legitimation in international systems/orders. In contrast to the core–periphery Roman Mediterranean, the eastern Indian Ocean represents an open, decentered, and pluralist multiplex order.

In this book, our focus is not so much on which system was more peaceful (although that can be the subject of a follow-up study), but on whether the two systems displayed discernibly distinct features over a reasonably long period, and on the different ways in which they established and managed order and provided public goods of security and trade. Briefly put, we investigate two main questions. First, what were the key differences in characteristics and structure between the Mediterranean and the Indian Ocean, especially when it came to the exercise of power and provision of public goods? A second question to be addressed relates to the spread of political ideas. Do the materially powerful or hegemonic actors seek to spread their ideas in the system? How does local agency influence the spread of ideas? Addressing these questions is key to understanding whether and to what extent the two systems represented two alternative models of international order, and which one might bear greater relevance to the post-Western world order which is now emerging. We undertake this extrapolative exercise in Chapter 4.[55]

Contributions of the Book

Divergent Worlds makes a number of contributions to the study of international relations in general and international orders in particular.

First, it advances the comparative study of systems and regions from a long-term historical perspective on the evolution of world order. Few available books provide such a broadly sweeping perspective on world order, comparable to what Francis Fukuyama's *Origins of Political Order* does for domestic political systems. For example, Henry Kissinger's 2014 book *World Order*, while valuable (see Chapter 1), is of limited historical depth and is rather American-centric. Indeed, available books on the comparative history of international systems/orders with implications for world order are usually written by Western writers and tend to be Western-centric. They highlight the contributions of Western cultures and civilization and downplay those of non-Western civilizations as noted at the beginning of this introductory chapter. In some cases, these texts accentuate the negative features of non-Western civilizations, presenting them as backward and static. A good example is Niall Ferguson's *Civilization*. While a few works by Western scholars, such as John Hobson's *Eastern Origins of Western Civilizations*, acknowledge the contribution of non-Western civilizations, there is no such work on world order written from the vantage point of regions outside of the West.[56]

A second contribution is to the comparative study of international systems. While itself a rarity, mostly undertaken by scholars from the English School of IR theory, there has been no comparative study of international systems featuring maritime international orders, especially one that treats the Indian Ocean and Southeast Asia as an international system. Interestingly enough, however, there is a body of work by historians that compares the Mediterranean with Southeast Asia to study the concept of "region-ness." Although political scientists and IR scholars have played no part in this debate, it is very relevant to the study of international systems, because it deals with the very issues which are central to international systems, including interaction capacity and outcomes (hegemony, anarchy, etc.). In this book, we offer the first comparative study between the Mediterranean and Southeast Asia as international systems from an IR theoretical perspective.

A third contribution of this book is to the literature on the spread of ideas, both rationalist and constructivist. Our explanation combines both material and ideational factors, but unlike the majority of work on individual international systems, we focus more on the role of ideas than of material forces. We agree with Judith Goldstein and Robert Keohane that "[u]nderstanding the impact of world views on general politics or foreign policy would require a broader comparative study of cultures."[57] While much work has been done on the role of ideas, most of it concerns contemporary cases. Historical investigations into the diffusion of ideas have been rare, those of non-Western cases of diffusion rarer still. Studies of ancient systems focus on the balance of power, leading to a focus on material forces such as military and economic power, and administrative capacity and organization.

In comparing historical international systems and orders, Stuart Kaufman, Richard Little, and William Wohlforth acknowledge the role of "intersubjectively agreed norms of international behavior"[58] in constraining hegemony and ensuring diversity and stability in an international system. But the primary focus of their volume is on the distribution (balance) of power—as they put it, "time's pendulum swinging between balanced and unbalanced distributions of power"—rather than on the distribution of ideas.[59] It is this "swinging" which is "the basic starting point of any theory of international relations."[60] Moreover, to the extent they focus on norms of international behavior, it is not to study how these norms come about or how they spread. By contrast, we focus on important questions about ideas: What role did ideas play relative to material forces? Relatedly, what was the impact of material versus ideational forces in shaping the international system? Whose ideas mattered?

Finally, this book contributes to international relations theory and more generally to redefining the discipline, or its progress into the field of Global International Relations (Global IR). A key aspect of Global IR is to broaden its sources beyond the Western world and its classical philosophical traditions. It highlights the Indian Ocean and Southeast Asia as a classical international system, which has been neglected by IR theorists, including those of the English School. This book thus enriches our understanding of the precursors to the modern Westphalian system at a time when demand for such investigations is growing. Such an effort is also important at a time when China and India are reemerging as major powers in the Indian Ocean and the world at large, because it is in this region that the contrasting "international" roles and influences of Asia's two major classical powers were fully demonstrated. As the pivotal region between them, Southeast Asia was a natural ground for their interaction then, as it might be now again.

Structure of the Book

While *Divergent Worlds* compares the Mediterranean and the Indian Ocean, the greater focus of the book is on the Indian Ocean, especially its eastern part. We use the classical Mediterranean as a point of comparison or contrast, because, as discussed earlier, this region has been extensively used as an ideal type of international order by scholars, especially of IR. Hence, discussing the nature of this idea type sets the stage for the rest of the book. But our major focus is on the eastern Indian Ocean. The remaining chapters of the book proceed as follows. Chapter 1 lays out the theoretical framework of the book, which not only covers conceptual clarifications about "hegemony," "empire," "hierarchy," and "primacy" but also discusses the theoretical explanations about the relationship between hegemony and international order and provision of public goods. In Chapter 2, we lay out the key features of the classical Mediterranean order (~sixth century B.C.E.–third century C.E.) in terms of its structure or power and authority, especially the Roman imperium as it operated in relation to its constituents or tributary states. We also discuss the dominant flow of ideas in that order, in this case led by classical Greece, or what is known as Hellenization.

In Chapter 3, we provide a similar analysis of the classical Indian Ocean (~first–fifteenth centuries C.E.), examining the structure of authority and the flow of ideas led by China and India, respectively, as well as the crucial role played by the Southeast Asian players in shaping these interactions. In Chapter 4, we briefly discuss the more contemporary history in the Indian Ocean. After providing a short overview of the entry of the European powers into the Indian Ocean (toward the end of the fifteenth century) and the period of Anglo-American ascendancy (after the nineteenth century), we focus on more recent developments. We draw in sharper detail the idea of a pluralistic and decentered international system and order which challenges not only the idea of hegemonic stability theory or liberal hegemony, but also the current dominant ideas about how to organize the "Indo-Pacific" region. Finally, the concluding chapter revisits the major theoretical arguments and empirical findings of the book.

CHAPTER ONE

Power, Ideas, and International Systems/Orders

A CENTRAL QUESTION ABOUT international order and stability is who creates and maintains it. In international relations literature, there is a fair amount of debate over this question. The noted scholar-journalist Fareed Zakaria writes that "[a]mong scholars and practitioners of international relations, there is one predominant theory about how and why international peace endures. It holds that the most stable system is one with a single dominant power that maintains order."[1] But Robert Keohane, one of the most influential scholars of international cooperation, offers a different, although not wholly opposite, view of a vital ingredient of international order: "The dominance of a single great power can contribute to order in world politics, in particular circumstances, but it is not a sufficient condition and there is little reason to believe that it is necessary."[2] Keohane argued that international cooperation forged through multilateral institutions among nations can continue after the decline of the hegemon that was initially responsible for creating it, because once created, institutions tend to be self-sustaining.

In this chapter, we present a more radically different view. We argue that stability and cooperation, and the provision of public goods in the international system, neither begin nor continue with hegemony. Our goal is to construct a theoretical framework for studying the role of power and ideas in the provision of public goods in international systems and orders. First, we define the concepts of international system, international order, hegemony, empire, primacy, and hierarchy (suzerainty). Second, we discuss IR theories, especially the Hegemonic Stability Theory (HST), that link hegemony with the provision of public goods, especially trade and security. Third, we discuss the concept of hegemony in contemporary discussions of the LIO and the limitations of that order in explaining change, especially toward a post-Western world. Finally, we present our alternative conceptual framework, arguing for security and trade in nonhegemonic systems, or in the absence of a hegemon.

International System and International Order

At the outset, we need some clarification about the meaning of the terms *international system* and *international order*. The definition of international system follows that of the world system. F. S. Northedge defines a system as a "regulated and orderly set of relationships between the parts such that they form a coherent but complex whole."[3] Hedley Bull and Adam Watson view an "international system" as a "group of independent political communities" in which "the behaviour of each is a necessary factor in the calculations of others," and differentiate it from an "international society," in which a group of states "not merely form a system ... but also have established by dialogue and consent common rules and institutions for the conduct of their relations, and recognize their common interest in maintaining these arrangements."[4] But the distinction between system and society can be blurry.[5] Most international systems feature some element of dialogue, rules, institutions, and common interest. The difference is a matter of the degree to which the frequency of the dialogues, thickness of the rules, robustness of the institutions, and depth and durability of the common interests vary.

Buzan and Little propose identifying international systems in terms of three sources: interaction capacity, process, and structure.[6]

Interaction capacity "focuses on the system-wide capability of units to maintain contact with each other by moving goods, people, and information around the system." It concerns the movement not just of physical systems such as caravans and ships but also of social systems such as "norms, rules, and institutions." *Process* refers to "the types of interaction that actually take place (e.g., fighting, political recognition, trade, identity formation, transplantation of flora and fauna)."[7] In other words, there are different types of interunit interactions in a system—politico-military, politico-economic, and politico-cultural. For Buzan and Little, a "full" international system includes all three types of interactions.[8] Finally, *structure* "concerns the principles by which the units in a system are arranged, and the effects of those arrangements on the behavior of the units (e.g., anarchy, market, international society)."[9]

Another key concept for this book is international order. In a well-known formulation, Bull defines international order as "a pattern of activity that sustains the elementary or primary goals of the society of states, or international society."[10] The goals toward which the pattern of activity is geared were identified by Bull to include preserving the state system, maintaining the sovereignty or independence of states, establishing relative peace or absence of war as the normal condition among states, limiting violence, keeping promises, and protecting property rights.[11]

The term *international order* is often conflated with the related concepts of "world order" and "global order." Bull argues that while "international order" refers to relations among states only, "world order" also brings nonstate actors into the picture and covers "social life among mankind as a whole."[12] The term *world order* is also sometimes applied to a single civilization's cultural attributes, worldviews, and distinctive modes of managing interstate relationships: hence the term *Chinese World Order.*[13] Then there is also the term *global order*, which Andrew Hurrell defines (using the term *global political order*) as a "world made up of separate, sovereign states which are, in turn, linked through various kinds of political practices and institutionalized structures."[14] But this seems rather similar to the term *world order*, albeit underscoring the increasingly "global" nature of interactions and interdependence among states.

Moreover, the distinction among "international," "world," and "global" orders is not sharp and clear-cut in theory and practice. Many conceptions of international order also include nonstate actors (Bull's criteria for how an international order becomes a world order). And the terms *international* and *world* are easily mixed up. For example, the term widely used to describe the post–World War II international order, the *Liberal International Order*, is often used interchangeably with the *Liberal World Order*. As Amitav Acharya has argued, however, the Liberal Order was never really worldwide in scope. Rather, it functioned mostly as a transatlantic club, with the limited participation of a few other nations like Australia, while the majority of nations, including China and India, stayed out of it for large parts of the Cold War.[15] And the term *global order* remains aspirational.

Kissinger's observation that "[n]o truly global 'world order' has ever existed" is especially pertinent here, although the British empire and American-led order came close.[16] In Acharya's view, creating a truly global order requires overcoming identity divides between the "West" and the "Rest," and the former's recognition and respect for the agency of the latter in building the current international order (as well as historical orders, the theme of this book).[17] Yet, the West–Rest divide, while blurring in economic and military terms, remains alive in political, ideological, and policy terms, as shown by Western rhetoric and the non-Western response to the Russia–Ukraine war.[18]

We do, however, differentiate between international systems and international order. While international system is a broad framework or arrangement of political, economic, and cultural relationships among states, an international order refers to the outcome of those relationships viewed in terms of stability and other goals desired by actors, such as trade, political legitimation, and cultural and religious learning. In other words, a system refers to units—states or empires—in a connected or interdependent relationship, but it does not necessarily tell us about the outcome of that relationship, that is, whether it produces greater predictability, stability, peace, and other desirable outcomes. In contrast, order is not just about a structure but also has some function and purpose. Scholars have associated order with a security purpose, or "dominant patterns of security management."[19] Order is also about stability. The *Oxford English Dictionary* defines world order (which can easily apply to international order) as "an international set of arrangements for preserving global political stability."[20]

Whatever term one may use, order is something more than system. It is important to stress the functions of order, not just its structure. This can be confusing, as order can also simply mean a given situation or configuration of institutions and arrangements in a large part of the world at a given period of history. Order in this sense is "a description of a particular status quo."[21] According to the *Macmillan English Dictionary*, world order means "the political, economic, or social situation in the world at any particular time and the effect this has on relationships between different countries."[22] But this tells us little about the functions or outcome of these arrangements, or to what end they were created and maintained.[23]

To put it differently, the notion of an international system refers to a structure in which the units are fairly interdependent, whereas international order relates to the goals or functions of that structure in achieving some desired outcomes. But the two are linked: some features of a system are closely related to the type and quality of the order; one which is especially important to this book is the reliance on coercion to provide public goods or the transmission of ideas and culture. Although a Rome-centered core–periphery hegemonic order existed in the Mediterranean for the benefit of Rome (and Italy), the decentered and multiplex order of the classical Indian Ocean provided more equitable benefits to the actors that maintained their politico-cultural diversity while obtaining simultaneous advantages from maritime trade.

But order is not the same as peace. Rather, it refers to stability. Karl Deutsch and David Singer define it as the "the probability that the system retains all of its essential characteristics; that no single nation becomes dominant; that most of its members continue to survive; and that large-scale war does not occur. And from the more limited perspective of the individual nations, stability would refer to the probability of their continued political independence and territorial integrity without any significant probability of becoming engaged in a 'war for survival.' "[24] As we have seen, Bull's definition of international order also speaks to the relative peace or "the absence of war . . . as the normal condition" among states as well as "limitation of violence." But the key word is "relative."

But we offer an expanded notion of international order. While it refers to the absence or relative paucity of "large-scale war," it also goes beyond survival to other elements, including rules. We accept Muthiah Alagappa's notion of international order as "rule governed interaction," "whether interstate interactions conform to accepted rules."[25] Moreover, we include in order economic openness including freedom of commerce, acceptance of religious and cultural diversity, and nonviolent ways of achieving political legitimation, especially legitimation through ideas and norms. Indeed, this book gives more play to the role of ideas and norms that shape international order, including practices and institutions of stability management. Hence our understanding of international order follows recent constructivist scholarship in giving emphasis to ideas, norms, and legitimacy in conceptualizing international order.[26]

To sum up, in this book we use the term *international order* to describe the Indian Ocean and the Mediterranean areas. These were certainly not "global" in scope. In recent centuries, with the expansion of Europe through imperialism and colonization, both regions acquired global importance and are more connected with each other than ever before. But we do not think either area represents the "social life of mankind as a whole," that is, all of the globe. Similarly, neither area was of a global scope, especially in the precolonial period. And while mindful of the overlap between "international" and "world," we focus on regionwide cultural and political practices and interactions, rather than individual civilizations. Hence *international order* seems more appropriate than *global order* for the purposes of this book.

We are conscious that the term *international* may be inappropriate for both regions, since it describes structures and interactions that prevailed before the rise of the sovereign nation-state. But this has not prevented scholars from using "international" to describe systems and orders in the premodern period.[27] While we acknowledge that the modern Westphalian sovereignty is much more legalistic and institutionalized than pre-Westphalian ones, whether in Europe or elsewhere, this did not mean classical states did not have any sense of sovereignty.[28]

In the following two chapters we show that both the classical Mediterranean and the classical Indian Ocean were "full" international systems, as interunit interactions included politico-military, politico-economic, and politico-cultural processes. However, these interactions produced very different outcomes: a hegemonic order in the Mediterranean and a nonhegemonic and decentered order in the Indian Ocean. To make this point, we now turn to the term *hegemony*.

Hegemony

Hegemony is one of the most commonly used but contested approaches to understanding the role of power in the making of international order. Most debates about hegemony revolve around two key questions: (1) Is it material and/or ideological, or both? And (2) what are the functions of hegemony and how does a hegemon provide collective goods, through force/caprice or sacrifice/benevolence?

It is necessary to clarify some key concepts. The first and most important one is hegemony. In international relations literature, the concept of hegemony is imprecise and contested. Part of the reason is that it is conflated with "hierarchy," "empire," and "primacy." According to the *Merriam-Webster Dictionary*, hegemony refers to the "preponderant influence or authority over others" and the "social, cultural, ideological, or economic influence exerted by a dominant group."[29] For John Mearsheimer, "a hegemon is a state that is so powerful that it dominates all other states in the system."[30]

Later conceptions of hegemony moved it beyond material capabilities. The most important reformulation relies on the Gramscian notion, which rejected traditional Marxism's emphasis on coercion while focusing on consent and went beyond economic factors to ideological ones. Hegemony is achieved through both coercion and consent, but consent is more important. For Robert Cox, hegemony implies "dominance of a particular kind" in which a "dominant state creates an order based ideologically on a broad measure of consent, functioning according to general principles that in fact ensure the continuing supremacy of the leading state . . .

but at the same time offer some measure or prospect of satisfaction to the less powerful."[31] Consent is achieved through ideological consensus.

International institutions play an important role in achieving consensus and legitimizing hegemony. For Cox, global and regional institutions both reflect and consolidate hegemonic power.[32] Weaker actors remain passive and accept the hegemon's preferences due to the benefits they receive. Furthermore, a hegemonic order appears universal, or is presented as universal. "To become hegemonic, a state would have to found and protect a world order which was universal in conception . . . an order which most other states . . . could find compatible with their interests."[33] As will be discussed in the next section, the liberal institutionalist view of Liberal Hegemonic Order, developed by G. John Ikenberry, applies this Gramscian and Coxian notion of hegemony to LIO, but leaves out coercion altogether.

The notion that hegemony is based on consent calls attention to the role of ideas, since ideas play a crucial role in legitimizing hegemony so as to make it consensual. But while many scholars accept that hegemony is both material and ideational, ideational factors are less emphasized or used to a limited degree. Although Cox argued that "material relations and ideas are inextricably intertwined to co-produce world orders," his own position is deeply conditioned by historical materialism, with transnational production conditioning political, ideological, and military relations.[34] Hence his redefinition and broadening of hegemony offers a limited and conditional view of autonomy to ideational forces.

Moreover, such an ideational conception of hegemony is really about ideology. Ideology is a key instrument of legitimation. Ideational hegemony is not the same as ideological hegemony. Ideological hegemony is closely related to power, or material hegemony, even soft power. It also connotes harm. Thus, "[i]deological hegemony occurs when an individual takes part in reinforcing power structures and societal ideas willingly, even when these structures and ideas are harmful or silencing for those without access to power."[35] "Ideology" is not the same as "ideational." Ideology is always an adjunct of power. All ideologies are ideational, but not everything ideational is ideological. Ideational influence or even dominance does not imply harm, and is more voluntary. And it is not linked to material power. It can occur without imperialism/hegemony (classical Indian versus classical Chinese influence in Southeast Asia). Sometimes, materially weaker states can have ideational influence over stronger ones (classical Greece over Rome).

The term *hegemony* is often conflated with a variety of international orders. *Empire* is a more commonly used term.[36] But there are differences between hegemony and empire. The former can exist without the latter. The United States today is not an empire, but is often referred to as a hegemon. Moreover, empires have territorial boundaries, even if they are not strictly defined or enforced. Hegemony is more fluid and indeterminate. One popular perspective is that while empire involves direct control or dominance, hegemony implies indirect dominance. Another perspective, offered by Michael Doyle, holds that in an empire, the leading power shapes both the domestic and foreign policy of another state, while in a hegemony, it controls only the latter.[37] But this view is not accepted by everyone who uses the term *hegemony* to study international orders.

Empire has contemporary relevance to IR. Some scholars hold that empire is not only more common through history than Westphalian "anarchical" systems, but also that imperial systems continue to have resonance in the current international order. As Tarak Barkawi and Mark Laffey put it, the "Westphalian models of the international obscure the role of imperial relations in world politics." If one views international relations "as a 'thick' set of social relations, consisting of social and cultural flows as well as political-military and economic interactions," then such relations "often take place in a context of imperial hierarchy." Hence "retrieving" the idea of empire as an analytic category "offers a way out of the 'territorial trap' set by Westphalia and alerts us to a range of phenomena occluded by IR's central categories."[38]

Another relevant concept here is hierarchy. Kenneth Waltz defines a hierarchical order as a system in which "political actors are formally differentiated according to degrees of their authority."[39] Barry Buzan and Richard Little offer more clarity by defining hierarchy as a "political structure in which units relate in a *subordinate-superordinate* relationship [emphasis added]."[40] But this is too general. Indeed, some conceptions of hierarchy are too all-encompassing. David Lake, for example, distinguishes among four types of hierarchical institutions: spheres of influence, protectorates, informal empires, and empires.[41] While this differentiates hierarchy from Westphalian "anarchy," it becomes too broad a category to have much analytical usage. The real indicator of hierarchy is the absence of direct control or the preservation of the relative autonomy of the weaker or subordinate actors, which is the case with empires. In the end, it comes down to the degree of control/autonomy.[42] David Kang holds that "hegemony is overarching and more intrusive" than hierarchy. He adds that while hegemony "focuses the bulk of its attention to the largest power," "hierarchy is more concerned with the interaction of states up and down the hierarchy. . . . In hierarchy, independent sovereign states accept the central position of the largest in the system but are fully functional on their own terms."[43]

Sometimes hierarchical orders are conflated with suzerainty. Suzerainty, defined literally as "the right of a country to partly control another," may imply widely varying degrees of control through a variety of means.[44] Like hierarchy, suzerainty refers to the relationship between a superior power and a weaker state. Although the word *vassal* is often used to describe the position of the weaker state in a suzerain system, the weaker state maintains its sovereignty. However, it is limited in being able to take independent action in foreign policy, and sometimes in the domestic sphere, without the consent of the superior power. The notion of superiority in a suzerain system can be in terms of material power or cultural prestige or both. While suzerain systems are different from empire, since no direct political control is involved, the superior state may offer protection to the weaker state and confer legitimacy on its ruler. While this may also be true of a hierarchy, suzerainty is much more limiting of the domestic and foreign policy autonomy of the weaker state.[45] In other words, suzerainty is much more intrusive for the weaker state than hierarchy but less intrusive than empire, although the degree of autonomy of the weaker state can vary from case to case. Furthermore, hierarchy is mainly symbolic and mostly reliant on cultural prestige, as well as being driven by a desire on the part of the weaker state to emulate the political and economic system of the superior state, while obtaining economic and diplomatic privileges such as in trade and diplomatic recognition.

Although hierarchical systems are found in all civilizations, one of the most well studied examples is the Chinese tributary system that is believed to have lasted for centuries, most notably from the Tang to early Qing dynasties.[46] This order was underpinned by a belief that "China was the superior centre and its ruler had duties toward all other rulers as his inferiors."[47] However, as has been argued recently, this idea of hierarchy did not imply Chinese "centrality."[48] This notion of hierarchy was in marked contrast to the European system of nation-states that were "equal in sovereignty and mutually independent within the cultural area of Christendom."[49]

Hierarchical orders like the Chinese tributary system are sometimes presented as more benign than empires. This might seem so, but it is not necessarily always the case. As Acharya has argued in response to Kang's depiction of East Asia's hierarchical order: while the Chinese order contained benevolent ideas such as the "impartiality" of the emperor (that China did not "discriminate among foreign countries and treated everyone equally"), this did not mean that everyone was "equal to the emperor, but [only that] they were equal in the eyes of the emperor."[50] Moreover, despite claims about its inclusiveness and peacefulness, the "Chinese world order actually operated on the basis of a pragmatic realpolitik, with power and security being major considerations and force being an important instrument."[51]

Hence, sometimes the Chinese accepted the equal status of neighbors that they could not conquer or control by force, as was the case with the Han dynasty's relationship with the Xiongnu federation, the Tang's relationship with Tibet, and the Song's relationship with the Mongols, who would ultimately defeat the Chinese. When the power gap was large, the Chinese did resort to the use or threat of force. The Ming emperor Yongle invaded northern Vietnam, and the Ming also maintained an "aggressive policy towards China's neighbours overseas" as explained in Chapter 3.[52] The famed voyages of Ming admiral Zheng He included show of force and military intervention in conflicts in Sumatra and Sri Lanka.[53] Although the Chinese order did not create an empire as vast as the later empire of the European powers, under both Han and later rulers (Yuan and Qing) China did incorporate formerly independent Xinjiang and Yunnan into the Chinese empire. Hence Andrew Nathan and Robert Ross aptly note that "[t]he Chinese are capable of peace as well as war."[54]

Finally, there is the more contemporary notion of primacy. But sometimes, hegemony and primacy are not distinguishable. Barry Posen views "primacy" as "essentially hegemony."[55] Like hegemony, primacy requires a preponderance of material power.[56] Joseph Nye, one of the main believers in American primacy, carefully distinguishes primacy from hegemony and defines the former as the "disproportionate (and measurable) share of all three kinds of power resources: military, economic, and soft."[57] But how much does soft power matter in this equation? Can a nation establish primacy only or mainly through soft power? While one can find some important differences among concepts such as hegemony, empire, hierarchy, and primacy that link power, ideas, and international orders, from the preceding discussion one thing stands out. As Mark Beeson notes, "All of these approaches are united by their efforts to explain the pivotal role played by the most powerful state of a specific era in underpinning particular international orders.[58]

After highlighting this, we now move to discussing some of the theories of international order that see hegemony as an important and even essential condition of international order, with order viewed in terms of security/stability. But our notion of stability, as discussed above, covers not only the physical security of states, but also the stability of commerce, and associated rules and norms, that supports the maintenance of an international system and order. Here two theoretical perspectives are especially important: Hegemonic Stability Theory (HST), and Liberal Hegemony or Liberal Hegemonic Order (LHO). Although developed at different stages by different scholars, these two are closely related: both take "hegemony as the most likely condition for international stability."[59] Zakaria, as cited above, merely restates the views of many others, such as A. F. K. Organski, for whom "[a]t any given moment the single most powerful nation on earth heads an international order."[60] He adds, "the periods of known preponderance are periods of peace."[61] Both theories link a preponderant power and the

provision of international public goods, including but going beyond security and commerce.

From Hegemonic Stability to Liberal Hegemony

While HST is often presented as a general theory of international
order, its specific focus is to link hegemony with public goods. The
theory is originally traced to American economist Charles P.
Kindleberger in his 1973 book *The World in Depression: 1929–
1939*.[62] Kindleberger argued that the economic chaos that afflicted
the world during the early-to-mid-twentieth century could be
blamed in part on the fact that no nation had a globally dominant
economy. It is often forgotten that Kindleberger neither advocated
hegemony as a desirable international order, nor viewed it as something that is possible to create. Quite the contrary.[63] But his explanation of why the Great Depression might have occurred was
raised by IR/IPE scholars to the status of a macro-theory or meta-
narrative linking international stability with a preponderance of
power by a single nation. Moreover, while Kindleberger was concerned mainly with economic order, his view was transformed to
associate hegemony with all sorts of things, including peace and
stability, economic welfare, and institutional efficacy.

At its core, HST holds that "cooperation and a well-functioning world economy are dependent on a certain kind of political
structure, a structure characterized by the dominance of a single
actor. ... Both Great Britain in the nineteenth century and the
United States after World War II helped bring about an interdependent and overall peaceful world."[64] Like Britain, the United
States benefited from free trade, while offering incentives to lesser
states which in turn benefited from access to the U.S. market and
security protection under the American security umbrella. However, to a far greater extent than British hegemony, HST became a
narrative about the emergence and consequences of American
hegemony. It served as a principal focal point for legitimizing U.S.
hegemony, and though initially a theory of political economy, extended to all aspects of the U.S.-led international order.[65]

HST has been a major influence on American discourses about
emergence, persistence, and change in the contemporary international

order.[66] Isabelle Grunberg suggests that the endurance of HST had to do with the fact that it is "comprehensive" or "so elegant while at the same time encompassing so much."[67] She likens HST to a "fantasy" that captured the "American political imagination" and that "lingers in the mind long after it has proved fallacious."[68] But the theory was "updated" from the British era to capture the much larger role of international institutions that emerged in the post–World War II period. It has been used to explain the U.S. role in the creation of new economic and security institutions like the International Monetary Fund (IMF), the World Bank, the General Agreement on Tariffs and Trade (GATT), and the UN after World War II. Indeed, the overall theory of international institutions and the concept of multilateralism were regarded as a unique product of U.S. hegemony. Multilateralism, as John Ruggie put it, is not an American *institution*, but an *American* institution.[69]

The criticisms of HST are too well known to bear repeating here. Some of its major criticisms cast it as a self-serving American concept, one that at worst ignores, and at best legitimizes, the unsavory or evil ideas and practices of British and U.S. hegemony, including colonialism, racism, economic exploitation, and rampant use of force, everywhere (before World War II), but especially in the non-Western world both before and after World War II.[70] Another major point of criticism is its limited ability to explain order and change in world politics, which requires an understanding of the contribution of other actors and forces such as decolonization. Duncan Snidal argues that HST should be "viewed as a beginning rather than a reliable conclusion to international politics."[71] Our position in this book is that HST (or the dominance of a single power) provides a very limited window to understanding the beginning, continuation, and conclusion of international orders, whether of the past, the present, or the future.

This is because HST is underpinned by a tendency to view certain contemporary Western ideas and practices as a timeless and universal standard, while ignoring or dismissing non-Western principles and practices as aberrations or inferior in providing stability and facilitating trade. In other words, HST legitimizes the denial of non-Western agency in past and present international orders, including rule-governed interactions in areas such as freedom of the seas, great-power accommodation, and commitment to shared prosperity. Non-Western polities are cast as passive recipients rather than active creators of international orders.[72] Yet this is far from true, and making this point in the case of the Indian Ocean is a major rationale for this book.

Yet HST has left enduring legacies for international relations theory and practice. Indeed, it has consistently resurfaced through the past decades to make the same or similar explanations about the necessity of hegemonic power to create and sustain international stability and provide public goods. This has been especially the case with liberal internationalists such as G. John Ikenberry.[73] Ikenberry sees the post–World War II order as a "liberal hegemonic order" with "the acquiescence and support of other states."[74] He defines this order rather vaguely as an "order that is open and loosely rule-based," but sees it as a distinct product of U.S. hegemony, hence his terms "American-led liberal world order" and "American-led liberal hegemony."[75] Although Ikenberry seldom makes the link, and although his theory focuses on the multilateral institutions needed to manage and maintain it, his LHO is clearly built upon the old idea of hegemonic stability.

Like HST, the LHO is a deeply hierarchical system built on both American power dominance and liberal principles of governance. "The United States was the dominant state, but its power advantages were muted and mediated by an array of post-war rules, institutions, and reciprocal political processes—backed up by shared strategic interests and political bargains. Weaker and secondary states were given institutionalized access to the exercise of American power. The United States provided public goods and operated within a loose system of multilateral rules and institutions. American hegemonic power and liberal international order were fused—indeed they each were dependent on the other."[76]

Although Ikenberry conceded that the U.S.-led liberal hegemonic order was being challenged by the rise of unipolarity (at the time his book was being written), erosion of state sovereignty (due, for example, to globalization and emerging norms of humanitarian intervention), and shifting sources of violence from states to non-state actors (e.g., terrorists), he insisted that there are no alternatives to the order and that in the end it will become more inclusive and universal.[77] As he put it, "the rise of non-Western powers and the growth of economic and security interdependence are creating new constituencies and pressures for liberal international order."[78] To him, there are enough "constituencies that support a continued—if renegotiated—American hegemonic role."[79]

The concepts of LIO and LHO have attracted a great deal of attention. (In this book, we use the terms interchangeably, but prefer to characterize this understanding of order as LHO.) This debate has been too well covered in the literature to require further discussion here.[80] A few points will suffice, some of which reflect criticisms of HST.

To begin with, the LHO was never a truly "open" order, easy to enter and inclusive. For much of its history, it has been a selective club of Western nations.[81] Socialist and many non-Western countries either stayed out of it of their own volition or were kept out of it by Western leaders for their own instrumental and identity reasons. China and Russia were not part of the World Trade Organization; while India, despite being a member, was not an open economy. Politically, human rights and democracy posed another barrier to entry to the club by non-Western nations. During the Cold War the Soviet Union created its own politico-economic sphere which operated apart from the U.S.-led LHO. Furthermore, nations and groups of nations in various world regions related to the Soviet sphere with varieties of intensity, and some even created their own regional spheres of influence.

In addition, the LIO's claim that "[t]he British and American-led liberal orders have been built in critical respects around consent"— which reflects a palpable Gramscian understanding, as mentioned earlier—sidelines plenty of challenges to that order from actors who have not found it attractive or just, including many from the non-West.[82] The legitimacy of the LHO was further challenged and undermined by the Western liberal powers' colonial past, their military interventions in the developing world, the uneven spread of the benefits of free trade, and the negative impacts of neoclassical economic conditionalities imposed by multilateral economic institutions on debt-ridden developing nations. The LHO's legitimacy deficit meant that other nations were reluctant and not enthusiastic partners of the Western liberal powers.

Against this backdrop, the LHO did not perform according to the expectations of its proponents. The presumed beneficiaries of the LHO in the non-Western world had major grievances against it. Among these were their concerns about the imbalance of leadership in multilateral institutions, the critical core element of the LHO. Emerging powers such as China, India, and Brazil viewed its institutions, crafted as they were in the 1940s, as reflecting an outdated distribution of power and influence in the context of the late twentieth and early twenty-first centuries. The expectation that such powers, especially China and India, could be coopted into the LHO was perhaps too optimistic. This belief proved unfounded and unrealistic.

While Ikenberry saw the LHO as adaptable and lasting, he did not anticipate the possibility of a leadership retreat by the United States such as that initiated by the Trump administration. The latter, as well as Brexit, showed that the challenge to the LHO comes not just from other aspiring powers like China and India, but also from *within* the Western nations, specifically the leading members of the LHO.[83]

Beyond Hegemony: Alternative Conceptions of International Order

There have been various attempts and ways to redefine and broaden hegemony beyond material power or the ideological dominance of a single state. One attempt is to rethink the association between power, cooperation, and public goods by Keohane, who, as noted earlier, argued that once established under a hegemony, international institutions can continue to provide public goods under posthegemonic conditions. Duncan Snidal argued that a group of rising powers, however small, can take over the burden of maintaining international cooperation once a hegemon disappears.[84] Another important body of work focuses less on structural power and more on different types of leadership. One example is Oran Young's theoretical differentiation between different kinds of leadership.[85] In particular, Young's distinction between structural, intellectual, and entrepreneurial leadership has opened the door for a number of scholars to argue that nonhegemonic actors can indeed make a significant difference to the prospects for cooperation.

As David Rapkin contends, "states lacking structural power can exercise entrepreneurial and/or intellectual leadership to activate [or induce] . . . the structural leadership of those that possess it" by "establishing settings, framing issues and forming coalitions."[86] Similarly, pointing to important changes in the global order, especially the decline of the United States and the emergence of new issue areas, Andrew Cooper, Richard Higgott, and Kim Nossal look at "alternative potential sources of initiative and innovation in international politics."[87] While conceding that the structural leadership of the great powers is still significant, they argue that "other categories of leadership can be significant in catalyzing the processes of reform and change—especially those requiring considerable cooperation and collaboration—in a variety of issue areas on the international agenda for the 1990s. Such a role may be performed by appropriately qualified secondary powers in a way that may not have been the case in the past."[88]

Yet, for the most part, the effort to study what Rapkin calls the "pluralization of leadership" stops at the level of the middle powers.[89] The conceptual shift from power to leadership still assumes a hierarchical agency led by Western nations. Indeed, while criticisms of HST and the LHO proliferated, few provided an alternative framework for world order. Conventionally, when discussing the future of world order, scholars and policymakers use the language of polarity, the most commonly used expression being "multipolarity." We argue that polarity is not a very helpful concept for analyzing world order—both future world order and past world orders. As Stephen Brooks and William Wohlforth argue, "The very qualities that make the concept of polarity helpful for capturing some key differences in how international systems work render it unhelpful for assessing complexity and also changes within a given system. Use of the concept helps analysts understand why a world with one superpower is different in important ways from one with two superpowers or none, but it is too blunt an instrument to track change from one kind of system to another."[90] Moreover, the "use of the concept of polarity encourages dichotomous thinking—the world is either unipolar or multipolar (or bipolar)—and thereby feeds an artificial debate about whether everything is changing or nothing is changing."[91]

We accept these criticisms of polarity made by Brooks and Wohlforth, but further argue that, while polarity may be somewhat useful to describe the distribution of material power, it does not tell us much about other variables that are crucial to world order, such as the role of ideas and interaction patterns. In other words, the distribution of power alone is not a sufficient indicator of world order; the latter is a product of many other forces, including ideas, institutions, and interaction capacity. Moreover, polarity and hegemony are not mutually exclusive. As liberal theorists would themselves concede, the Cold War bipolarity was also a period of U.S. hegemony.

To this one might add reservations about the specific concept of multipolarity. Traditionally, according to Barry Posen, multipolarity refers to the "relatively equal distribution of capabilities . . . with three or more consequential powers."[92] Similarly, Zaki Laidi defines multipolarity as "a system in which power is distributed at least among 3 significant poles concentrating wealth and/or military capabilities and able to block or disrupt major political arrangements threatening their major interests," and where "a pole is an actor capable of producing order or generating disorder . . . which has influence on global outcomes beyond its own borders."[93]

Yet we live in a world in which the ability of "producing order or generating disorder . . . which has influence on global outcomes" lies not just with great powers (even among these, power distribution remains asymmetric rather than equal), but also with nonstate actors such as institutions, corporations, extremists, and social movements using material (wealth and military), nonmilitary (especially new technologies such as artificial intelligence and others which have at least a dual use), and ideational resources. Moreover, whereas past multipolarity was managed by the great powers through a balance-of-power system, including the nineteenth-century Concert of Europe, colonialism, and a few multilateral institutions, the contemporary world order has a multitude of global and regional institutions wedded to collective and cooperative security.

An alternative concept to polarity and multipolarity in conceptualizing the world order, one which is also radically different from the HST and LHO, is the notion of "multiplexity"—the multiplex world and the conditions that shape it.[94] Briefly stated, this concept describes a nonhegemonic world in which a variety of consequential actors or leaders (rather than powers) provide public goods in a growing number of issue areas through individual, bilateral, regional, and multilateral means. Multiplexity does not mean that asymmetries of power are absent. Hence it is not an "apolar" (Niall Ferguson) or "nonpolar" (Richard Haass) world.[95]

Multiplexity does not mean that distribution of power is unimportant. But it has some distinctive features, especially in relation to the traditional conception of multipolarity, which was derived from Europe before World War I. Hence, the consequential actors in a multiplex world are not just materially strong powers or great powers, as in the case of multipolarity or any type of world order defined in terms of "poles," but also others, including regional powers, international institutions, nongovernmental organizations, multinational corporations, and transnational networks.[96] At the same time, a multiplex world is highly interconnected, not only through trade but also through the flow of ideas and people (migrations), religious exchange, and cultural flows, although cultural diversity does not disappear. A multiplex world is

> [a]n international or world order in which no single nation or civilization dominates, which is *culturally and politically diverse yet deeply interconnected through trade, migration, and religious and cultural exchanges.*

In sum, a multiplex world has the following attributes:

- It is neither an empire, nor a hegemony of a single power, although power inequalities and hierarchies remain.
- It is not just the great powers that shape and dominate it, as in a multipolar system, but also regional powers, smaller polities (such as trading states or emporiums), international bodies, as well as people: preachers, merchants, and social networks.
- It is interconnected not only by extensive economic exchange as well as migration, but also by religious, linguistic, and cultural flows.
- Cultural, ideological, and political diversity do not disappear, but are respected.

- There are multiple local and subregional centers of power and culture.
- The spread of ideas and institutions occurs through localization, rather than outright imposition or wholescale adoption of foreign ideas. Foreign ideas and institutions do not displace or extinguish local identities, but may legitimize and enhance them.

Taken together, the multiplex system is a form of nonhegemonic international system and order. This is conceived broadly as a pattern of activity such as international rule making, institution building, and conflict management devised and carried out without the enduring leadership and controlling influence of the strongest power/s in a given international or regional system. NHIOs are not necessarily bereft of strong power/s. Disparities of power do not disappear. But the power and influence of the major actors either dissipates, is voluntarily abandoned, or is neutralized or socialized with the help of norms and institutions, often through the involvement and leadership of the so-called lesser actors. In essence, the notion of NHIO speaks to the agency of nonhegemonic actors, including states, civil society groups, and international organizations.[97] Such a system is decentered by definition in the sense that international authority does not emanate from a fixed center. At the same time, such decentered systems lack a central axis of hierarchy.[98]

The idea of a multiplex world draws on attempts to challenge traditional notions of hegemony. This idea directs attention to the possibility of a nonhegemonic international order, which not only existed in history but might well come about as the U.S.-led hegemonic order declines. Such an order may retain some features of the LHO, but would be different in many critical respects. It will be multicivilizational, decentered, and pluralistic, not only in the sense of a post-American but also a post-Western world. The historical comparative study of the Indian Ocean provides one of the most striking examples of such an order, in sharp contrast to the classical Mediterranean order. Moreover, the multiplex notion describes not only a historical order of the Indian Ocean but also a futuristic one for the Indo-Pacific, a term that subsumes the Indian Ocean and which is currently much in vogue.

CHAPTER TWO

The International Order
of the Roman Mediterranean
(~Sixth Century B.C.E.–
Third Century C.E.)

THE ROMAN MEDITERRANEAN CORRESPONDS with the paradigmatic hegemonic orders of IR theory discussed in
Chapter 1. This chapter provides a theoretical account
of the international history of the ancient Mediterranean. The association between hegemony and international order
that characterizes much theorization in international relations is a
universalization that draws from the Roman precedent. This account privileges material power and the materially powerful with
the making and shaping of international orders. To put it differently, ordering is a top-down process in this account as the hegemon establishes the practices governing social relations. In the
classical Mediterranean, it was Roman power—especially naval
power and the practice of sea control—that underwrote the security of the trading system. Even the flow of ideas in this system, the
twin processes of Hellenization and Romanization, reflected the
imperial power of Rome. The hegemonic Roman Mediterranean

was a core–periphery tributary system with Rome at the center, and *Pax Romana* was an outcome of military conquest.

Introduction

Early Rome (~500–200 B.C.E.) is best characterized as a "conquest state" that relied on booty and exercised "hegemony in an alliance system."[1] Rome gradually transformed into a "tributary empire" by the end of the Punic Wars.[2] Rome's destruction of Carthage and the subordination of the Hellenistic monarchies led to the establishment of its "effective hegemony" over the Mediterranean by the mid-second century B.C.E.[3] This imperial Republic (until 31 B.C.E.) has been likened to "a rentier state" because the burden of taxes shifted from Rome and Italy as "[w]ealth was looted and taxed by the state from the conquered peoples," even as "Italy as a whole grew richer."[4] The taxation system under the Principate (31 B.C.E.–284 C.E.) was similar to that under the imperial Republic although the subordinate polities transformed into imperial provinces.[5] This transition from imperial Republic to Empire transformed Rome's effective hegemony into "universal hegemony," and "tribute" continued "to be lifted out of local communities at the threat of use of force."[6] In other words, Rome was "an empire of domination."[7] In fact, it is *the* archetype that forms "a cognitive model" for the coercive exercise of power (see Fig. 1).[8]

However, "control could not depend upon coercion alone."[9] The Roman path from a city-state to a Mediterranean-wide empire went "hand in hand with" its Hellenization despite "changing views on the Roman ways of appropriating, translating, and diffusing Greek culture."[10] In other words, the Roman Mediterranean "had a high degree of cultural integration among the elites" through the process of Hellenization in which Greek culture served as a point of reference for all things Roman.[11] After all, Hellenization and Romanization were the "interrelated aspects of the same phenomenon," and Romanization or the development of Roman socio-cultural and political identity had a "Greek foundation."[12] Nevertheless, it was clear that Greek culture "was to be in the service of" the imperial power of Rome.[13] So even as the Romans enthusiastically Hellenized (and consequently Romanized),

Figure 1. Map of the classical Mediterranean (~sixth century B.C.E.–third century C.E.). (Produced for the authors by Oxford Cartographers)

they were also declaring, "We are not Greeks," from "as early as we can hear their voices."[14]

The aim of this chapter is to explain the role of power and ideas in the making and shaping of these two aspects of the international order of the Roman Mediterranean: its coercive tributary system and the Hellenization of Rome. Rome's emergence as a hegemonic power after the defeat of Carthage (~200 B.C.E.) saw "a steep rise (more than threefold) in seaborne trade."[15] The following four centuries witnessed "an intensity of traffic by sea that was not to be matched again for a thousand years."[16] Rome's domination over and expansion in the Hellenistic East recast the Mediterranean into "a Roman lake" (*mare nostrum*, "our sea") after the conquest of Ptolemaic Egypt in 31 B.C.E., as Rome came to control all the lands surrounding the Mediterranean.[17] Over the next two centuries, the Roman Empire and navy "guaranteed the safety of the seas from the Straits of Gibraltar to the coasts of Egypt, Syria, and Asia Minor."[18] Thus constituted, *Pax Romana* generated a hegemonic core–periphery world order in the Mediterranean with the city of Rome (and Italy) at the center of an imperial polity that saw the "transfer of revenue" from the provinces and clients to the imperial center in Rome (and Italy).[19] In addition to material wealth, Hellenization also meant the "wholesale transfer of [Greek cultural and human] resources" into the Roman center, and then on to other parts of the empire, given the twin and parallel process of Romanization.[20]

This chapter emphasizes two factors in the making of this hegemonic core–periphery order with Rome at its center. First, the practice of *sea control* was at the heart of the geopolitics of the ancient Mediterranean. Given that "the movement of resources," including trade, revenue, and food, "has always been an essential aspect of Mediterranean power," what was truly at stake for these polities was "the control of the integrating medium across whole tracts of sea."[21] Notably, this struggle over maritime trade routes in the Mediterranean can be traced all the way back to the archaic age (eighth–sixth centuries B.C.E.). Even the rise of the ancient Greek city-states in the eighth century B.C.E. "was intimately tied to the Phoenician expansion and to competition for trade routes."[22] When viewed thus, "Rome's success" appears "spectacular only in its completeness and duration," as observed by Peregrine Horden and Nicholas Purcell.[23]

Second and relatedly, such competition generated wars and large-scale movements of people. The consequent colonization and migration, and the coercion associated with these processes, did lead to cultural transformation shaped by the power asymmetries entailed in such contacts. The Hellenization of Rome should then be understood as the *appropriation* by an imperial power not just of the material spoils of its conquest, but also of the culture of the conquered to the degree that it augmented Rome's imperial power itself. After all, "appropriation does not happen incidentally, without conscious effort, but rather results from deliberate and purposeful actions on the part of identifiable actors or cultural forces."[24] It is also noteworthy that the Hellenization of Rome "had its reverse counterpart: an aversion to and contempt for Greeks."[25]

The rest of this chapter is divided into four sections. The first section explains why the ancient Mediterranean (~sixth century B.C.E.–third century C.E.) should be treated as an international system. More specifically, this section elucidates the structure of this system: its hierarchic/hegemonic and core–periphery arrangement. The next section explains the structure of power and authority in the classical Mediterranean and focuses on political-strategic and political-economic interactions. The emphasis here is on the practice of *sea control* and its interaction with the material and strategic factors in the making of the Mediterranean trading system. The third section explains the transmission of ideas or the process of Hellenization of Rome through the *appropriation* of Greek ideas. The fourth and final section concludes with the provision of public goods by the Roman hegemon in the Rome-centric core–periphery Mediterranean world.

Before proceeding, a brief explanation of the long temporal scope of this chapter is in order. To begin with, the Roman polity itself was particularly long-lived.[26] Importantly, the end of the Republic (509–31 B.C.E.) and the beginning of the Principate (31 B.C.E.–284 C.E.) "was not something objectively and explicitly marked by some public fact in our evidence . . . but something that we must infer circumstantially from a variety of facts and factual changes over the course of several decades."[27] Furthermore, given similar processes of economic expansion, J. G. Manning has argued that "there is little need to make a hard break between the 'Hellenistic' and 'Roman' in the 4th and early 3d [*sic*] century BCE."[28] While the maritime trading order certainly transformed from a polycentric system before the Punic Wars to one that was increasingly Rome-centric over time, we are simply trying to explain the impact of the interplay of material and ideational factors in the making of world orders, especially those related to the practice of sea control, for the ancient Mediterranean.

Similarly, in terms of cultural transformation, Angelos Chaniotis has referred to the period from Alexander the Great (336–323 B.C.E.) to the reign of the Roman emperor Marcus Aurelius (161–180 C.E.) as "one single historical period." According to him, it would be "misleading . . . [t]o call these processes of cultural convergence 'Hellenisation' for the Hellenistic and 'Romanisation' for the Imperial periods, as has been traditional," for the emergence of a "cultural *koine*" in the Mediterranean was a singular process in this "long Hellenistic Age."[29] In turn, Kostas Vlassopoulos sees the emergence of "a Mediterranean-wide global *koine* based primarily on Greek culture" as a continuous process spanning the archaic, classical, and Hellenistic periods during which Greek culture was globalized and glocalized.[30] Indeed, Arnold Toynbee has even described the Roman Empire as "the universal state of the Hellenic civilization."[31] Consequently, even as there were significant differences in the processes of cultural transformation over time in the Mediterranean as explained subsequently, the *Hellenization* of the Mediterranean under Rome was the culmination of these actions that began in the archaic period and must be viewed in the *longue durée*.

The Ancient Mediterranean as an International System

Given the "full" range of Barry Buzan and Richard Little's interunit interactions discussed in Chapter 1—politico-military, politico-economic, and politico-cultural/ideational interactions—the Mediterranean easily qualifies as an international system. It is perhaps the most important one of the classical period, and has received more than its fair share of recognition by IR scholars. For example, Adam Watson discussed Rome in his survey of ancient states systems to show that its Mediterranean world eventually moved toward the imperial end of his pendulum of systems.[32] Similarly, Daniel Deudney has argued that Roman legacies are "deeply woven into the fabric of balance-of-power theory," while Michael Doyle drew attention to Rome as an empire that brought "peace and material progress . . . borne by the chariot of imperial domination."[33]

In fact, some classical scholars have also used IR paradigms (from the realist toolkit) to study the classical Mediterranean to explain the rise of Rome. For Arthur Eckstein, republican Rome created "a system of unipolarity" by replacing "the long-standing multipolar anarchy" of the Mediterranean.[34] While Eckstein questioned whether the entire Mediterranean was "a single system" or a series of interconnected systems, Deudney considered the anti-Roman alliance between Carthage and Macedonia that was forged during the Second Punic War (218–202 B.C.E.) as marking "the full joining of the subsystems of the Western and Eastern Mediterranean."[35]

Buzan and Little have argued that "the idea of system is an analytical concept, [and therefore] analysts have the right to set the criteria for it with greater or lesser degree of stringency."[36] Since "[d]ense fragmentation complemented by a striving towards control of communications may be an apt summary of the Mediterranean past," according to Horden and Purcell, we consider the Mediterranean before the Carthaginian-Macedonian treaty (~200 B.C.E.) as a series of interconnected and interacting subsystems.[37] Prior to the rise of Rome as a naval power during the First Punic War (264–241 B.C.E.), the Mediterranean was divided into the spheres of influence of multiple competing powers. The Phoenicians controlled the western Mediterranean, the Etruscans dominated the north-central regions, while the Hellenistic empires competed in the east.[38] However, after Rome's emergence as a naval power and with its victory over Carthage in the Second Punic War, the Mediterranean eventually began moving toward a single system along with Rome's trajectory toward the imperial end of Watson's pendulum.[39]

Even after the creation of the Principate, Rome's universal hegemony was "composite" and "heterogeneous" because "universal empires did not require a uniform, generalized form of power."[40] Indeed, a "Roman emperor could be a *Princeps* in the senate, a pharaoh to Egyptian provincials or even Olympian Panhellenic Zeus to a league of Greek speaking elites in the Eastern part of the empire."[41] Similarly, Rome also took over the diverse fiscal systems of its subject polities instead of homogenizing revenue collection. Syracuse, Spain, Pergamum, and Egypt maintained their preexisting systems, although the revenue now began to flow toward Rome.[42] The universal empire was nevertheless extremely centralized and has been characterized as a patrimonial-bureaucratic empire because of the central role played by the monarch (and other elites).[43] Given its small bureaucracy of 150 civil servants and 150 senatorial and equestrian administrators, Michael Mann has even argued that the Roman "state was largely an army" given the crucial role played by coercion in the extraction of revenue.[44] Although the imperial government "was spread thinly," it "could be concentrated and applied with great intensity" given the state's coercive power.[45]

In other words, politico-military processes (including warfare and coercion) as well as politico-economic processes (including taxation and commerce) were crucial to the Mediterranean international system. However, the politico-cultural dimension was just as important, and it too pointed toward extreme centralization. Hellenization provided the ideational glue in the Roman Mediterranean. Elite unity in the Roman world was partly an outcome of this cultural transformation and identity formation. As observed by Mann, Rome's hegemony was "uncontested" in part due to elite cultural integration. Despite the violence of civil wars and succession crises, "[n]o contender seems to have been a provincial 'national' leader, attempting either provincial secession or conquest that would have involved establishing the hegemony of a province over the whole empire."[46]

Consequently, the structure of the Roman Mediterranean was hierarchic and pointed toward the formation of a core–periphery order ever since the city-state began to expand. As shown subsequently, the early city-state, embedded though it was in a polycentric Mediterranean, expanded through the formation of hegemonic alliances through which its allies contributed troops for whom they themselves paid.[47] Additionally, Rome expanded through colonization, wars of conquest, and the creation of client states. While Mediterranean trade (and taxation on it) was crucial for the Roman economy, the collection of booty, plunder, slaves, and tribute from the defeated and vanquished polities was also important.

Even as this tribute transformed into tax after the creation of the Principate, Peter Fibiger Bang prefers to use the language of tribute because it did not imply "negotiation and collaboration." For the Romans, "tribute became the mark of imperial subjection, whether made manifest by the imposition of regular (land) taxes or articulated in ceremonies of defeated foes offering the resources of their territories as gifts of submission to the imperial lords."[48] This tribute collection was "massively redistributive," both under the imperial Republic and the Principate, because Rome and Italy were exempt from land taxes after 167 B.C.E. and were not taxed again until the fourth century C.E.[49] According to Fernand Braudel, Rome was the "centre" of the Mediterranean world economy.[50] In addition to these material resources, Rome also appropriated the culture of the Greeks, as mentioned earlier. However, this process was imperial as opposed to cosmopolitan because Rome also destroyed the culture of others (such as Carthage) for imperial ends.

Under Rome, the Mediterranean became a coercively hegemonic international order. Although the term *hegemony* is Greek in origin (*hēgemonia*), and "there was a conceptual continuity, rather than any clear-cut contrast, between the ideas of hegemony and empire in classical Greece," it was the Roman practices of hegemony and empire that have served as models for others, especially in Europe, and have become the benchmarks for IR theory, as explained earlier.[51] While "Rome continued the inheritance of classical Hellenism," it was Rome that became the "inescapable example to reflect on."[52]

The geopolitical "integration" of the Mediterranean "reached its zenith under the Roman Empire, when it experienced political unification for the first and last time."[53] Furthermore, it was during "the centuries of Roman rule" that "safe and reliable transportation helped to integrate the entire Mediterranean into a single cultural and economic space."[54] The violence and protection offered to other polities by Rome (before their formal annexation), the eradication of piracy, and the safe transit for maritime trade through sea control were the major public goods offered by Roman hegemony. Rome's dominance culminated in the imperial peace of *Pax Romana* in the form of the "tight" control of *mare nostrum* after Rome's Mediterranean-wide conquest.[55]

It is well established in historical scholarship, in Gilpinian realism, and in the work of leadership long-cycle theorists that "trade is conducted within a geopolitical framework."[56] However, the anthropologist and historian Philippe Beaujard has argued that in addition to these strategic and economic factors, trading systems are also shaped by the "systems of ideas" governing such exchange.[57] Sociologists, economists, and historians have also stressed the crucial role of ideas in the making and shaping of social, political, and economic systems. According to Jack Goldstone and John Haldon, "the psychological-ideological systems that underpin forms of political and social power" play an "important and causal role" in socio-political systems.[58] Similarly, Douglas Irwin and Kevin O'Rourke have noted that "ideas sometimes matter in history," even as "many economists dislike the notion."[59]

Since "material and ideational relations" are "generative of both actors and the ways in which power is exercised," the economic and military factors interact with ideas to create and maintain the trading system.[60] Notably, the ideas that underpin such interactions influence the degree of coerciveness in the creation and maintenance of the international order.[61] The Roman Mediterranean, then, emerged out of the military and economic interactions that provided security to Rome (and its expanding empire), enriched the Roman (and Italian) core, and was underpinned by the Hellenization (and Romanization) of the empire's elites. Hegemony, hierarchy, and imperium should then be seen as "a type of interaction or relationship," as opposed to "a trait" of the system.[62]

A brief note on the impact of geography is important before we look at the interplay of these processes. The Mediterranean is sometimes viewed as a "closed" sea. Indeed, the word *Mediterranean* itself "means that which is between the surrounding lands."[63] Some strands of IR scholarship argue that "open" regions tend toward balances (or system fragmentation), while hegemonies are possible in "closed" regions.[64] However, Greg Woolf has argued that "the Mediterranean was never a closed system" and that both "Jugurtha and Mithridates challenged Rome with resources drawn from outside the Mediterranean world."[65]

Even as the Mediterranean was somewhat "open" around its edges, the Romans successfully conquered all the surrounding lands. Notably, the "stopping power of water" did not work in the Mediterranean under the Romans.[66] The "complete political dominance" of the entire Mediterranean by Rome notwithstanding, such a political outcome had never occurred before the rise of Rome, "nor has it happened—in quite the same way—since."[67] In other words, geography was hardly decisive in generating Roman hegemony, either in the form of closing the Mediterranean or by limiting Rome's ability to project power over what became *mare nostrum*. How was the Mediterranean system actually created, and how was international order maintained in this world?

Power and Authority: Structure and Interaction
Political-Military

The early Republic found itself in the highly competitive and interconnected city-state network of the Italian peninsula that included the Campanians, the Samnites, the Etruscans, and the Italiote Greeks, in addition to Rome's immediate Latin neighbors. After the First Rome-Latin War of 493 B.C.E., Rome came to lead the Latin League of approximately thirty towns.[68] However, as late as 396 B.C.E., Rome had only managed to capture its Etruscan rival Veii, which was barely twelve miles away.[69] In the meanwhile, Rome was already engaged in a commercial rivalry with Carthage.

It is noteworthy that the earliest two treaties between Rome and Carthage (signed around 509 and 348 B.C.E.) were concerned with commerce raiding, and even "defined ... where Roman ships might and might not go."[70] While there is some evidence of a small Roman navy in the fourth century B.C.E., Rome's "preferred" mode of defense against enemies from the seas, "whether state enemies or pirates, was the establishment of *coloniae maritime* (maritime colonies)."[71] Rome established "five or six citizen colonies and some nineteen 'Latin' colonies" in Italy between 338 and 263 B.C.E., in addition to thirty-five more by the end of the second century B.C.E.[72] The colonization of the island of Ponza in 313 B.C.E. shows that early Rome did have some trappings of a naval power.[73] Rome had established several more colonies by 180 B.C.E., including in the territories of its Samnite rivals.[74]

However, it was the First Punic War that marked the emergence of Rome as a major naval power. The war was an outcome of the geopolitical contest between Carthage and Rome over developments in Syracuse and Sicily that had implications for the control of "the straits between Italy and Sicily."[75] During the war, the Carthaginians launched seaborne raids against Italy from bases in Sicily, Sardinia, and Corsica. In addition to Rome itself, the security of Rome's allies in southern Italy was also at stake, especially because they had only "recently come under Roman hegemony (in the 280s and 270s)."[76] While Rome took the war to Sardinia and North Africa itself, it was Rome's naval victory in 241 B.C.E. that granted it control over Sicily. In addition to paying a large war indemnity,

Carthage agreed to "refrain from sending ships to Italian waters," and both sides agreed "not to attack the other's allies."[77]

The First Punic War "broadened the Roman horizon considerably."[78] Not only had Rome stepped out of the Italian peninsula into Sicily, but it also soon came to control Sardinia (238 B.C.E.) and Corsica (236 B.C.E.), partly driven by the desire to prevent Carthage from using these islands as bases to attack Rome in the future. In the meantime, Roman expansion into the Greek city-states of southern Italy, especially Tarentum in 281 B.C.E., had also brought Rome into contact with the Greek world to its east, as Tarentum sought help from Pyrrhus of Epirus.[79] The Romans were also looking east toward Illyria and the Adriatic at a time when Carthage was building its base in the west in the Iberian Peninsula. Iberia had "rich gold and silver deposits" and provided Carthage with soldiers for its army.[80] During the Second Punic War, Carthage came close to destroying Rome itself under the leadership of Hannibal, who pushed into Italy after crossing the Alps (over land from his base in Spain). "In the peace, Carthage retained its civic existence and a restricted territory in Africa and paid a large indemnity, but it was no longer a major power."[81]

What is noteworthy is that after Hannibal, Rome's "existence as a state" was never threatened.[82] The anti-Roman Carthaginian-Macedonian alliance has been referred to as a "jackal alliance" as Macedonia did not extend any help to Hannibal.[83] Nevertheless, Rome turned east and, with some exceptions, "made war every year" until 16 C.E.[84] Not surprisingly, the dominant view of Roman expansion as "defensive imperialism," first articulated by Theodor Mommsen in the nineteenth century, has now been "comprehensively demolished."[85] As Rome expanded into the Greek East, it was now more interested in "plunder, disrupt[ing] local hegemonies," and leaving "the region in control of its allies."[86] After Roman victories over the Seleucids and the Peace of Apamea (188 B.C.E.), the Seleucids were no longer a significant naval power in the eastern Mediterranean.[87] By 168 B.C.E., Rome had also defeated Macedonia and divided its territory into "four republics."[88]

Meanwhile, the Ptolemies of Egypt had continued to maintain friendly relations with Rome since 273 B.C.E., and remained neutral throughout the Roman wars in the Greek East.[89] In 168 B.C.E., the Romans also forbade the Seleucids from invading Egypt.[90] With the final destruction of Carthage after the Third Punic War (149–146 B.C.E.), Rome had "no potential adversary anywhere in the Mediterranean basin that could constitute a first rate threat to Roman power."[91] Nevertheless, Augustus (31 B.C.E.–14 C.E.) "added more territory to Roman rule than any other figure in Roman history."[92] As a consequence of Roman expansion, all the remaining naval powers of the Mediterranean were eventually destroyed and subordinated (or annexed)—Corinth (146 B.C.E.), Rhodes (88 B.C.E.), and finally Egypt (31 B.C.E.)—thereby transforming the Mediterranean into a Roman lake.

While Roman "militarism and aggressive decision making" did play a role in Roman expansion, these factors cannot explain the Roman quest to coercively dominate the Mediterranean after the elimination of Carthage as a major power in the aftermath of the Second Punic War.[93] After all, such militarism was characteristic not just of Rome but of all Mediterranean polities. Even more perplexingly, Rome created a "permanent navy" only with the establishment of the Principate in 31 B.C.E.[94] Not only did Rome not have a permanent navy in the centuries of its relentless expansion, as fleets were then "commissioned for particular needs," but it was Rome's naval allies, "primarily Greek polities and a few Etruscan polities of Italy," that had played a major role during the Punic Wars.[95] Similarly, Rome's Rhodian allies had also contributed significantly to Rome's victory against the Seleucids.[96] Even the permanent fleets of the Principate under Augustus "were manned primarily by non-Romans who came from cultures with a strong naval heritage."[97] While the permanent naval fleets did support expansion under the Principate—Mauretania (41–42 C.E.), Lycia (43 C.E.), and Thrace (46 C.E.)—thereby "giving Rome control of the whole Mediterranean seaboard," "large-scale naval warfare" in the Mediterranean had become "obsolete, at least for the next couple of centuries."[98] While Rome's aggressiveness was partly rooted in economic factors as discussed subsequently, Rome's political-strategic interactions did entail a crucial practice: sea control.

In the case of Rome, conquest, colonization (through settlers) and sea control were deeply intertwined from the very beginning of the Republic. It was "the need to control the seaways and the affiliated Italian trade routes that induced the Romans" to pursue colonies through settlers.[99] Early Rome was already in competition with Carthage for maritime trade, as noted earlier, and the first Roman colonies also began to appear in the fourth century B.C.E. As such, these settler colonial networks also performed a security function as they reduced the need to permanently station troops in the colonies. At the same time, they boosted commerce with Rome.

However, there was nothing inevitable about this practice of sea control as other options were certainly available, at least in theory, especially after the elimination of Carthage as a major power. At least one such alternative involved strategies to improve economic performance instead of relying on conquest.[100] There is some evidence that Ptolemaic Egypt may have pursued the path of state-backed agricultural expansion (including through the introduction of cash crops), in addition to pursuing technological innovations such as the use of water-lifting devices.[101]

A second alternative included commercial networks not backed by naval power. Notably, Roman trade with the western Indian Ocean world was not backed by the coercive naval power of any state. This is important simply because Rome suffered a massive trade deficit with the Indian Ocean region.[102] Instead of being backed by naval power, the management of the Rome–India trade saw several organizational, financial, and legal innovations.[103] (By contrast, "targeted projection of armed force and the maintenance of a thin security apparatus in strategic locations on land and on the water" did promote the economic integration of the Atlantic "rim" with the Roman Mediterranean, and "eventually squadrons of Roman warships even patrolled the Atlantic coasts of Spain, Gaul [France], and Britain—'The Outer Sea.'")[104]

As a third alternative, it was also possible to be a sea power and not pursue an empire or a hegemonic role. Hellenistic Rhodes "provides an example of a state" with a maritime commercial orientation and naval power but one with the notable absence of "an empire."[105] However, even as Rome "had no ambition to become a naval power" until 300 B.C.E., a possible fourth alternative, it went down the path of naval "dominance."[106] The Romans even pursued "preventive and indeed provocative action against states they perceived as possible threats" after the First Punic War.[107] So even as Rome "met no rival that threatened its own immediate security" after the destruction of Carthage, Rhodes, Egypt, and others were eventually conquered.[108]

Rome was certainly socialized during its encounter with Carthage, as "the Phoenicians represented a powerful model for the conduct of trade."[109] Consequently, competing centers of maritime trade were destroyed and "refounded by the Romans themselves."[110] Notably, Cato specifically opined that "Carthage must be destroyed," a fate that also befell Corinth among others.[111] Such destruction was followed by a form of "social engineering" by Rome through "the dispatch of colonies" to occupy such lands.[112] According to Bang, Rome effected economic change in the Mediterranean through exceptional brutality and a ruthlessness that is "difficult to exaggerate."[113]

Given that the social structure of the Mediterranean was informed by the practice of sea control, ambitious polities like Rome aspired to nothing less than "the control of seaborne mobility" itself.[114] The expanding Roman Republic sought to control "all landing spaces" in and around the Mediterranean, as opposed to controlling the seas per se "through engagement between ships at sea."[115] Even after the conquest of the entire Mediterranean, Rome kept a watchful eye through the creation of a permanent navy that included two fleets in Italy (at Misenum and Ravenna) and three provincial fleets in Syria, Alexandria, and Pontus (while creating other provincial and local fleets as needed). The presence of the Roman navy at both ends, in Egypt (Alexandria) and at Rome (Misenum), ensured the safety of the all-important grain trade.[116]

Importantly, "the modern notion of control of the sea, or even of the so-called sea lanes, should not be "simply transposed to the ancient world."[117] After all, the "idea of 'patrolling' in the western Mediterranean and the Adriatic from these ports which is often encountered in modern scholarship, is simply anachronistic and impracticable for oared warships."[118] Given the "limited range of these oared warships," long-distance warfare was not possible in and of itself.[119] "The best situation was to establish bases that were only a day's voyage from one another."[120] Consequently, the practice of sea control in the Mediterranean was about controlling the nodes of connectivity on the northern and southern shores, and on the islands separating them. This form of control was very crucial in a region where major polities depended on trade for staples such as food.

The ancient Mediterranean practice of sea control was then about control over oceanic activity, as opposed to seeking ownership of the ocean itself.[121] While the Mediterranean was "a realm to be conquered and controlled," the sea itself was "beyond . . . ownership," even as "the things that were separated from it could become objects of rights."[122] It is in this sense that Rome sought to control the Mediterranean, and the "very unity of the Empire rested on the control of the Mediterranean" by a single power.[123] Although "low level coastal piracy" continued in the Mediterranean, the Roman conquest of all of the surrounding lands ensured that maritime trade remained undisturbed until the Goth and Scythian naval attacks after the mid-third century C.E.[124]

Since "trade and commerce can be regulated, limited, promoted, or disrupted," the social practices associated with trade matter and can have dramatic consequences "on the configuration of social and political relations" of a trading order.[125] The practices embodied in the "norms" and the "deep rules" of world politics are generally seen as "a secondary aspect" in "the Western tradition" due to "the dominance of military institutions and coercion in the political history of the western Eurasian world."[126] This is problematic because the practices related to sea control, conquest, and colonization were a part of the "social fabric" of the trading world of the Mediterranean.[127]

Political-Economic

According to David Abulafia, the "question of whether trade comes before the exercise of naval power is perhaps a chicken and egg problem" for the ancient Mediterranean.[128] Indeed, "mercantile contact and colonial settlement" were the core features of "the Mediterranean throughout the pre-Roman age" going back to the Mycenaean civilization from a millennium before the rise of Rome.[129] After the First Punic War, Rome "consciously" developed a strategy of sea control and "decidedly" pursued conquest.[130]

Trade was crucial for wealth generation and for the political survival of the Roman polity, under both the expanding imperial

Republic as well as the Principate, as it was linked to booty, slaves, and resources (especially food and mineral wealth). Control of the trading zones in the central and western Mediterranean was an important cause of the Punic Wars between Rome and Carthage.[131] Roman expansion into Sicily after the Punic Wars was also linked to Sicily's importance in the grain trade at that time. Rome also restructured the political economy of the wider region. The forced appropriation of agricultural regions in the vanquished polities, and the resettlement of Romans (and Italians) in these regions, were widely practiced. Approximately 1–2 million slaves were "imported" from the conquered regions into Italy from 225 to 30 B.C.E., and "tens of thousands of Italian peasants" were moved overseas, where they were given "bigger individual plots."[132]

The immense scale of the slave trade—which may have reached 4 million by 200 C.E.—converted parts of "Italy and Sicily into veritable slave societies."[133] Notably, "slavery may not have dominated production outside Italy" in the Principate.[134] However, slavery was linked to Roman warfare and political economy: "successful warfare produced slaves who could work the land, and slave labour on the land freed farmers to go to war."[135] Not surprisingly, the defeat of Veii in 396 B.C.E. "was remembered as an event accompanied by the mass enslavement of the defeated."[136] Later, when Rome "enslaved some 150,000 people from Epirus in northern Greece in 167 BC, its own official citizen numbers were only 313,000."[137] Natural reproduction, along with the politics of citizenship and manumission, continued to ensure a steady supply of slaves even after the wars of expansion had slowed down under the Principate.

Rome was "enriched" by its incessant wars.[138] Not only were plunder and raiding common, but Rome's extraordinary expansion across the Mediterranean meant that "a steady stream of movable wealth began to flow into Rome and Italy."[139] The First and Second Punic Wars had nearly depleted the Roman treasury, and large indemnities were therefore imposed upon Carthage. The Romans received 3,200 talents from Carthage after the First Punic War and an additional 1,200 talents when they came to control Sardinia in 238 B.C.E. After the Second Punic War, Carthage was made to pay 10,000 talents over fifty years.[140] Since it is "difficult for modern readers to grasp the enormous amount of this transfer of wealth" expressed in talents, it is noteworthy that 3,002 talents "could have paid for twenty-five legions in 150 BC."[141] At this time, a legion included 4,000 legionaries and 200 cavalry, but it could be expanded to 5,000 legionaries and 300 cavalry during crises and wars.[142]

The expanding Republic also extracted economic rents from subordinate polities as a form of protection money from rival claimants (including Rome itself). Bang has referred to this "economic force" as "predatory imperialism" under the Republic, which gave way to a more "routinized" form of extraction through tax collection after the establishment of the Principate (as the subordinate polities were transformed into Roman provinces).[143] What is noteworthy is that these "rents" and later "taxes" were high enough that this burden was levied entirely on the "defeated subjects," as Rome and Italy were exempt from land taxes for almost four centuries after 167 B.C.E.[144]

To put it differently, war and the extraction of material resources (trade, food, slaves, rent, and taxes) were interactive processes. "As it was the Romans who usually started the wars ... we find a circular process that contributed to the permanency of warfare."[145] Furthermore, "Rome's military victories during this period became nearly costless, in an economic sense, as conquered nations footed the bill for further expansion" through "booty, slaves, and indemnity."[146] For example, Rome was enriched through the mining revenues from the Spanish and Macedonian gold and silver mines. While exact figures are hard to come by, Carthago Nova in Spain, which was captured by the Romans in 209 B.C.E., produced 35 tons of silver per annum, or approximately 1,500 talents.[147] Similarly, the "reopening of Macedonian bullion mines" in 158 B.C.E. "was a very significant occurrence."[148] The consequent "increase in production of Roman denarii" resulted in an "expansion of monetary liquidity in Italy" and further boosted the economy.[149]

The conquest of Carthage, Sicily, and Sardinia had meant that grain cultivation in Italy was already declining even before the conquest of Egypt in 31 B.C.E.[150] Later, its status as the granary to supply free grain to 200,000–250,000 Romans was so important that "Egypt, though a Roman province, always remained peculiarly bound to the personal control of the Emperor."[151] Approximately

15 percent of the state's revenues were spent in supplying this wheat to Rome.[152] This grain trade was the economic motor of the long-distance trade in the Mediterranean that "allowed the economy to lift off the ground."[153] Many other major cities also depended on imported grain. Tariffs on this trade in grain, which also boosted the exchange of other commodities, including olive oil, metals, and wine, "yielded the treasury more than any other source save the tribute of conquered provinces."[154] Not surprisingly, "Rome perceived the empire as existing for the benefit of Rome [the city] and perhaps Italy."[155] Along with the flow of material resources, Greek culture was also "transferred" to Rome. How was the flow of Greek culture patterned in the ancient Mediterranean?

The Transmission of Ideas in the Mediterranean: Hellenization and Romanization

The wholesale importation of Greek culture by the Romans "creates the formidable problem of the inverse flow of culture and power," since it was the imperial power that adopted the culture of the conquered.[156] It was the Romans who appropriated most aspects of Greek culture, including literature, philosophy, religion, art, architecture, and aspects of law and politics.[157] This "total penetration of Greek into Roman culture" meant that "well-educated Romans could be counted on to be bilingual in Greek" for "the next five hundred years" from the second century B.C.E. onwards.[158] This change in the Roman approach toward the Greeks in the third century B.C.E. is a puzzle because the Roman interest in Greek culture "was intermittent and often of secondary importance" until then and "Roman attitudes towards Hellas lacked continuity or systematic formulation."[159] This is not insignificant because Rome had been in commercial contact with the Greek world since the Bronze Age, as noted above, in addition to being in indirect contact via the Etruscans.[160]

How are we to understand this process of Hellenization, which is traditionally defined as "the spread of Greek culture and its adoption by non-Greek peoples"?[161] Moreover, the process of Hellenization is "usually seen as active."[162] However, this "Hellenocentric approach" that assumes the "superiority of Greek culture over

Roman" is no longer acceptable "as it has little to do with the historical attitude of Romans towards the Greeks."[163] Recent scholarship has emphasized that the "transfer of ideas" is not about "cultural influence operating arbitrarily."[164] Since the "zones of contact" are "sociopolitical spaces," we cannot explain the spread of culture without paying attention to the power and agency of the actors involved.[165]

It was only with Rome's imperial expansion into southern Italy (home of the Italiote Greeks), Sicily (home to Greek city-states like Syracuse), and the Hellenistic world that Rome became enamored with Greek culture. However, the expansion of the imperial Roman Republic was temporally synchronous with the Hellenization of the eastern Mediterranean under the Hellenistic kingdoms. In turn, these processes can themselves be seen as a continuation of the Hellenization of the Mediterranean during the archaic and classical periods, especially as they relate to the developments in southern Italy and Sicily. Since Rome entered an already Hellenized Mediterranean as it stepped out of Italy before *appropriating* this culture, it is important to understand the Hellenization of Rome in the *longue durée*, as mentioned at the beginning of this chapter. Therefore, this section explains the Hellenization of the ancient Mediterranean through three interconnected processes beginning with *colonization* during the archaic and classical periods, followed by *hegemonic socialization* during the Hellenistic period.[166] The Hellenization of Rome was, then, the culmination of these prior trends that led to the *appropriation* of Greek culture by the all-conquering Romans.

Greek Colonization in the Archaic and Classical Periods

The spread of Greek civilization throughout the Mediterranean is one of the central features of the history of the archaic period. According to Mogens Hansen, approximately 279 Greek "colonies" and 129 "Hellenized communities" were founded between the eighth and fourth centuries B.C.E. (of which 72 colonies were founded during the classical age, during the fifth and fourth centuries B.C.E.).[167] This was a period of constant movement of the Greek communities, and city-states or *poleis* were appearing and disappearing all the time along the coasts of the Mediterranean and the Black Seas. While this phenomenon is often called "colonization," it refers to the migration of the Greeks and the cultural Hellenization of the indigenous communities. Indeed, by the fourth century B.C.E., approximately "40 per cent of all ancient Greeks" lived "outside Greece" as a result of these processes.[168] Not surprisingly, according to Plato in the fourth century B.C.E., "we [Greeks] live between the River Phasis [around the Black Sea region] and the Pillars of Hercules [or the Strait of Gibraltar] ... making our homes around the sea just as ants or frogs do around a pond."[169]

Given the vast number of such *poleis* during the archaic age, it is "practically impossible to make watertight generalizations" for their establishment.[170] There were multiple causes for the spread of Greek communities around the Mediterranean and the Black Seas in the archaic age; the traditionally emphasized reasons include overpopulation and land shortage in Greece, along with the commercial ambitions of the Greeks. However, recent scholarship has also emphasized intra-Greek rivalries, warfare, and expulsion leading to emigration.[171]

Since the Phoenicians "dominated" Mediterranean trade prior to the archaic age and had established their own "colonies" in this wider region, it has been suggested that "the most important factor" in this "expansion" of the Greeks was related to commercial competition with the Phoenicians, which was ultimately linked with "who had effective control of the sea."[172] Tamar Hodos has emphasized this competitive dimension with the Phoenicians in the Greek colonization of Sicily, North Africa, and northern Syria.[173] By 600 B.C.E., the Greeks "massively outnumbered the Phoenicians in the west Mediterranean and Greek urban forms were having a much bigger impact on west Mediterranean populations."[174]

However, Greek colonization and the formation of new *poleis* were not tantamount to imperialism. Most colonial *poleis* were "politically independent," although many maintained strong cultural links with the *metropolis* or mother city.[175] The emigrant Greeks in the colonies "reproduced the same cults, calendars, dialects, scripts, state offices and social and political divisions as in their mother cities," at least initially.[176] Notably, this colonization was not necessarily state-led or state-backed, and "reinforcements" often came from multiple *poleis*.[177] Many scholars prefer to use the original Greek word—*apoikiai*—for such settlements, given the modern baggage associated with the term *colonization*. *Apoikiai* means "a home away from home" or "emigrant community," and these population movements and migrations were permanent.[178]

Cultural feedback from the colonies to the *metropolis* also existed. For example, certain forms of urbanism were "developed first in the colonial world and then influenced developments back home."[179] In fact, the emergence of the *polis* in "its Classical sense of 'city-state' can be traced back to c.734, when Syracuse was founded [in Sicily] by some Corinthians."[180] However, the colonial *poleis* were not politically subordinate to the *metropolis*. In fact, some colonial *poleis* even fought wars with the *metropolis*, as demonstrated by the battle between Corcyra (colony) and Corinth (*metropolis*) in the seventh century.[181]

Nevertheless, the colonial *poleis* were not established in empty lands. "Lands often described as 'empty' were empty only in the eye of the beholder, or authors legitimizing the Greeks' claim, in particular, to territory or foreign shores."[182] For example, the native Sikels of Sicily were "expelled to make room for the Greeks" during the foundation of Syracuse.[183] Other colonial *poleis* in Sicily (Himera, Gela, and Camarina) were also founded after the expulsion of the locals, as were colonial *poleis* elsewhere, like the one on the island of Naxos.[184] In other parts of Sicily (and around the Mediterranean), many *poleis* were in fact Hellenized communities of the locals who were acculturated "over a long period through immigration of individual Greek settlers and through interaction with neighbouring Hellenic communities," thereby making *strategic interaction* a parallel process of Hellenization during this period in addition to colonization.[185] It was the Phoenicians and Etruscans, "rival settlers, rather than native populations of each hinterland, that for several centuries would prove to be the Greeks' strongest competitors."[186]

While it is true the "cultural 'Hellenization of the barbarians' was at no time consciously planned," "the Greek *apoikiai* were highly conscious of being Greek communities and of being part of the Panhellenic world."[187] Earlier understandings of Hellenization

viewed the role of the recipients as passive, especially in the western
Mediterranean. According to John Boardman, "[i]n the west the
Greeks had nothing to learn, much to teach."[188] However, recent
scholarship has been critical of such views. For Hodos, Boardman's
"essentialist view" implies that "Greek culture (itself viewed as
somewhat static) overwhelmed others ... with no consideration of
agency, nor of reciprocity."[189] Similarly, Sara Owen is critical of this
"one-way influence" that is ultimately rooted in notions of Greek
"cultural superiority."[190]

Emphasizing the agency of the local/indigenous populations,
newer theories of Hellenization emphasize "hybridity," "middle
ground," and "communication and negotiation" between the immi-
grant Greeks and the locals.[191] In Sicily, different indigenous communities adopted different material, social, and political strategies
to deal with the immigrants, and acculturation included elements
of competition, emulation, and even mythological integration.[192]
Similarly, it was local socio-political changes at Thasos in Thrace
that initiated contacts with foreign cultures prior to the migration
of the Greeks. Furthermore, "there was at least some Greek integration into the existing ritual landscapes" in Thasos.[193]

Although the recognition of local agency is an important contribution in understanding the processes related to transculturation,
Hansen has argued that "confrontation between the local inhabitants and the Greek colonists" occurred in almost "every single
case" of Greek colonization and the founding of *poleis*.[194] Furthermore, relations with the locals could change over time, and at Meg-
ara Hyblaia, "Greeks came into conflict with non-Greeks after
an initial phase of peaceful coexistence."[195] Nicholas Purcell has
explained this "aggression" between the migrants and the locals by
noting that Greek colonization was "the continuation of agrarian
domination by elite groups in new environments" (as opposed to the
"political hegemony" of the *metropolis*).[196] For example, Greek colonists "did not crop plants known to the locals" in the Pontic region;
"instead they brought with them and planted familiar crops."[197] Consequently, the contest for this "land for settlement and agriculture"
with the locals was an important feature of Greek colonization.[198]

This emphasis on the territorial dimension of Greek colonization is best understood in contrast with the parallel process

of Phoenician colonization. Phoenician communities "did not dominate—culturally, politically, or economically—the societies in which they cohabited and with whom they interacted, and this is perhaps the most fundamental difference between the Phoenician and Greek overseas settlements."[199] As noted by Johann Arnason, "Carthaginian domination does not seem to have resulted in a 'Punicization' of North Africa or the Iberian peninsula."[200] Since the Phoenicians were ultimately interested in dominating commerce and commercial networks, their colonies were in fact established on the margins of the lands already settled by local communities. Not surprisingly, the Phoenician communities "disappeared over time, probably absorbed by the locals."[201]

By contrast, "the whole colonial world" had become a part of Hellas or the realm of Greek culture.[202] It was the non-Greeks who were incorporated into the Greek civilization. "[T]here are very few known cases where Greek colonists adapted themselves to the local language and culture and finally stopped speaking Greek or feeling themselves to be Greek."[203] Even in places like Iberia, where the agency of the locals has been emphasized and where "middle ground" was sought, the indigenous people "experienced the Greek approach as a use of power," and these parts of Iberia became a part of Hellas.[204] Elsewhere, power asymmetries were exercised in their gendered form through intermarriage with native women in places like Massalia (southern France) that resulted in the Hellenization of local communities.[205]

The Eastern Mediterranean: Hegemonic Socialization and Hellenization after Alexander's Conquests

Unlike the western Mediterranean, the eastern Mediterranean was not Hellenized in the archaic age except along specific coastal stretches, as the Greeks encountered equally powerful but older civilizations in that region. For example, Greek mercenaries had been employed by the Egyptian pharaohs since the seventh century B.C.E. However, Greek settlements there were "under strict Egyptian control," and intermarriage between the Greeks and locals was forbidden.[206] The eastern Mediterranean was Hellenized after its conquest by Alexander the Great (336–323 B.C.E.) through hegemonic socialization, or the imposition of Greek culture on local societies by the conquest states of his successors: the Seleucids and the Ptolemies. The Macedonian case itself is slightly different, for the process of Hellenization there had begun before Alexander. However, hegemonic socialization was at work in Macedonia too.

Whether or not the Macedonians were Greeks has been a long-running question in scholarship. While it is now recognized that "Macedonian was a Greek dialect," it is also known that the other population groups speaking different languages predated the Macedonian speakers in that region, and that they were "either expelled or reduced to a subordinate position and eventually assimilated by the conquering Macedonians."[207] From the fifth century B.C.E. onwards, the Macedonian kings (not the people) tried to import Greek culture. Under Philip II (359–336 B.C.E.), Attic, the Athenian dialect of Greek as opposed to the Macedonian dialect, was used for written documents and public inscriptions in Macedonia.[208] This semi-Hellenized polity at the frontier of the classical Greek world eventually took over the culture of Greece under Philip and his son Alexander the Great "by diplomacy and conquest."[209]

Beyond Greece, Alexander's conquest of Persia and Egypt has been referred to as the " 'big bang' of Hellenistic 'globalisation.' "[210] Importantly, Alexander's campaigns were followed by the setting up of garrisons in these conquered territories, where "a Greek-speaking population" also continued to live.[211] In other words, "Alexander's conquest opened . . . [these lands] to Greek immigration," and the Seleucids wanted "to create *Greek* colonies and to install citizens of Greek cities in Phrygia, in Pisidia, and even in the Persian Gulf region."[212] With the promotion of Greek culture by the ruling elite of the Hellenistic monarchies, many non-Greek locals "had strong incentives to attain power and wealth through acquiring the Greek language, Greek names, Greek education or Greek cultural practices" through the process of hegemonic socialization.[213] While some non-Greeks became "completely Hellenised," the Seleucid domains experienced a "more or less stable diglossia" of Greek and local languages like Aramaic with "people using different languages in different communities for different purposes."[214]

Meanwhile, "the Ptolemies created a basic distinction between Greeks and Egyptians," with different legal, judicial, and taxation systems, even as some Egyptians and other non-Greeks could at times be classified as Greeks for administrative purposes.[215] However, in their "brand new, purpose-built capital-city" Alexandria, "native Egyptians, like the Jews, had their own quarters and were clearly a minority."[216] While the Ptolemies came to rule a two-millennia-old wealthy polity in Egypt and "were treated as both Egyptian pharaohs and Hellenistic monarchs," Cleopatra was probably the first Ptolemy to have known Egyptian, and she became the ruler of this kingdom after two and a half centuries of Hellenistic rule.[217]

Greek remained the language of the political elite and of education in Egypt until its conquest by Rome (and thrived for several centuries thereafter as well). Although the Hellenization of the locals "was not complete or uncontested" (as shown by the use of different administrative systems and linguistic registers), Greek was clearly the language of politics there, and ethnic Greeks and Hellenized locals staffed the upper echelons of government and society in the Hellenistic kingdoms.[218] In other words, when Rome entered the eastern Mediterranean, it stepped into this Hellenized world, "the bequest of the conquests of Alexander."[219]

Appropriation: Hellenization and Roman Imperialism

The process of the Hellenization of Rome was rooted in considerations of politics and prestige. Unlike the process of hegemonic socialization in the Hellenistic world in the wake of Alexander's conquests, "the Romans did not force their culture" on the peoples of the territories that they dominated and conquered.[220] Rome's imperial dominance over the Hellenistic world notwithstanding, it was the Romans who adopted the culture of the subject people. According to the Roman poet Horace in the first century B.C.E., "Greece, the captive, took her savage victor captive, and brought the arts into rustic Latium."[221] However, this civilizing narrative was created by the Romans themselves, in part to serve the ideological agenda of Roman imperialism.[222]

The Roman polity had encountered Greek culture from its very beginnings, as noted earlier. "But this stirred no obvious interest by Rome in the lands of the Greek East."[223] Rome began to pay attention to Greek culture only after its expansion into the world of the Italiote Greeks to its south. Initially, "the hellenization of Roman Italy had expressed itself in material culture" that was achieved through the loot and booty acquired from Tarentum (272 B.C.E.), Volsinii (265 B.C.E.), and "by a veritable flood of Greek art after the capture of Syracuse in 211."[224] Similarly, Rome's victory over Macedon in 168 B.C.E. also produced a booty of 20,000 volumes of Greek knowledge from the library at the royal palace at Pydna.[225] Considerations of prestige also promoted the Hellenization of Rome. Prior to the conquest of Macedonia, Rome was not considered a beautiful city "in its public or private spaces."[226] Rome learned about the "aesthetics of power," both material (such as monumental architecture and public art) and ideological (such as the imperial quest to promote *humanitas* or "liberal values"), from the Greeks.[227]

However, Rome had no interest in being "culturally colonized" by the Greeks.[228] The Romans themselves vigorously debated the Hellenization of Rome. The "most celebrated luxury-hating, anti-Hellene of the Republican period" was Cato the Censor, who worried about Rome's moral decline through imported luxuries.[229] Similarly, there were enthusiastic Hellenizers like Cicero, "one of the primary apostles of Greek intellectual culture at Rome," who believed that the Romans had much to learn from the Greeks.[230] The civilizing myth of the rustic Romans by the cultured Greeks noted above needs to be understood in light of these intellectual debates in Rome.

In fact, the Romans were "orientalizing" the Greeks (in a manner implied by Edward Said) through such debates and critiques of Greek luxuries to assert their military dominance.[231] Even as Cato was himself "steeped in Greek language, history, and culture," he was ultimately more worried about the "destructive character of many Hellenistic models born within the courts of Alexander's successors" for the republican institutions of Rome itself, instead of agonizing about Greek culture per se.[232] "Hellenization and [imperial] power" went together because it was the Romans who were "deciding who should exercise the authority of regulating the process of acculturation, when, and how."[233]

As Tim Whitmarsh has noted, the Hellenization of Rome itself was never in question; "the only debate . . . was over *how* it was to be inserted into an imperial framework."[234] The Roman appropriation of Greek culture was about imperial dominance, as it was about Rome having "robbed" Greece of its culture.[235] After all, "the Greeks the Romans knew the best were domestic slaves, employed artisans, and diplomats" with whom they interacted during imperial expansion.[236] This imperial assertion of Roman power over Greece through Hellenization has been characterized as "imperial Hellenism" because neither was Rome's "rightful dominance over Greece" questioned nor were its "art-plundering generals" criticized, even as the Romans vigorously debated *how* to Hellenize.[237] There are two other important facets of this Roman appropriation of Greek culture. First, Rome's respect for Greek culture "was focused upon the past—rather like the British in India [in the nineteenth century], they viewed contemporary Greece as decadent."[238] Second, and relatedly, "Hellenism was largely confined to the cultural and intellectual sphere, and located in a complementary, dyadic relationship with Roman military and political supremacy."[239]

At a more pragmatic level, as Rome expanded into the Hellenized world to its east, there were more Greek speakers in the imperial Roman Republic from the first century B.C.E. than Latin speakers.[240] These educated Greeks (especially traders, geographers, and imperial administrators) could be made to serve the imperial ends related to the expanding Roman polity. Since "Greek was understood throughout the [Mediterranean] world," it was better "for Romans to be celebrated in the world language."[241] Given its "public character," Greek literature, especially rhetoric—"the most important intellectual discipline in ancient Western history"—was also useful for Roman imperial administrators, as it was advantageous during the debates in Rome's senatorial and public assemblies.[242] Consequently, the absorption of Greek philosophy did not change "the political views of the Romans who adopted" Greek thought, instead "it bolstered and sustained those views."[243]

An important political reason driving Hellenization was the role of Rome's Italian allies. Rome's imperial expansion under the Republic was jointly pursued with the Italian allies, as discussed above. However, the exclusiveness of Roman citizenship before the Social War (91–87 B.C.E.) meant that the allies (especially the Italiote Greeks) looked toward Greek culture—a quasi-universal

culture in the Mediterranean with which they had had close interaction, just like the Romans—to express their participation in the
imperial enterprise. "The Italians became Roman on the condition
that Romans became Italian. Both sides found the point of cultural
convergence in Hellenism."[244] As the Roman elite became "Greek
culturally, the mass of the Greek-speaking population of southern
Italy overnight became Romans *legally*."[245] Extension of Roman citizenship clearly meant the weakening of local (Greek) political
identities.

However, culture is not unitary, so the Romans (and Italians)
could Hellenize without becoming less Roman or Italian.[246] "Roman
traditions claimed no purity of lineage. Distinctiveness of blood or
heritage never took hold as part of the Roman self-conception."[247]
From its very beginnings, the Roman identity had been constantly
transformed through the appropriation of some of the cultures that
had been conquered. The destruction of Veii in 396 B.C.E. had made
its patron deity, Juno, into a Roman divinity, "not a defeat of the
other's god but an appropriation of it."[248] Consequently, the "influx
of Greek culture forced Romans to think about what it was to be
Roman."[249]

According to Bang, the Romans "entered the game of competitive emulation with the Greeks."[250] Cicero Latinized Greek philosophy while a Greek, Livius, is believed to have invented Latin
literature. Similarly, even as the Romans emulated Greek art and architecture, they enriched it with their own technological innovations
(such as the use of cement and Puteoli stone).[251] At the same time, the
Romans also rejected some aspects of Greek culture altogether, such
as music and gymnastics.[252] Hellenization and Romanization were,
then, parallel processes because the Hellenization of Italy occurred
simultaneously with the "spread of Roman roads and control."[253]
In Rachel Mairs's words (summarizing Andrew Wallace-Hadrill),
"Rome's Hellenization is important in understanding the Romanization process in the western provinces, where Greek culture, imported
from the Greek East to the Roman center, was reconstituted and re-
imported to the provinces as an essential part of the Romanization
'package.'"[254]

The civilization of the Roman Empire was, then, "dual"—
Hellenic and Latin/Roman—as opposed to "composite."[255] Fur-

thermore, there was a profound asymmetry between them as the dominant direction of cultural change was from Greece to Rome.[256] However, the parallel processes of Hellenization and Romanization did not necessarily represent inclusivity and cosmo-politanism. These cultural processes were "ultimately imperial-ist."[257] While Rome may have adopted the older and venerable Greek civilization, it also destroyed the much older Punic civiliza-tion with the destruction of Carthage. Not only did the Romans "demonize the Carthaginians," but "Hannibal himself served as a bogeyman for many generations of misbehaving Roman chil-dren."[258] Similarly, only those aspects of Egyptian culture were adopted—such as ruling Egypt as a pharaoh—that allowed Rome to administer that province effectively. The Hellenization of Rome was about appropriation related to "the practical and historical suc-cess" of Rome as an imperial power.[259] While Rome's Greek sub-jects now identified themselves politically with the Roman imperium despite their erstwhile imperial role in the Hellenistic monarchies, they did so through Greek politico-cultural sym-bols.[260] By contrast, despite enthusiastic Hellenization, "Rome never became a Greek city."[261]

Not only did Rome create a "sustainable tributary economy," but the cultural Hellenization of Rome also meant that this core–periphery order was both material and ideational.[262] "The [ide-ational] goal was the imposition and performance of distinction [at the level of elites], not the forging of cultural homogeneity [throughout the empire]."[263] This cultural process was clearly Rome-centric as Hellenization was an act of imperial appropriation. It is also important to note that "Roman power . . . tended to mar-ginalize and later eliminate local languages" other than Greek.[264] As noted by Anthony Pagden, almost "no trace" remained of "any pre-Roman literature, oral or written, or any pre-Roman history of the peoples at the heart of the empire in the western Mediterranean and northwestern and central Europe. . . . The same was true of the Roman settlements in North Africa."[265] After all, it is an empire that is known by the name of the city at its center. So what were the public goods provided by the empire that ensured its relative stabil-ity over the centuries?

The Roman Core–Periphery System and
the Provision of Public Goods

There were two key structural attributes of this Rome-centric system. First, Rome's "predatory imperialism" reorganized land and labor in the Mediterranean as wealth began to flow into the city (and Italy). This process has been referred to as "one of the greatest transfers of wealth in history."[266] Not only did Rome and Italy not pay any land taxes after 167 B.C.E., but the indemnities that Rome extracted after its incessant wars "were [also] spent mostly in Italy."[267] The institution of slavery was an integral feature of the Mediterranean economy. Additionally, the confiscation of agricultural land in the defeated polities by Roman colonizers meant that "Roman citizens became the owners of large estates in the provinces and the conquering elite of the Romans gradually acquired wealth commensurate with their conquest of the Mediterranean basin."[268]

Second, this core–periphery order was linked to Rome's hegemonic alliances that can be traced back to its expansion under the early Republic. Rome imposed "permanent and unequal treaties" on its opponents beginning with the Latin League.[269] As subordinate allies, Rome's opponents not only supplied it with troops at their own cost, but also limited their relations with foreign powers other than Rome itself. Furthermore, allied troop contributions were relatively high: they supplied between half and two-thirds of all troops during the second century B.C.E.[270] As noted above, Rome's maritime allies like the Italiote Greeks, Etruscans, and Rhodians had played a significant role in the creation of the Roman *mare nostrum*. With the allies as oarsmen and the Romans as marines, "the secret to Roman success lay not so much in the maritime transformation of Roman culture but in the ability of the Romans to attach themselves to those polities and cultures that did have strong naval traditions."[271]

This core–periphery international structure became "tighter" under the Principate. Economically, the needs of the city of Rome (especially grain) and the military dictated the patterns of trade around the Mediterranean.[272] The massive standing army of nearly 300,000 soldiers and the large permanent navy were also recruited from the provinces.[273] In fact, service in the military was also a vehicle of Romanization.[274] As the subordinate polities transformed into provinces, Roman law was imposed, albeit unevenly, throughout this "ecumene," where a "collective identity" emerged at the elite level.[275] Even as "an illusion of local autonomy" was maintained in the provinces, "local institutions, cultural and religious practices, and power networks were deprived of any political significance."[276] For example, the Greeks in the eastern Mediterranean "cared little for the niceties of the Roman republican constitution" and "treated the emperor simply as a king" after incorporating him into their own traditions.[277] Similarly, while the emperor ruled Egypt as a pharaoh and relied on local temple elites, it was clear that power lay in Rome.

This Rome-centric order was supported by the infrastructure of Roman public goods: protection (which included the implicit threat of violence), suppression of piracy, and sea control as a motor to shape Mediterranean trade. However, it should be noted that the provision of these functions was deeply implicated with the Roman understanding of power and peace. "It used to be widely held that ideas exercised relatively little power in the Roman world, but fewer now believe this."[278] According to Wolfgang Spickermann, "ancient Mediterranean empires saw themselves as peacekeeping powers," and we should try and understand *Pax Romana* in these terms.[279]

The Romans had a very distinct understanding of peace. "It was the product of victorious war, something imposed on the vanquished, the product of surrender, humiliation, and the breaking of the enemy's spirit."[280] In turn, this idea of peace was associated with the idea of power that implied "supremacy as resting on" the issuing of "orders that must be obeyed."[281] In other words, this idea of power went beyond territorial control and other material resources in possession. According to Polybius, the Romans approached power in the sense that implied that others could not afford to "disobey" Rome.[282] (Polybius, the Greek historian of Rome in the Hellenistic period, had had a first-hand experience of Roman power given that he was among the mass deportees of Greek and Macedonian elites sent to Italy after the defeat of Macedonia in 167 B.C.E.)[283] Such an articulation of power and the imposition of consequent peace and protection (of allies and dependents) show Rome's attitude "to express their hegemony . . . being explored through the language of peace."[284]

Consequently, a decade after the Second Punic War, when Carthage offered to pay off its entire war indemnity to Rome that was scheduled for periodic payments over fifty years, Rome declined. "Continuous long-term payments emphasized the submission of the former enemy and gave repeated reminder of her defeat, a lesson to other powers who might be recalcitrant or belligerent."[285] Similarly, while Pompey's victory against the pirates in 67 B.C.E. is legendary, Rome had not even begun "to try to suppress piracy until the very end of the second century BC."[286] In fact, piracy in the eastern Mediterranean was at least partly a result of the disarray brought about by Roman expansion in that region in the first place.[287] Even after Pompey, there was a "lack of will" in Rome to completely eradicate piracy (although it was certainly brought under control), for it would have removed "a source of slaves."[288]

Finally, the creation of the Principate also meant that Rome had to rethink its practice of sea control because it had literally conquered all the lands surrounding the Mediterranean. *Pax*/peace was now "to be established over the expanse of empire rather than in relation to an opponent."[289] Consequently, Rome did what it had been doing for centuries: it appropriated "the Hellenistic ideas of world domination" to express the Roman *pax* "in terms of Roman *imperium* over the *orbis terrarum* and *terra marique*," or control over all land and sea.[290] The ancient Greek idea of *oikoumene* or "the inhabited world" had already been applied to the Romans by Polybius in the second century B.C.E.[291] While the Hellenistic monarchs had sought to *rule* over all land and sea, the Romans justified their conquests as bringing *pax* over all land and sea.[292] However, this Roman peace over *mare nostrum* was the result of conquest and was maintained by the presence of a permanent navy.

CHAPTER THREE

The International Order of the Classical Indian Ocean (~First–Fifteenth Centuries C.E.)

T HE TRADING SYSTEM OF the eastern Indian Ocean (or maritime Asia) emerged in the absence of a coercive hegemonic actor. Since the dominant theories of international relations hold that hegemons create international order, they are unable to account for the making and shaping of this order that thrived and survived for centuries despite the rise and fall of several Chinese dynasties as well as many Southeast Asian and Indian polities. In this chapter, we develop a theoretical account of the classical Indian Ocean over the *longue durée* to demonstrate that the stability of commerce was underwritten by the combination of the decentralized practices of the large and small actors of this system. In other words, there was no hegemonic naval power exercising sea control in this maritime world. While Chinese empires were certainly important, it was Southeast Asia's *local initiative* that played the crucial role. Furthermore, despite China's material and economic power, especially during periods of the large empires, Southeast Asian polities (with the partial exception of northern Vietnam) actively looked across the Bay of Bengal toward India for the ideas that informed the region's politico-cultural formations. We argue

73

that the classical Indian Ocean is the paradigmatic case of a nonhegemonic, decentered, and multiplex international order that challenges the dominant view that hegemons make and shape orders.

Introduction

The international order in the classical Indian Ocean was created with the active agency of the local Southeast Asian polities, along with various Indian polities (connected via the Bay of Bengal) as well as the Chinese empires/polities (which looked toward the South China Sea). This oceanic corridor between the manufacturing powers of China and India was arguably the most dynamic part of the global economy by the beginning of the Common Era (and remained so until the Industrial Revolution [~1800]).[1] Notably, no empire or hegemonic actor controlled this entire maritime expanse in the eastern Indian Ocean. It was Southeast Asia that connected the core economies of China in the east with that of India in the west (with the latter being a multicentered core), thereby playing a crucial role in the maritime Asian system (see Fig. 2).[2]

Despite asymmetries with its Asian neighbors, it was the Austronesian peoples of Southeast Asia who had pioneered the shipping routes to China and India in the prehistorical period, "and around the beginning of the Common Era, they carried goods between China and India" on Southeast Asian ships.[3] In the absence of a hegemonic navy patrolling maritime Asia, the local agency of the Southeast Asian polities was crucial in the making and shaping of this system. Consequently, Southeast Asia was hardly a periphery of the Chinese and Indian cores; it was in fact pivotal. This is especially so, because the Chinese and Indian cores did not enrich themselves through the exploitation of Southeast Asia that remained politically, economically, and culturally vibrant. As shown in this chapter, even the so-called Chinese tributary system did not result in the flow of wealth to China at the expense of others as happened in the Roman tributary system discussed in Chapter 2. The political and commercial benefits in maritime Asia were more evenly distributed. Thus configured, the classical eastern Indian Ocean (~first–fifteenth centuries) is representative of a nonhege-

Figure 2. Map of the classical eastern Indian Ocean/Southeast Asia (first–fifteenth centuries C.E.). (Produced for the authors by Oxford Cartographers)

monic and decentered international order, perhaps the paradigmatic case for such a multiplex order in the classical world.

Although Southeast Asian polities did pay "tribute" to China, it represented "ceremonial presents" that provided the political/ritual façade for trade with China.[4] It did not constitute taxation of the sort levied by Rome in the Mediterranean. While recognizing a loose form of Chinese primacy implied in such relationships, the Southeast Asian societies adopted "Indic ideologies and [socio-political] practices ... from the necessity to better control the flow of goods" to and from their own ports.[5] China's leading geopolitical position notwithstanding, it was Indic ideas that were far more influential in Southeast Asia, outweighing Sinic ideas. In other words, the Chinese tributary system was itself embedded within larger maritime Asian networks that were actively created by the Southeast Asian polities.

Southeast Asia *Indianized* by adopting and adapting "key elements of Indian religious life, arts, and language as well as law and statecraft."⁶ The Indic idea of the *mandala* ("circle") to organize their political organizations (or state-like entities) was also borrowed by the Southeast Asians. The region experienced a wave of Indianization everywhere with the partial exception of northern Vietnam where Sinic ideas held sway. However, "even there Indic elements were not insignificant" as explained subsequently.⁷ Unlike Chinese imperialism in northern Vietnam, the Indianization of Southeast Asia was a peaceful process. According to Hermann Kulke and Dietmar Rothermund, it "is one of the greatest achievements of Indian history or even the history of mankind" because "[n]one of the other great civilisations—not even the Hellenic—had been able to achieve a similar success without military conquest."⁸

The aim of this chapter is to explain the role of power and ideas in the making and shaping of the international order in the classical eastern Indian Ocean: its open, nonhegemonic, and decentered trading system, and the Indianization of Southeast Asia. This chapter emphasizes two factors. First, unlike the Roman Mediterranean, the practice of *sea control* was absent from the geopolitics of maritime Asia. The Chinese empires used the tributary system and resorted to "political manipulation" to manage this trading order at the Chinese end of this maritime world.⁹ On the other hand, even as the Southeast Asian polities depended on the sea for commerce and travel while fighting wars and engaging in acts of piracy for the control of maritime wealth, they sought the "[c]ontrol of nearby seas" or of *local* waters only, as opposed to controlling the entire long-distance maritime trade routes straddling the region and beyond.¹⁰

Since the "whole archipelago was a crossroads," there was no single politico-commercial center in Southeast Asia because "where exactly the merchants congregated was never a given conclusion, and indeed changed over time."¹¹ Consequently, the networks of connectivity fluctuated with the power of the *mandalas*, and the resultant order in maritime Asia was a function of "the accretion of decentralized choices."¹² Given this diversity of political actors that legitimated their statehood on different ideas—Southeast Asian *mandalas*, Chinese empires, Sinic Dai Viet (after 938–939), and Indic polities that interacted with Southeast Asia (and with China via Southeast Asia)—and the important role played by merchant diasporas as explained later, a multiplex order existed in Southeast Asia.

In effect, there was no single centric power or hegemonic power in the classical Indian Ocean. The safety of the sea lanes was the result of "shared management" by different actors.[13] The various Chinese polities as well as the maritime *mandalas* were motivated by different reasons to look after their local seas. The international order in this decentered world was clearly dynamic, and the intense "interpolity competition" in Southeast Asia was related to controlling the local waters for "access to foreign prestige goods," as opposed to dominating the trade routes via sea control.[14] The "seas remained open" in maritime Asia despite the absence of a maritime hegemon keeping this passage open.[15]

Second, and relatedly, as Southeast Asian polities competed, they looked toward Indic politico-cultural models, especially ideas like the *mandala* and the associated concepts of the *cakravartin* (universal/ paramount) ruler, *rajadhiraja* (the Raja of Rajas), and *maharaja* (Great King). The process by which "elements of Indian civilization penetrated Southeast Asia . . . unevenly and serendipitously, creating hybridities of endless variation" is best understood as *localization*.[16] Unlike Chinese imperial expansion in the region now corresponding with contemporary northern Vietnam that "truncated an indigenous development of a state society in the Red River delta" after 111 B.C.E., state formation that was already underway elsewhere in Southeast Asia began "gaining momentum" beginning in the first century C.E. "with the adaptation of state ideologies borrowed from India."[17]

In contrast to the Mediterranean where Hellenization was linked with colonization, hegemonic socialization, and imperial appropriation as discussed in Chapter 2, the Indianization of Southeast Asia was not backed by overseas imperialism in the Indic mold, nor did it emerge out of Indic politico-economic hegemony or state-backed religious-cultural evangelism. Furthermore, unlike Greek notions of cultural superiority or the Roman imperial perception of Greece as decadent, the Indianization of Southeast Asia "was not of much interest to the Indian mainland—neither an object of political ambition nor a source of cultural hubris."[18] This was in spite of the fact that India "loomed so large in the Southeast

Asian *imaginaire.*"[19] As observed by the seventh-century Chinese Buddhist scholar Xuanzang, "People of distant places generally designate the land they admire as India."[20] Centuries later, the *Nagara-Kertagama*, the fourteenth-century Javanese politico-cultural text, could identify only two "renowned" places in the world: Java and India.[21] Indic political models that were perceived as being universal were actively localized by the Southeast Asians.

The rest of this chapter is divided into four sections. The first section explains why the classical eastern Indian Ocean centered on modern Southeast Asia should be treated as an international system. The following section elucidates the structure of power and authority in maritime Asia by focusing on its political-strategic and political-economic interactions. Despite the presence of maritime conflict, maritime Asia was the largest trading system of the premodern global economy. The third section focuses on the Indianization of classical Southeast Asia through the *localization* of Indic politico-cultural ideas. Southeast Asia was not a mere periphery of an Indic ecumene; instead, Southeast Asia was a co-creator of this social system. The fourth and the final section focuses on the decentered order in maritime Asia and the practices of shared management in the provision of public goods that kept the trade routes open even in the absence of a hegemonic navy.

The Classical Eastern Indian Ocean as an International System

Classical Southeast Asia was a region of *mandala* polities. The *mandala* refers to the realm of authority of a ruler whose power radiated out from a center and included other such rulers who were lower in the hierarchy.[22] While being unbounded in theory, the power of the ruler nevertheless diminished with distance from the center, and eventually ceased to matter or overlapped with the edges of other powerful rulers from neighboring *mandalas*. The identity of the central realm was not fixed, and the number of subordinate rulers also varied across time and space. Consequently, *mandala* rulers "coerced as well as wooed" as they competed for followers, and the *mandalas* "expand[ed] and contract[ed] in concertina-like fashion."[23] Throughout the classical period, Southeast

Asia was literally the realm of "hundreds" of *mandalas*, and some of the larger ones were "nested amid hundreds of smaller ones."[24]

In general, historical Southeast Asia has been ignored in the IR theoretical scholarship, as discussed in the Introduction. More recently, some scholars like Hendrik Spruyt have treated classical Southeast Asia as "a distinct regional system."[25] However, Spruyt did not specifically analyze Southeast Asia as a maritime system, which is a chief focus of this study. Furthermore, even as Spruyt acknowledged the "Indianization of Southeast Asia," he did not explain how and why Southeast Asia Indianized, and gave undue primacy to religion in the making of its socio-political order. Other scholars tend to club classical Southeast Asia with East Asia—with China at the center—in a "closed" region.[26] Some have even argued that this larger region was "not in regular constant contact or cultural or social relations" with other parts of the world.[27] While Spruyt only paid cursory attention to Southeast Asia's trade connections with India and China, the region's political, commercial, and cultural links with the Indian Ocean world are completely ignored by scholars who focus on East Asia as a closed region.

By contrast, following the lead of Southeast Asian and global historians, we treat classical Southeast Asia as an "open" region.[28] The Southeast Asian states/societies evolved "in communication with adjacent Asian civilizations in India and China."[29] The peoples of maritime Southeast Asia had been trading "with India by 500 BCE and China by 400 BCE."[30] For Southeast Asian polities, "a single continuous 'sea' " linked the eastern Indian Ocean with the South China Sea.[31] Given the old Southeast Asian cliché that "the sea unites, the land divides," the geographical edges of this maritime world were literally and figuratively fluid.[32] In fact, this maritime region stretching from the South China Sea to the Bay of Bengal via contemporary Southeast Asia exhibited the full range of Buzan and Little's politico-military, politico-economic, and politico-cultural interaction processes to qualify as an international system, as discussed in Chapter 1.

Hoogervorst has argued that the cultural links between India and Southeast Asia "were preceded by centuries of commercial interaction," and that "contacts with wealthy foreign merchants, frequently from South Asia, played an important role in the process of state formation" in Southeast Asia.[33] While long-range overseas military encounters were relatively rare between the Indian sub-continent and Southeast Asia, they did occur. The south Indian Pallavas militarily intervened in Takuapa in the Thai-Malay penin-sula in the ninth century for reasons related to the diversion of maritime trade.[34] The most important known examples of Indian military campaigns in Southeast Asia were the attacks carried out by the Cholas (in 1017, 1025, and the 1070s), allegedly to retaliate against Sriwijayan interference in Chola trade with China.[35]

Southeast Asian polities also sent expeditions into South Asia. Tambralingga (Nakhon Si Thammarat) in the Thai-Malay penin-sula attacked Sri Lanka in 1247 and may have controlled its north-ern regions until 1258.[36] A triangular politico-military contest existed between polities in Sri Lanka, Burma, and the Thai-Malay peninsula between 1000 and 1200.[37] Pagan and Arakan also raided Bengal for "skilled artisanal workers" after the twelfth century.[38] What is noteworthy is that this pattern of known South–Southeast Asia military encounters dates from centuries after the beginning of Indianization (~300 C.E.). Moreover, with some exceptions like the Chola attack, they were limited to relatively low-level raids, es-pecially when compared with Roman expansion in the Mediterra-nean or even the Chinese military forays into Southeast Asia.

In 112 B.C.E., the Han emperor Wudi sent "a fleet of 200,000 marines" to Guangdong "in the powerful maritime kingdom of Nanyue" that included parts of contemporary northern/central coastal Vietnam.[39] Later, in 41–42 C.E., "a naval fleet of over 2,000 multideck warships was sent to Jiaozhi" to reoccupy northern Viet-nam, which remained in the orbit of various Chinese empires until 938–939 C.E.[40] Beyond naval warfare along the Vietnamese coast, the "first firm historical evidence for the presence of Chinese fleets in Southeast Asia and beyond comes as late as the thirteenth cen-tury."[41] While these later Chinese naval forays into Southeast Asia are subsequently discussed, it is noteworthy that the envoys of Em-peror Wudi sailed beyond Nanyue to Huangzhi/Kanchi in south-eastern India "on board Austronesian ships" despite Han China's impressive naval capabilities.[42]

Funan was probably the first Southeast Asian polity to receive Chinese envoys (from the Wu state around 240 C.E.).[43] The Chinese envoys in Funan met an envoy from the Murunda rulers of eastern

India. They questioned the Murunda envoy "in detail about the customs of India, and on their return [to China] ... they claimed to have visited or heard about more than a hundred kingdoms in the Southern Seas."[44] In the fourth century, the Linyi polity in central Vietnam presented a memorial to the Chinese Jin state "written in a foreign script, apparently Indic, the earliest reference to the use of any script in Southeast Asia."[45] That the world beyond northern Vietnam was an Indianized realm of hundreds of *mandalas* was well known to the Chinese polities from the earliest times.

Funan in the Mekong region was "the earliest true Indianised state of Southeast Asia (1st–7th centuries CE)," and the intense cultural exchange between India and Southeast Asia meant that "a package of state concepts and Indian religions (both Buddhism and Brahmanism) was adopted and adapted by Southeast Asian societies and their rulers, together with monumental and iconographic props, and last but not least, the usage of Sanskrit and writing (first for Sanskrit, soon for vernacular languages)."[46] In Majapahit in east Java, the last of the major Indianized states of Southeast Asia that survived until the 1530s, "Sanskrit poets from India were welcome guests" until the late fourteenth century, and Sanskrit inscriptions were still being composed "as late as 1447."[47]

Given the strong politico-cultural links between India and Southeast Asia in this period (~first–fifteenth centuries), Sheldon Pollock has argued that "it makes hardly more sense to distinguish between South and Southeast Asia than between north and south India, despite what present-day area studies may tell us."[48] Similarly, in terms of commercial and trading links during this period, "peninsular maritime India and Southeast Asia formed more of an integrated zone than did southern and northern India" according to Richard Smith.[49] However, commercial links with China were crucial because China was the single largest economic actor, especially during periods of the large empires: Han, Sui, Tang, Song, Yuan, and Ming. From the Bay of Bengal to the South China Sea, the classical eastern Indian Ocean can then be thought of as a "dynamic, pulsing, multi-layered, and fluid" system with Southeast Asia at its core.[50] Since a pan-Southeast Asian indigenous empire has never existed and given the absence of a hegemonic navy exercising sea control, maritime Asia had a decentered structure.

Until the Mongol-Yuan maritime invasions in the thirteenth
century, no Chinese polity had tried to politically incorporate
Southeast Asia (beyond Vietnam) or to dominate the sea routes.
After the Mongol-Yuan failure to do so, "Zheng He's expeditions
could have been the prelude . . . to control over the trade networks
of the Indian Ocean, but this did not happen."[51] As such, the absence of coercive hegemony in the eastern Indian Ocean cannot be
reduced to geography or to "the stopping power of water."[52] After
all, imperial Japan did bring all of maritime Asia under its hegemonic domination during the Second World War for approximately three years (1942–1945). It also made military forays into
the adjacent regions of India while already controlling parts of
southern and eastern China. So how did the classical Indian Ocean
trading system maintain its decentered structure?

Maritime Asia was created bottom-up by the local Southeast
Asian actors (although the role of various Indian groups, and later
the Chinese, was also important). Patterns of maritime connectivity enabled by monsoon winds had generated this eastern Indian
Ocean system, which was "an environmentally unified space."[53] According to a Chinese source from the third century C.E., Southeast
Asian ships, probably from what today is Indonesia, were more
than fifty meters long, and could carry 600–700 passengers along
with 600 tons of cargo.[54] By the eighth century C.E., they could
carry more than 1,000 people.[55] Under the Tang (~600–900 C.E.),
Chinese ships may have even ventured beyond Southeast Asia to
southern India's Malabar coast.[56] However, "it is not always clear
that those sailing in Chinese ships were necessarily Chinese."[57]
While Indian merchants also traversed these waters from the pre-
historic period, Southeast Asian players were the most important
agents of connectivity.[58] Beyond this general process of connectivity, what kinds of interactions existed in maritime Asia?

Power and Authority: Structure and Interactions
Politico-Military

The Chinese had long recognized that "the Indian Ocean and the
'southern ocean' of Southeast Asia formed a single stretch of water,
united by a single system of communications."[59] The envoys the Wu

state sent to Funan in 240 C.E., as noted above, also wanted "to view first hand the nature of [maritime] trade . . . and seemingly as well to evaluate whether conquest down the coast beyond Ton-kin would be worthwhile."[60] Conquest was ruled out, for the Chinese found no rivals (and China chose to trade with this region through the practices of the tributary system, as discussed below).[61] The Chinese thought of Southeast Asia "as a realm of 'squirming worms,' a politically unstable realm that was not generally worthy of Chinese concern."[62]

The Chinese perception of Southeast Asian polities as unstable was a "cultural judgement." After all, Southeast Asian political systems based on *mandalas* were deemed unstable only by different Sinic "standards of government."[63] Nevertheless, Chinese expansion toward Southeast Asia stopped after it became clear that "there were no threats from maritime enemies."[64] On the mainland, Dai Viet (which became independent in 938–939 C.E.) and the polities in contemporary Yunnan (Nanzhao and Dali) existed as a buffer between the Chinese empires and the rest of Southeast Asia. This is in spite of the fact that the Tang had started mass production and export of ceramics for foreign markets in the eighth to ninth centuries, and Song ships in the eleventh century even "ventured directly to Southeast Asian ports."[65] In the *longue durée*, "closer attention was paid to more distant places (such as India) than to some neighboring regions (such as Cambodia)."[66]

Although the "Southeast Asian demand for manufactured goods" had "provided an important stimulus to the economy of southeast China in the late Song period," and a Chinese navy was created in 1132, it "never operated beyond China's coastal waters."[67] The Song navy was a defensive force against the northern Mongols. By the end of the thirteenth century, Chinese polities had the largest navies in the world. The Song had an estimated 13,500 warships, while the Mongol-Yuan had 17,900 warships.[68] When the Song were finally conquered, the "decisive battle" with the Mongols was the naval battle at Yanshan in 1279.[69] By then, the Mongol-Yuan dynasty had already conquered Dali to outflank the Song in 1253. Interestingly, the Mongols bestowed the Indic title of *maharaja* upon the ruler of Dali, a *mandala* polity at the edges of the Sinic and Southeast Asian worlds.[70] The early Ming had to reconquer that region in 1382 to establish their authority.[71]

Although the Mongol-Yuan expeditions to Southeast Asia failed, the early Ming sought to outdo their Yuan predecessors. However, the Ming navy, which was also the largest in the world in the early fifteenth century, may have only had an estimated 5,500 warships.[72] Based on the size of the fleet, ship design, and ocean-going activities, Gang Deng has argued that "the climax of the Chinese sea- and ocean-going activities occurred in Song-Yuan times, not in Ming," despite "Zheng He's spectacular multiple voyages to the Indian Ocean."[73] Although Zheng He was unsuccessful in controlling the sea routes, it is clear that unlike Rome, which was at least partially motivated to look at the seas due to its rivalry with Carthage, China did not unleash its naval thrust into the south to meet any challenge posed by putative rivals, as there were none. Notably, the borders established by the Mongol-Yuan between China and Southeast Asia "have remained more or less the same to the present day."[74]

Although China did not perceive a strategic threat from the southern seas, it was still concerned about "piracy on the high seas and rivalries among the maritime kingdoms," for they could disrupt Sino–Southeast Asian commerce.[75] However, instead of attempting conquest or sea control through the deployment of a hegemonic navy, China managed its maritime interactions through the tributary system. The ideology of the tributary system emphasized "a civilizing mission" that called for the "peaceful transformation of strangers" and "the winning over of enemies" through the virtuous example of China's cultural superiority.[76] The rituals of submission associated with the tributary system were believed to confirm "the admiration for Chinese civilization."[77] Notably, the Sinocentric Chinese rulers believed that "the southern barbarians would eventually become part of the Chinese cultural realm" even as their politico-cultural moorings lay westward toward India.[78]

Nevertheless, the Chinese empires did employ a mix of "economic enticement, military intimidation, and skillful diplomacy" to attract tribute-bearing subordinates.[79] However, "the ideal policy" toward the states of the southern seas devoid of strategic threats was "control by loose reining (*chi-mi*)" and "winning their confidence through kindness (*huai-jou*)."[80] When practical considerations warranted the pursuit of other policies on occasion, the language of the tributary system was flexible enough to ensure the continuity of the virtuous Sinocentric worldview.

To begin with, it should be noted that the trading system flourished for centuries even before China acquired a large oceangoing navy during the Song under the rubric of the tributary system. After losing northern China, the Southern Song "redefined" the Sinocentric worldview to refer to the territories of this truncated empire as the embodiment of "the core values of this civilization," while continuing to record trade missions as tribute-bearers even as reliance upon maritime taxes was crucial for the state's finances, as discussed in the next section.[81]

With its "great state" ideology, the Yuan understood tribute to mean political "submission to a great power," in this Mongol version of *tiānxià*.[82] According to this concept, "there is nothing natural about the boundaries of a political territory, and . . . the goal of rulership is to enlarge the realm through conquest."[83] The Mongols literally aspired to world conquest.[84] Despite having the largest navy in the world, not only did the vast Yuan navy fail to conquer Southeast Asia, but "the naval domination of a sizeable section of the maritime routes, much less the whole, was [also] simply unobtainable."[85]

As ethnically Chinese, the early Ming tried to outdo the Mongol-Yuan through the so-called *tiānxià da yi tong* ("unifying all-under-Heaven") doctrine by bringing the entire eastern Indian Ocean world under the Sinocentric tributary system (and even sought to extend it to East Africa and the Persian Gulf).[86] Although the Zheng He naval expeditions did attempt to control and regulate maritime trade in Southeast Asia and the Indian Ocean, China's very different dependence on maritime trade (especially when compared to Rome) meant that this objective failed.[87] In any case, Zheng He had no theory of sea power.[88] Furthermore, the Zheng He "encounters" were an exception as they "differed significantly from those of previous periods and were never replicated again by any future court in China."[89]

China tried to influence this system through the practices of the tributary system: by allowing only certain foreign polities to send merchants and receiving them via the protocols of tributary relations; by identifying specific Chinese ports that they could visit; by determining the frequency of their visits; by allowing some goods to be traded (but not others); and by imposing restrictions on the prices of many of these goods.[90] However, China did not collect any customs dues, akin to Roman practices in Rhodes, in any of its Southeast Asian tributaries.

The Chinese empires had two primary goals in "managing" this system, one economic and the other ideological. First, China was less concerned with "confirming Chinese regional sovereignty over the maritime passageway" than with seeking tributary trade "to supply China's marketplace demand for Indian Ocean products, and therein increase the volume of taxable international trade taking place in China's ports."[91] Second, China sought the ideological confirmation of the Sinocentric worldview, as explained above. In other words, China never sought to rule the seas as Rome did. The Yuan expeditions were motivated by political conquest, while the Ming fleets sought "to incorporate the countries of maritime Asia within the tribute system" and "were not seeking territories to conquer or sea lanes to monopolize."[92]

Although the indigenous momentum toward state formation was crucial in Southeast Asia, "long-distance sea trade itself played a key role in stimulating political development which eventually led to the formation of states."[93] Given the importance of maritime trade for state formation and the presence of hundreds of *mandala* polities that rose and fell, commercial rivalries and warfare were endemic to classical Southeast Asia. On the mainland, the "heavily Indianized" Champa polity of central/southern Vietnam was a constant irritation to the northern/Chinese empires (but hardly an existential threat).[94] In the fifth century, Champa launched "almost annual raids" into this southernmost part of the "Chinese administration" that even saw "some southern Chinese people . . . absorbed by Champa and culturally 'barbarized.' "[95] However, Champa itself was a *mandala*, a network of "separate, even rival, polities," as opposed to a single kingdom.[96]

In addition to military tensions with the southern end of the Chinese empires, and later its intense rivalry with Dai Viet after the latter's independence, Champa was in a rivalry with Angkor. Notably, Angkor tried to expand at the expense of Champa to seek the South China Sea trade during the Song.[97] Simultaneously, Angkor also expanded toward polities in the Thai-Malay peninsula. In 1012, Angkor may even have entered into an entente with the Cholas prior to the attacks on Sriwijaya in the Strait of Melaka.[98] As such, claims of Sriwijaya's *control* of the Strait of Melaka are probably exaggerated, although it certainly exercised some form of *mandala*-like influence there. If Sriwijaya "was attempting to impose its authority over its neighbors, fragmentary references to blood, battle, and victory on several Palembang inscriptions suggest considerable resistance."[99]

Despite frequent warfare, a pan-Southeast Asian empire did not emerge, as noted earlier. This was at least partly related to the nature of the *mandala* political organization and the associated practices of warfare in classical Southeast Asia. Given the open-ended *mandala* polity, "controlling people remained more significant than policing fixed territorial boundaries."[100] The political ecology of premodern Southeast Asia, with its relatively low population density (compared to the nearby China and India), contributed to this because it made "flight rather than fighting" a distinct possibility.[101] Fleeing smaller *mandalas* dependent upon seaborne trade could (re)establish themselves in newer locales with relative ease while avoiding political domination.

Since a *mandala* required a dominant ruler as well as one or more lesser rulers, "victories rarely, if ever, led to permanent obliteration of local centers either by colonization or through the influence of centralized institutions of government."[102] In turn, this allowed the lesser rulers to overthrow the dominance of the center when the opportunity arose, while trying to create an alternate *mandala* with itself at the center. Consequently, "the object of warfare" was "to increase the available manpower, not to waste it in bloody pitched battles."[103] So even as wars were often brutal, and slavery and piracy also existed in the region, the center of a *mandala* only tried to control nearby and local waters.[104] Not surprisingly, Southeast Asian polities vigorously competed for such maritime trade.

The Southeast Asian polities also actively tried to influence the tributary system to their own advantage. In 430 C.E., the Ho-lo-tan polity of Java sent a tribute mission to China seeking "protection from afar" after complaining about attacks from neighboring polities. This Southeast Asian polity was seeking access to the Chinese market without any "trading restrictions" in its competition with others in and around Java.[105] For reasons that are not fully documented, Ho-lo-tan did not send any other tribute missions after 452 C.E. Given that China did not have any naval presence in Southeast Asia at that time, China's instructions to others, even if they were issued, were probably not always obeyed. At the same time, this example also demonstrates that most Southeast Asian polities were probably only able to control their local waters as opposed to controlling the entire sea lanes through the region, given that hundreds of such *mandala* polities existed to China's south, and because the practices of warfare also had limits in Southeast Asia, as discussed above.

Even the presence of the Chinese navy in Southeast Asian waters in later centuries did not disrupt this general pattern, whereby Southeast Asian polities sought to manipulate the tributary system to their own advantage. "In 1279, a small Mongol fleet carrying envoys who sought Javanese submission to Mongol authority was driven back by Javanese naval forces" of Kertanagara of the Singasari kingdom.[106] A few years later, Kertanagara also disfigured the faces of the Yuan envoys when they asked for submission again. In 1292–1293, the Yuan sent 1,000 ships and 20,000 soldiers along with cavalry in an expedition to Java.[107] However, they found Kertanagara dead after being defeated by the Kadiri kingdom. Meanwhile, Kertanagara's son-in-law established the Majapahit kingdom and submitted to the Mongols, only to defeat Kadiri before ousting the Mongols themselves.[108] After the rise of Majapahit, "trade was increasingly harder to control for anyone."[109] Even in the absence of *Pax Sinica*, trade flourished.

In the intervening centuries between Ho-lo-tan and Majapahit, the Sriwijaya polity may have attempted to control the trade between the Indian Ocean and the South China Sea by trying to dominate the Strait of Melaka. The Sriwijaya *mandala* entered into a tributary relationship with China, "suggesting that those who utilized Srivijaya's ports were given preferential treatment when entering Chinese ports."[110] However, it would be far-fetched to argue that Sriwijaya dominated the trade between Southeast Asia and China, for the Javanese Heling kingdom as well as Champa sent far more tribute missions to China than Sriwijaya under the Tang.[111] It is nevertheless true that Sriwijaya "used violence when necessary" in the Strait of Melaka "to make passing ships call at its harbour and pay duty."[112] However, the success of the Sriwijayan *mandala* with the port-polities of this strait "may have been linked by some kind of treaty or commercial agreements to limit competition, rather than a hegemonic system based on force."[113]

Sriwijaya's subordination to China was far from decisive to its success. Commercial motives meant that Sriwijaya also engaged in ritual diplomacy with important Southeast Asian polities like Angkor, and with the Pala (Bengal) and Chola powers across the Bay of Bengal.[114] Not only did the Sriwijayan rulers think of themselves as Buddhist *cakravartins* (or universal monarchs), a Sriwijayan ruler even referred to himself as the "King of Ocean Lands" in an embassy to China sent in 1017.[115] However, the Chola invasion of the Strait of Melaka exposed the hollowness of such claims in 1025. One of the most significant outcomes of this invasion was Chola control of the Kedah port of the Sriwijayan *mandala* at the northern end of the Strait of Melaka.[116] (The Cholas did not control the southern edges of this strait, and consequently did not control the Strait of Melaka either.)

Although Sriwijaya lost its claim (pretense?) to hegemony in the strait after 1025, "trade continued to grow."[117] In other words, even if Sriwijaya had temporarily exercised some form of control in the strait that had fostered commerce, hegemonic control over this crucial maritime waterway was not necessary to make the trading system work because maritime trade flourished both before and after the existence of Sriwijayan influence on this waterway.

Therefore, even as Chinese empires may have adopted the Sinocentric view of thinking of Sriwijaya as a vassal that was "policing the seas" on their behalf to keep the "trade routes to China open," it was in fact the "rulers inside and outside Southeast Asia" who "independently and for their own interests"[118] protected the constantly fluctuating stretches of their local seas to make the trading system run. As some locales got disturbed in Southeast Asia time and again, newer (re)connections emerged, and trade continued in this most dynamic part of the global economy. In effect, it was the combination of multitudes of local initiatives as opposed to hegemonic control of the sea routes that made the maritime Asian trading system.

Politico-Economic

Well into the Song period, the various Chinese empires played a "passive" role in China's maritime trade with the *Nanhai* (southern seas) region.[119] Despite interest in the Indian Ocean mentioned above, early China played the role of "the recipient economy, awaiting ships and goods to arrive at its shores," and "relied on foreign shipping and merchants to acquire and transport Chinese products" to the outside world.[120] Early Chinese elite believed that commercial endeavors distracted "from the activities fundamental and indispensable to the survival of the state," and also led "to a maladjusted society."[121]

However, there was always a demand for the commercial products that came from these southern seas (spices and metals), for items of religious (Buddhist) significance, and for the "rare and precious objects" from the south that "played an important part in legitimizing their [China's] status."[122] Consequently, China used the so-called tributary system to manage this commercial relationship, while keeping it under close state supervision (but only at its Chinese end). Indeed, the "tribute system paralleled, or was in symbiosis with, a network of commercial trade relations."[123] It provided a "ritualistic facade of the Chinese emperor's superiority" and became the way of acquiring "southern luxuries while avoiding the semblance of trade."[124]

This " 'passive' era of Chinese merchants came to an end" in 1090 under the Song when "the Chinese merchants began to ply the waters on their own ships," and "the government started to permit Chinese ships to depart from basically any port in China."[125] While China had now begun playing a more active role, "the firmly entrenched interests" of the other merchants "were not shaken a bit by [the] Chinese participating in shipping and marketing," as the Chinese traders continued to remain "a minor sharer" among others.[126] While Chang Pin-tsun has emphasized the role of South and West Asians in the Sino–Southeast Asian trade from the eleventh to the fourteenth centuries (especially under the Yuan), Kenneth Hall has argued that this regional trade "was in the hands of Southeast Asians and Southeast Asia–based traders."[127] Even as there was some variation over the centuries, China was just one player among many along these regional trade networks. China did not dominate this trading system despite having the world's largest economy and the world's largest navy from the Song onwards.

In practice, different Chinese empires had different motivations in looking toward the sea. In the late eighth century, the Tang may have sent a diplomatic mission "crossing the Indian Ocean to the 'Abbāsids, probably intending to contain the Tibetans with the assistance of the Arabs."[128] After the An Lushan Rebellion in the mid-eighth century, the Tang had turned toward "maritime commerce as an option to address its fiscal problems."[129] The Tang were also mass producing ceramics for foreign markets as noted above, and Guangzhou had a foreign population of 100,000–200,000 traders of West Asian, South Asian, and Southeast Asian origins.[130] As impressive as these figures are, the "fiscality of T'ang China remained rural," as only one-sixtieth of its revenue came from commerce, while the rest came from agriculture.[131]

By contrast, the Song approached maritime trade as a means to earn revenues. Maritime trade in the early years of the Southern Song contributed up to 20 percent of the state's cash revenues, increasing to 70 percent by the end of the twelfth century.[132] The Southern Song simply wanted to maintain a monopoly on commerce for generating wealth through taxation on maritime trade at specific Chinese ports, and therefore private trade was encouraged.[133] Notably, Angela Schottenhammer has characterized the Southern Song's policy as "relatively free trade."[134] Southeast Asian demand for Chinese ceramics also provided a boost to the Chinese economy at that time. Even as ethnic Chinese traders began to finance their own shipping and voyages to the southern seas during these centuries, and many even settled abroad permanently, the Southern Song did not promote their commercial interests overseas despite having the world's largest navy.

Although the Song navy was defensively oriented toward the Mongol threat from the north, it is noteworthy that Rome's overland challenges from several "barbarian tribes" (and later Parthia) did not limit its maritime exploits or diminish Rome's Mediterranean hegemony. Even as relative power favored the Song in relation to Southeast Asia, they did not venture south politico-militarily. This is noteworthy because the Chinese economy may have in fact become "poorer" on the whole due to consuming the perishable goods from the southern seas that "disappeared from circulation," while paying for them in hard currency that also left China (even as the state's revenues increased for a while).[135] As early as 965, the Song instituted laws, including executions, to prevent the drain of cash from China.[136]

This drain of money from China also happened under the Yuan, who instituted "even stricter controls on the use of precious metals in trading," and later introduced "paper currency" into the region "that increased the dependence of foreign merchants on the Chinese government."[137] Meanwhile, the Yuan were "easy on matters of trade and tribute," practiced "relatively free" private trade, and even supported "the 'open seas' (*kai hai*) policy."[138] However, they were influenced by the Mongol ideology of the great state mentioned above.

Not surprisingly, the Yuan launched "the largest naval campaigns in pre-modern world history" and tried to subdue Southeast Asia.[139] "Despite such efforts, the focus for the Qubilai thrust was still meant to be the Indian Ocean region."[140] For the Yuan, Champa was "a pivotal region for the dominance of trade between the South China Sea and the Indian Ocean," and they also sent embassies to southern India seeking submission.[141] While these campaigns failed dramatically even as they affected regional geopolitics, the Yuan naval thrust was driven by political ideology, not economics, and they did not attempt to restructure the trade patterns in Southeast Asia.[142]

In contrast to both the Southern Song and the Yuan, the early Ming regulated all trade through the formal tributary system. Their trade and diplomatic outreach "was directed toward Southeast Asia, and more importantly India, at the core of the Indian Ocean."[143] However, the Ming wanted to outdo the Yuan to bring this entire zone formally under the tributary system, and even to expand it. Consequently, they launched seven spectacular naval expeditions "to display the wealth and power" of the empire and to "spread awe" in the eastern Indian Ocean world—and, of course, to seek tribute.[144] Despite the coercion entailed in these missions, the Ming was motivated by very different objectives compared with its Song-Yuan predecessors as well as Rome.[145] In the words of Schottenhammer,

[The Ming] did not consider the exploitation of foreign wealth as a means of national enrichment, seeking to establish politico-economic circumstances and relations in foreign countries through *exclusive* exploitation, [or] through the removal of natural or human resources [and their transfer] into their own domestic value production.[146]

This does not mean that the Chinese empires were incapable of demonstrating the brutality of the Romans. For example, Southeast Asian "K'un-lun slaves" certainly existed in imperial China, although their economic role was very different from that of slaves in the Roman Empire.[147] Nevertheless, the participation of foreign lands in the formal Chinese/Ming tributary system meant that they received gifts of greater value than they had presented to the Chinese emperor, in addition to the right to trade at specific ports in China. As such, formal "tribute" with its emphasis on rare and precious gifts was very different from the "rents" extracted by the Roman Republic in the ports of subordinate polities through the management of their customs dues or as protection money, let alone from the "taxation" under the Principate. By contrast, the "Ming drew most of its revenue from the land tax and gave as little thought to taxing trade as it did to protecting it."[148]

Finally, the Ming naval expeditions were not launched to support ethnic Chinese traders in the region. In fact, the ethnic Chinese settled in Southeast Asia "frequented Ming ports as 'foreigners.' "[149] While the Chinese certainly participated in regional trade during the Song, Yuan, and the Ming, it was dominated neither by the ethnic Chinese nor by the Chinese navy/state. Regional trade remained in the hands of local merchant groups in the eastern Indian Ocean, although they were now joined by their Chinese counterparts.

On their part, the Southeast Asian *mandalas* "never came to regard trade as an end in itself" because "[w]ealth was merely an instrument of power."[150] State (trans)formation in this *mandala* world was linked to the "acquisition by local chiefs of prestige and luxury goods from trade and the redistribution of some of these amongst clients," since it "provided the basis for the exercise of economic influence and political authority in Southeast Asia."[151] The rulers of the Southeast Asian *mandalas*—the *cakravartins,* the *maharajas,* and the *rajadhirajas*—were the *primi inter pares* ("first among equals") of such redistribution networks.

Given the sheer size of China and its prestige products like silk, Southeast Asian traders "understood that the best means of access to the huge market of China was to present themselves as tribute-bringers from a barbarian kingdom, particularly one that was recognized at the Chinese court from older documents regardless of whether it represented any continuing reality."[152] This was particularly so because the Chinese court recorded all mercantile missions as diplomatic missions sent by Southeast Asian rulers who recognized the superiority of the Chinese emperor.[153] Preferential access to Chinese ports was certainly advantageous in terms of intra-Southeast Asian geopolitics, for it offered privileged access to the Chinese market. Consequently, these "tributaries" emerged as important centers for local (intra-Southeast Asian) trade between China and Southeast Asia.

However, these Chinese tributaries were Indic-style *mandala* polities. Southeast Asia's turn toward India was partly related to the fact that India was the chief producer of one of the most important prestige goods of the premodern world: cotton textiles. However, India—which was home to many large and small polities, not unlike Southeast Asia itself—was hardly a political or economic hegemon. Stephen Dale has argued that the so-called Silk Road was a "Cotton Road" in the "reverse direction."[154] According to John Guy, "there is evidence" that India's textile trade with Southeast Asia "was established practice by at least the first century AD, when Indian merchants were establishing themselves in the region."[155]

Furthermore, India and the Indianized states of Southeast Asia "sold cotton cloth to China at an early date in the Christian Era, and . . . certain kinds of Indian cotton cloth continued to be sold in China well after the Chinese cultivation of cotton and production of cotton cloth blossomed in the late thirteenth and early fourteenth centuries."[156] Indeed, the Javanese Ho-lo-tan's embassy to China in 430 C.E. mentioned above included Indian cotton cloth.[157] Although the Southeast Asian polities competed vigorously for trade in the eastern Indian Ocean, this commercial exchange occurred in the absence of *Pax Sinica* or a hegemonic navy exercising sea control. While China resorted to the practices of the tributary system to manage the trading system, the Southeast Asian polities turned toward Indic political ideas. How can we explain this process of cultural transformation?

The Flow of Ideas: Indianization and Localization (First–Fifteenth Centuries C.E.)

The Indianization of Southeast Asia—the extensive diffusion of Indian culture and ideas which had a profound and transformative impact on the culture, society, and politics of classical Southeast Asia—and the term "Indianization" have been intensely debated over the past century or so.[158] The "externalist" paradigm stressed the civilizing influence of Indian culture on the primitive societies of Southeast Asia and gave primacy to Indian agency through colonization and the establishment of Indian colonies. Such ideas were championed by colonial European orientalists and the nationalist Indian advocates of the Greater India Society, all of whom were steeped in imperialist thinking related to the civilizational influence of dominant cultures on lesser cultures.[159] In reaction to this paradigm, and in parallel with growing recognition of Southeast Asia as a coherent region in the postwar period, Southeast Asianist scholars championed the "autonomous" paradigm. One of the most extreme cases of this view was J. C. van Leur, who emphasized Southeast Asia's civilizational indigenism and dismissed the Indian "world religions and foreign cultural forms" as "a thin flaking glaze" under which Southeast Asia's "old indigenous forms" continued to exist.[160]

Recent scholarship has dismissed both these extreme positions. To begin with, Pollock has noted that "a stable singularity called 'Indian culture,' so often conjured up by Southeast Asian indigenists, never existed."[161] Furthermore, there were no ancient Indian colonies in Southeast Asia. Although the spread of Indian culture to Southeast Asia happened via overlapping politico-religious and commercial networks, most Indians in Southeast Asia were sojourners over this millennium (even as occasional/individual migration may have certainly occurred during these centuries). While there is some archaeological data for early Indian settlements in Khao Sam Kaeo on the Thai-Malay peninsula in the

fourth century B.C.E., the first "written evidence" of semi-perma-
nent Indian communities in Southeast Asia dates only from 1088
(with this reference related to Barus in Sumatra).[162]

In the future, population genetics may revise our views on
these movements. For example, the foundation story of Funan
based on the marriage between an Indian brahmin and a local
princess may be rooted in Indian migration to Southeast Asia.[163]
However, most admixture between Indian and Southeast Asian
populations occurred in the past 500–1,000 years, centuries after
the beginning of the Indianization process according to current
genetic evidence.[164] As per current sociological evidence, it is unlikely that there was any large-scale Indian immigration to Southeast Asia, especially one backed by Indic polities during these
centuries (~first–fifteenth centuries).

Furthermore, it was the Southeast Asians who actively borrowed Indic ideas to bring administrative and ideological "coherence" to the rising "Southeast Asian Buddhist and Brahmanical
states."[165] However, active Southeast Asian agency should not imply
a passive Indian role on the maritime circuits of the Indian Ocean.
Since Indic state ideologies took multiple forms—Hindu (both
Saivite and Vaisnavite) and Buddhist—the Indic agency came in the
form of the persuasive powers of enterprising entrepreneurs who
advocated specific Indic traditions that could be adapted to meet
local needs. However, it was Southeast Asia that attracted such Indic
agents of persuasion, or the Southeast Asians may have themselves
visited India in search of suitable models. This process of transculturation was not rooted in Indian imperialism, whether military,
economic, or cultural. The possible exception here is the Cholas,
who may have promoted Hinduism in Kedah, although this process,
like the Chola invasions, occurred centuries after the beginning of
Indianization. The Chola promotion of Hinduism was also highly
circumscribed in its geographic scope in Southeast Asia.[166]

Like the externalist view, the autonomous paradigm has also
been challenged. O. W. Wolters had already warned decades ago
that "broad generalizations about a 'Southeast Asian' culture should
be avoided" because they risked essentializing the region.[167] More
recently, Victor Lieberman has argued that "states and cultures
arose much earlier" in India and "provided a civilizational tem-

plate" for Southeast Asia, "which looked towards India for cultural and political models."[168] Furthermore, archaeological evidence indicates that contacts between India and Southeast Asia began in the second half of the second millennium B.C.E., and that from the mid-first millennium B.C.E. these contacts were "sustained" as opposed to "intermittent."[169] In other words, by the time of the Indianization of Southeast Asia in the early first millennium C.E., economic and cultural contacts had led to sustained interactions and "familiarization" across the Bay of Bengal over many centuries.[170]

However, advanced agriculture, metallurgy, seafaring, maritime trade, and urbanism already existed in Southeast Asia when the wave of Indianization began.[171] Therefore, not only is the prior characterization of Southeast Asia as a primitive region before the impact of Indian civilization erroneous, but the centuries-long familiarization across the Bay of Bengal also demonstrates that this transculturation was "an act of pure free will" on the part of Southeast Asia.[172] As a consequence, the Southeast Asians "did not become Indians. They became new versions of themselves."[173] Used thus, the term *Indianization* can now be used "without hesitation" to refer to "the period after the 4th century," when "advanced states were formed [in Southeast Asia] on the basis of an Indian model under the influence of Buddhism or Hinduism."[174]

Given this understanding, two new models have emerged to explain the Indianization of Southeast Asia—Pollock's "Sanskrit cosmopolis" and Kulke's "convergence theory." For Pollock, the Sanskrit cosmopolis was a "quasi-global formation" that included "all of South and much of Southeast Asia" for a millennium, where a common cosmopolitan order existed that made "similar claims about the nature and aesthetics of political rule: about kingly virtue and learning, the *dharma* [ethics] of governance, and a peculiar universality of dominion in a world of plural universalities."[175] In this cosmopolitan realm, the Sanskrit language was used to represent the aesthetics of political power in a common idiom, while vernacular/local languages were used for the mundane tasks of governance. On the other hand, Kulke has argued that the socio-economic and political "convergence" on both sides of the Bay of Bengal "required and enabled similar solutions to similar problems of social change," and therefore it was the "social nearness" between India

and Southeast Asia that promoted this social change "under, un-
doubtedly, Indian influence in Southeast Asia."[176] Indianization was,
then, a parallel and simultaneous process on both sides of the Bay
of Bengal.

While both these models are the leading explanations of the
Indianization of Southeast Asia at present, they are not without
shortcomings. Pollock's model has been criticized for being top-
down (or an elite-driven process), while recent scholarship has also
emphasized the role of artisans and shipmasters as opposed to the
political/commercial and religious elite, who were the carriers of
the high culture.[177] Similarly, an excessive emphasis on Sanskrit de-
tracts from the influence of Pali (used by the Theravada Bud-
dhists), Prakrit (the language of the common folk in north/central
India), and Tamil (spoken in south India), for these languages also
influenced Southeast Asia.[178] Most important, Daud Ali has critiqued Pollock for an excessive focus on the Sanskrit literary
aspects of Indianization while ignoring the processes of state
(trans)formation in Southeast Asia.[179]

In turn, even as Kulke's theory is precisely about the processes
of state (trans)formation, he did not explain how the common cultural substratum on both sides of the Bay of Bengal emerged in the
first place. In fact, Pierre-Yves Manguin has even asked if Southeast Asia "Indianised before Indianisation," since Southeast Asia's
contacts with India predate Indianization by centuries.[180] However,
it is also possible that processes of cultural exchange were underway across the Bay of Bengal much earlier because there are hints
of "Austronesian settlements in India during the first millennium
BCE."[181] Furthermore, there were different degrees of Indianization across time and space in different parts of Southeast Asia during the first fifteen centuries of the Common Era.[182] Nevertheless,
it has been observed that Kulke's convergence theory "provides a
sociological complement" to Pollock's Sanskrit cosmopolis.[183]

While an argument that integrates both these models is still
awaited, especially one that can explain the variance in time and
space across this vast realm, it is noteworthy that both Pollock and
Kulke have emphasized the process of localization in Southeast
Asia. Localization is a process of "idea transmission" in which borrowed foreign ideas are made local (through discourse, framing,

grafting, and cultural selection) to make them congruent with local beliefs, while simultaneously changing the locals' identity and behavior.[184] Kulke has explicitly noted that his convergence theory "tries to explain the spread of Indian culture and its congenial acceptance and localization in Southeast Asia."[185] Similarly, Pollock has noted that this process of transculturation involved "a thoroughgoing reconstitution of the cognitive landscape" through "wholesale toponymic transformation" in Southeast Asia that reproduced the names of prominent Indic kingdoms, rulers, and natural features locally.[186] This allowed Southeast Asia to "be in the Sanskrit cosmopolis and simultaneously remain at home."[187]

The Southeast Asians actively localized Indic ideas. Not only did the Southeast Asians pioneer the shipping routes to India and then continue to play an active role in the process of cultural transmission as the shipmasters in the process of connectivity, it was the Southeast Asian rulers who had "summoned" Indian brahmins to their courts to legitimize their rule.[188] While some Indian brahmins may have been present in Southeast Asian capitals, it has recently been suggested that most brahmins in Southeast Asia were in fact Indianized Southeast Asians (as opposed to Indians) who had studied at the religious centers in India (or with Indian brahmins in Southeast Asia).[189] Furthermore, "Southeast Asian patterns of rulership never shifted to unconditional Brahmin primacy," as happened in India itself during the second half of the first millennium, when Buddhism remained politically prominent in Southeast Asia (and eventually predominated).[190] In contrast to India, where Buddhism did encounter Brahmanical violence, there is "no record of violence between adherents of Hinduism and Buddhism" in Southeast Asia.[191]

Nevertheless, Southeast Asia itself changed in this process of Indianization. To begin with, monarchs with Indic names began appearing in the Southeast Asian *mandalas*. The oldest known Sanskrit inscription in maritime Southeast Asia is that of King Mulavarman of eastern Kalimantan from the early fifth century. Not only is Mulavarman an Indic name, but the inscription also gives the name of his father, King Asvavarman, also an Indic name, and that of his grandfather, King Kundunga, probably a local name.[192] While the inscription talks about gifts to brahmins, it also refers to "traditional

Austronesian practices ... in the guise of Sanskrit terms," thereby demonstrating the localization process.[193] Elsewhere, the Champa polity invoked Campā from the Sanskrit politico-religious text, the *Mahabharata*, while Thai Dvaravati reproduced Dvārakā from the same text.[194] Meanwhile, the Siem Reap was known to the Khmer as the holy river Ganges, while the Khmer rulers with Indic names styled themselves as *cakravartin* rulers.[195]

The Indianized kings of these Southeast Asian polities funded the construction of monumental Hindu-Buddhist architecture, including Angkor Wat (the largest religious/Hindu structure in the world) and Borobudur (the largest Buddhist temple). However, "these places may in fact have been seen by their inhabitants not as Annam or Laos or Sumatra but as existing inside a Bhāratavarsa [India]."[196] In other words, these Southeast Asian holy places were not "surrogates" of some authentic "India" but "an extension of the same landscape."[197] The "India" they were living inside was the ideal politico-cultural realm of Sanskrit/Indic literature as opposed to an actual polity. The Chinese Buddhist monk Xuanzang and the Javanese text *Nagara-Kertagama* mentioned above were probably referring to this ideational India (as opposed to an actual polity in the Indian subcontinent).

While taking inspiration from the Sanskrit politico-cultural literature and legal texts, the Southeast Asians localized these Indic codes.[198] Such toponymic mimicry and localization of the politico-cultural literature was happening on both sides of the Bay of Bengal (or in India itself), as explained by Kulke. Importantly, these processes were near-simultaneous. It was King Rudradaman's Junagarh rock inscription of 150 C.E. in Gujarat that heralded the beginning of the Sanskrit cosmopolis as it marked "a true break in cultural history" by using a sacral language for political purposes for the first time "in a public space."[199] Meanwhile, the first Sanskrit inscription from outside the subcontinent, the Cham inscription of Vo Canh, near contemporary Nha Trang, "has been dated between the second and fourth centuries."[200] Not only was this inscription more or less contemporary with the appearance of such inscriptions throughout the subcontinent, it was also "at least as advanced linguistically and stylistically as the contemporary epigraphs within India."[201] Moreover, it has "nothing whatsoever to do

with India. Rather, it refers to the gift, or tribute, of white ele-
phants offered by the [Cham] king to the Chinese court."[202]

So even as Southeast Asia changed, "the cultures of Java and
Cambodia were not hybrid"; instead, the Southeast Asians "retained their distinctive character" as they were changing to conform to local needs.[203] Not surprisingly, certain aspects of Indian
culture that did not resonate with the locals, such as the brahmanical vision of a caste society, were never adopted in Southeast Asia.
Elsewhere, the spread of Indic ideas amplified the local in Southeast Asia. For example, in fifth-to-sixth-century Funan, the cult of
Siva was used to "unify local deities" as the Khmer rulers tried to
exert political authority over their expanding territorial realm by
incorporating local gods. The cloaking of the local in "Indian garb"
meant "exalting the old while revering the new," and therefore In-
dianizing while remaining Khmer.[204]

Additionally, *relocalization* was another characteristic of this Indianized world. This is probably most clearly visible in the prolifer-
ation of India-derived scripts across the region. The origins of the
Burmese, Thai, Lao, Khmer, and old Javanese scripts can be traced
back to the Indic Brahmi script. However, by the eighth century
Sanskrit, "the one self-same cosmopolitan language, undeviating in
its literary incarnation, was being written in a range of alphabets almost totally distinct from each other and indecipherable without
specialized study."[205] In other words, different Southeast Asians relocalized the same aspect of Indian culture at different times in different places according to local sensibilities. The other important
dimension of this relocalization process is the fact that the vector of
ideational flow did not always run from India to Southeast Asia.
Some Southeast Asian polities, such as Dvaravati in eastern Thailand, borrowed and *relocalized* some politico-cultural ideas from the
Indianized Khmer (and not directly from India).[206]

Finally, Southeast Asia was not a cultural periphery of India, as
ideas *circulated* from this Indianized world back to India itself. For example, the imperial cult of the Cholas of southern India "centered on
their massive temples," and their "great tank at Gangaikodachola-
puram" was influenced by the practices at Angkor.[207] At the same
time, it should be noted that the Indianized kingdoms of Southeast
Asia were *centers* in their own right, given that their political statehood

was expressed in the same politico-cultural idiom as in India itself, and because all of them sought to replicate ideal Indic-style polities. Not surprisingly, Indian Buddhist masters like Atiśa went to study with Southeast Asian Buddhist masters like Dharmakīrti in the tenth century, and Indian Buddhist pilgrims traveled to Prambanan in central Java to worship at a Buddhist temple there in the ninth century.[208]

Nevertheless, there was a degree of asymmetry in the India–Southeast Asia relationship. While the process of politico-cultural convergence "was almost simultaneous from one shore of the Bay of Bengal to the other—within one or two generations (to the advantage, of course, of the Indian Subcontinent)," it is not known if any Indian rulers expressed their politico-cultural ideas in any Southeast Asian language or invoked Southeast Asian gods to mark their statehood.[209] Although this asymmetry is an important factor in the academic study of India's interaction with Southeast Asia over the *longue durée*, it should not be overlooked that the cultural circulation noted above meant that the politico-cultural order at any given point in time during these centuries was decentered.

While no Indian polity "pretend[ed] to universal rule in Southeast Asia" specifically, all the major and minor rulers of India and Indianized Southeast Asia had universal aspirations in general in the form of the *cakravartin* ruler.[210] This geo-cultural space was, then, an anarchy of *mandalas* where every polity aspired to centrality, even as the norms limiting warfare/coercion and the practices of attracting subordinates were widely diffused. Every *cakravartin* ruler tried to produce such centrality through the creation of ideal Indic political realms. These Indic/Indianized *cakravartins* coexisted with the Chinese "Son of Heaven" in a decentered world where every ruler thought of himself as the central actor. While all aspired to universality, they were masters only of their finite locales even as they varied in size.

In this world of multiple universal centralities, all aspirational, there is no reason to give centrality to Chinese empires. Given that prominent Chinese Buddhist monks like Yijing studied in Sriwijaya in the seventh century, David Henley has argued that, official Chinese rhetoric notwithstanding, the Chinese approached Southeast Asia and India "not as bearers of what they regarded as superior civilization, but as seekers of sacred knowledge."[211] At the same time, there is also no need to give centrality to the Indian/subcontinental polities over Indianized Southeast Asian polities at any given point in time. After all, India itself was a decentered politico-cultural realm, especially after the collapse of the Gupta empire (~320–500 C.E.), which did not rule all of the subcontinent in any case. Furthermore, different parts of Southeast Asia borrowed different aspects of Indic culture from multiple centers in India: South India, Bengal, Gujarat, the Gangetic plains, and so on.[212] There was no monolithic Indian culture emanating from a single point of origin over these centuries, let alone a political process of Indianization backed by a subcontinental polity.

Furthermore, there were periods when Southeast Asian polities were politically and culturally at least as sophisticated as, if not more sophisticated than, their Indian (and Chinese) counterparts. For example, at the beginning of the thirteenth century, Angkor, the capital of the Khmer *mandala*, was "probably the largest city on earth outside China" according to Peter Sharrock.[213] However, others believe that Angkor was the largest city in the world before the Industrial Revolution.[214] Similarly, even as "the largest Chola temples were five times the size of anything that preceded them," the Khmer temples "dwarf[ed] their Indian contemporaries."[215] If anything, the politico-cultural order in this Indianized world then represented "peer-polity interactions" among multiple *cakravartins* who practiced cultural pluralism in a realm with multiple religions and languages where none of the boundaries, including political, were absolute.[216]

While most of Southeast Asia Indianized during this period, northern Vietnam was *Sinicized* through a very different politico-cultural process. Northern Vietnam was transformed through *hegemonic socialization* by imperial China, and it "constituted a colony of the Chinese empire for nearly one thousand years under the Han, Sui, Tang, and intervening dynasties."[217] The "Chinese wanted to assimilate the Vietnamese and instill Chinese values, customs, and institutions."[218] Even then, Sinicization was countered by Indianization in northern Vietnam despite the absence of Indic/subcontinental imperialism in Southeast Asia.

Initially, the Austroasiatic (Mon-Khmer) people of Linyi emerged "as an 'independent' polity in ... the southernmost district of the Eastern Han Empire," and then underwent "self-Indianization" between the fourth and seventh centuries, before intermixing with the Indianized Austronesians of Champa to their south.[219] As mentioned earlier, the Chinese empires had a troubled relationship with Champa. Champa fought in these locales while also engaging in cultural exchanges. Consequently, "[e]ven during the Chinese period, Indic/Southeast Asian influences had counteracted the Sinicizing pressures to some extent."[220]

After the advent of an independent Dai Viet in the tenth century, the northern Vietnamese state emulated Chinese state rituals and institutions. Therefore, "it was apparently not uncommon [in the early centuries after independence] for southern Chinese to emigrate to Vietnam and enter government service there" because "the two monarchies [China and Dai Viet] were interchangeable enough."[221] However, "the mandala concept [also] applies to Vietnam (Dai Viet) in the early centuries."[222] Even "while establishing itself as a Sinic patrilineal line, the ruling Ly [dynasty of Dai Viet] also in 1057 began their own royal cults to Indra (De Thich) and Brahma (Phan Vuong)," "consciously called up their direct links to India," and invoked the Mauryan-Indian Buddhist emperor Aśoka (~268–232 B.C.E.), who was regarded as the ideal *cakravartin*.[223]

In the meantime, the Song (in 1075–1076), the Yuan (in 1250 and again in 1278), and the early Ming (in 1406–1427) tried to reconquer Dai Viet but failed. At the same time, the rivalry between the Dai Viet and Champa for maritime trade continued. There was a tense geopolitical equilibrium between Dai Viet and Champa, and the Cham came close to destroying Dai Viet toward the end of the fourteenth century (~1360–1390).[224] In 1415, when Dai Viet was under Ming occupation, a period that coincided with Zheng He's maritime voyages, the Cham ruler Virabhadravarman performed his consecration (*abhiseka*) ritual, and "re-established Vijaya [Champa] at the centre of a thriving Indic domain . . . marking the new age in Indic terms."[225] It was only following its bureaucratic reorganization after the end of Ming occupation that the re-Sinicized Dai Viet, now supported by the newly reestablished Confucian ideology, was finally able to defeat Champa decisively in 1471 through the use of Chinese-style firepower.[226] Throughout the classical period, imperial China's politico-cultural influence beyond northern Vietnam was "negligible," although Southeast Asia actively localized Indic culture in the absence of imperialism and coercion.[227]

The combination of the practices entailed in the Chinese tributary system and the Indianization of Southeast Asia produced a decentered order in maritime Asia. Given their different ideational world and commercial links across the Indian Ocean, the Southeast Asian polities were hardly the peripheries of a Chinese center despite the rhetoric of the Sinocentric court (and the texts that it produced). If anything, it was the Chinese tributary system that was just one component of a larger, decentered Asia. Imbued with their Indianized worldview, the *mandala* polities of maritime Asia actively managed their trade relations with China to collectively produce the public goods of this trading system.

The Decentered World of the Eastern Indian Ocean and the Provision of Public Goods

A dynamic and interactionist multiplex order existed in the classical eastern Indian Ocean. This regional order was not the product of superior Chinese imperial/material power, or some essentialist version of the tributary system. Nor did Indic ideas spread "naturally" into an ideational vacuum in Southeast Asia. This order was in fact an outcome of Southeast Asia's active agency in fostering connectivity with Chinese and Indian polities, and the consequent material and ideational interactions that ensued. The multiplex order in the eastern Indian Ocean was a highly robust and resilient order that lasted for centuries even in the absence of a grand design. It did not depend exclusively on any single polity, not even imperial China. Although the rise and fall of Chinese empires may have changed the modes of interaction with China (at the Chinese end of the system), the maritime interactions across this vast space continued. As one local *mandala* disappeared, another assumed its nodal position in this interactive and interconnected world.

It was the underlying ideational factors that made this order sticky and long-lasting. According to Hedley Bull, all international orders have a purpose or goals that sustain the pattern of interactions, as discussed in Chapter 1. A shared normative understanding of order had historically emerged in the classical eastern Indian

Ocean that was supportive of the twin goals of making the trading system run while maintaining distinct politico-cultural identities. These norms were embedded in both—the ways in which the *mandala* states sought to manage their politico-military and politico-economic relations, and the rules that governed their trade and cultural intercourse.

Furthermore, while wars were hardly absent in the classical eastern Indian Ocean, they were not system-destroying. As explained above, the very nature of the *mandala* polities put limits on warfare, and bureaucratic and territorial incorporation of the defeated polity was not the dominant practice. Although motivated by entirely different interests and ideologies, even the large-scale naval expeditions by imperial Chinese polities and the Cholas did not destroy the system, although they did change the fate of some *mandalas*. While inter-*mandala* warfare and the Chinese/Chola expeditions were governed by different logics, their combined effect was to ensure the twin systemic goals of continued maritime trade and the maintenance of the distinct politico-cultural identities of the regional polities, thus ensuring what Karl Deutsch and David Singer termed systemic "stability," as discussed in Chapter 1.

In the absence of a hegemonic navy or the practices of sea control, the decentered world of maritime Asia was based on the shared management of this trading system. The different actors in this maritime world pursued multitudes of practices out of their own self-interest. These practices were tantamount to the "rules" governing this trading world. China provided access to its large market while injecting prestige commodities like silk textiles by manipulating the rituals of the tributary system. The Southeast Asians actively connected maritime Asia even as they vigorously competed. The eastward-oriented Indic polities also injected important goods like cotton textiles, while Indian merchants joined their Southeast Asian counterparts along these networks. Later, the addition of Chinese traders in maritime Asia beginning with the Song happened in the absence of coercion, and they coexisted alongside preexisting traders. The multiplex order of this trading system emerged from the interaction of all these decentralized practices, which were undertaken by different polities in the pursuit of different functional and social needs.

Although China did exercise a loose form of primacy through the tributary rituals, it did not play a hegemonic role. First, there was no hegemonic peace or *Pax Sinica* in this maritime world, as indicated by the examples of warfare mentioned above. In fact, several wars were initiated by different Chinese empires themselves. In the absence of a Chinese navy in Southeast Asia prior to the Yuan, the Chinese empires attempted to manage regional security only rhetorically. For example, not only was Champa a continual menace for the Chinese empires to their south, but China also sought to discipline Champa in 1167 through "refusal to accept tribute from the Cham court" instead of eradicating Cham "piracy."[228] Later, even though the Ming had a powerful navy, China only made a partial attempt to eradicate Asian piracy. While the Ming navy did suppress piracy by destroying Chen Zuyi's fleets in Palembang in 1407, the returning fleet in 1417 encountered Japanese piracy on the Chinese coast.[229] Ultimately, it was local actors like Sriwijaya that tried to control piracy in their own local waters.[230] Security of trade in maritime Asia emerged out of the accretion of such individual efforts. No single naval power controlled the maritime routes stretching from the South China Sea into the Bay of Bengal.

Second, China was not *the* economic center of this trading system. As mentioned earlier, India itself was a multicentered core. Furthermore, Southeast Asia was not an economic periphery of these cores. In fact, Southeast Asia played the pivotal role of connecting maritime Asia with its traders and ships. After China started manufacturing oceangoing vessels under the Song, the Chinese built upon the shipping techniques of the Southeast Asians, and these hybrid Sino-Southeast Asian ships then continued to sail these waters along with local Southeast Asian ships.[231] Additionally, Southeast Asia injected its own commodities into the system (spices and metals).

These Southeast Asian products did not constitute the raw materials for the manufacturing industries of the Chinese and Indian cores. The Southeast Asian demand for Chinese goods was also crucial, and it even provided an important stimulus for the Song, as noted above. More important, maritime Asian resources did not flow into China at the expense of the region. In fact, some Chinese empires became poorer with the outflow of cash into Southeast Asia. The benefits of the Chinese tributary system were more equitable because it was simply one part of a wider maritime commercial network in the eastern Indian Ocean. By contrast, given the direction of the flow of revenue and the very different meaning of tribute there, it was in the Rome-centric Mediterranean that a "tributary" economy actually existed.

Third and finally, maritime Asia did not fall under China's cultural domination. According to Charles Kupchan, hegemonic powers "seek to extend to their expanding spheres of influence the norms that provide order within their own polities."[232] While the Mediterranean did Hellenize/Romanize, as explained in Chapter 2, China made "no attempts to Sinicize" Southeast Asia.[233] Given its own unique history, northern Vietnam did Sinicize. Outside of northern Vietnam, no polity in Southeast Asia emulated China's domestic political model. Throughout this truly decentered region, it was Indic ideas that spread through the process of localization (as opposed to Indic imperialism). In sum, despite power asymmetry with China and the spread of Indic politico-cultural ideas, it was Southeast Asia's active *local initiative* in the security, economic, and ideational realms that collectively produced a nonhegemonic international order through the shared management of maritime Asia.

CHAPTER FOUR

The Rise of the Indo-Pacific and the Return of Geopolitics

T HE RISE OF CHINA and the growing rivalry between China and the United States have increased the importance of maritime Asia. However, given the strong association between hegemony and international order drawn from the Roman Mediterranean, this rivalry is widely perceived as a clash between competing hegemonies. But the idea of a pluralist and decentered order developed in this book better captures the emerging geopolitical configuration in the Indo-Pacific. As explained in this chapter, where we extrapolate our findings from the previous chapter on the classical eastern Indian Ocean, the local initiative of the Southeast Asian states (individually and collectively) is actively shaping the regional order along with the regional norms rooted in the so-called ASEAN [Association of Southeast Asian Nations] Way that are also being extended into the Indo-Pacific. In turn, these norms are influencing and conditioning politico-military and politico-economic interactions across this vast space, thereby playing a formative role in the making of the international order in the Indo-Pacific. Southeast Asian states reject hegemony and are coengaging the United States, China, and other consequential players like India and Japan. Although motivated by different reasons, all these powers are collectively producing the public goods of trade and security through the shared management of maritime Asia. We argue that the future of the Indo-Pacific has resonances with the nonhegemonic classical Indian Ocean, where multitudes of local initiatives are collectively producing an open and multiplex order.

The Indo-Pacific

According to Aaron Friedberg, the Indo-Pacific region connecting the Pacific and the Indian Oceans "is the central front" of the ongoing Sino-American contest, which "is likely to be a protracted military rivalry."[1] Indeed, the United States recognizes the Indo-Pacific "as the world's center of gravity."[2] Similarly, leading Chinese scholars like Wang Jisi have also observed that the world's "economic and political center of gravity" has been shifting to "the Asian mainland and the regions where the Indian and Pacific Oceans merge."[3] Not surprisingly, China is modernizing its navy for contingencies "in the two oceans region . . . the western Pacific Ocean and northern Indian Ocean," even as China does not use the Indo-Pacific nomenclature.[4] Importantly, this oceanic space corresponds with the eastern Indian Ocean discussed in Chapter 3.

Not surprisingly, the emerging regional order in the Indo-Pacific has become the subject of a major debate. There are two important views regarding the emerging order in the Indo-Pacific because of this looming Sino-American contest. First, invoking the so-called Thucydides Trap, named after the ancient Greek historian, Graham Allison is of the view that China's rise is "undercutting America's status as a global hegemon." While Allison does not argue that war is inevitable, he sees considerable potential for it. Although the idea of the Thucydides Trap and the associated power transition paradigm have been widely critiqued, "they continue to dominate popular and academic discussions."[5]

The U.S. Department of Defense is fearful that a rising China is seeking "Indo-Pacific regional hegemony," as China wishes to "reorder the [Indo-Pacific] region."[6] While the United States is believed to have heretofore held the "command of the sea" that has underwritten "world trade," some scholars argue that the United

States and China are now in a contest for "maritime dominance" in the Indo-Pacific.[7] After all, China overtook the United States as the world's largest trading nation in 2013, displacing the United States from the top position it had held since the end of the Second World War.[8]

The second view posits an ASEAN-centered Indo-Pacific region led by the Association of Southeast Asian Nations. Indeed, the ASEAN Outlook on the Indo-Pacific (AOIP) envisions an "ASEAN-centered" region, whereby its "central role" shapes the economic and security architecture, and promotes peace and prosperity in the Indo-Pacific.[9] All the major powers of this region have endorsed ASEAN-centrality, at least rhetorically. ASEAN-led institutions such as the East Asia Summit (EAS), the ASEAN Regional Forum (ARF), and the ASEAN Defence Ministers' Meeting-Plus (ADMM-Plus) are expected to provide the mechanisms to manage regional issues in the Indo-Pacific.

However, the idea of ASEAN-centrality—though always tenuous and perhaps even mythical—has come under challenge in recent years by the Quad grouping of the United States, Japan, Australia, and India.[10] The Quad is an important component of the American strategic response to the rise of China. Consequently, Sino-American rivalry has led ASEAN to search for ways to redefine its centrality.[11] Nevertheless, given ASEAN's vulnerabilities to great power politics, it has also been suggested that ASEAN unity and neutrality may be more important than centrality.[12] Therefore, ASEAN must "downsize" to focus on issues within Southeast Asia rather than striving for centrality in the Indo-Pacific.[13]

We reject the notions of a Thucydidean power transition and that of ASEAN-centrality in this chapter. A hegemonic power transition is not in the making in the Indo-Pacific. Therefore, no hegemonic naval power exercising sea control is likely to emerge in the region. The belief that a hegemonic naval power that keeps the sea routes open is necessary for a maritime trading system is based on a generalization drawn from Roman history. However, it has no basis in maritime Asia.[14] At the same time, even as ASEAN-led mechanisms will have some role to play in the regional architecture, ASEAN will hardly be central. In fact, a decentered and multiplex system is in the making in the Indo-Pacific. Order in this region, especially the provision of public goods for the safety of the all-important sea lanes, will emerge from the accretion of the local initiatives of several actors, large and small, individually and collectively. As in the classical eastern Indian Ocean discussed in Chapter 3, regional public goods also will be provided through the practices of shared management in the contemporary Indo-Pacific and not through hegemonic or great power management.

The rest of this chapter is divided into three sections. First, we address the gap between the classical Indian Ocean and the contemporary Indo-Pacific by focusing on the brief history of the period after the European intrusion into this space (post-1498). In particular, we analyze the periods of presumed British and American naval hegemonies in the nineteenth and twentieth centuries that are believed to have occurred in "succession."[15] We argue that the politico-military, politico-economic, and ideational underpinnings of British and American interactions show that maritime hegemony over the past 200 years was fleeting and tentative, especially in the Indian Ocean. If anything, Britain and the United States were the *primi inter pares* among the naval powers, but not hegemonic. Furthermore, local agency continued to matter to regional order building in the Indian Ocean.

Second, our focus on the contemporary Indo-Pacific shows the deeply interactive and mutually reinforcing politico-military and politico-economic interactions taking place across the region. More specifically, we posit that U.S.-China rivalry is not a competition of competing hegemonies but a quest for relative position and a geopolitical contest over access to this oceanic space. Third, we show that these politico-military and politico-economic interactions are being actively influenced and shaped by the regional norms embedded within the ASEAN Way, and that Southeast Asia is actively shaping the regional order.

We argue that while China has attenuated American dominance in maritime Asia, this is unlikely to result in Chinese hegemony. At the same time, renewed American hegemony is also unlikely. The absence of a hegemonic power exercising the command of the sea will not result in maritime disorder. A decentered and nonhegemonic regional order is in the making in the eastern Indian Ocean, with overlapping layers of governance at the subregional and regional levels through bilateral, minilateral, and multilateral initiatives. The eastern Indian Ocean will also be an "open" space given the (re)entry of some extraregional (European) actors.[16] Most important, we highlight the agency of the Southeast Asian states, especially for coengaging all the major powers while rejecting hegemonism.

The Indian Ocean after 1500

The period after the Portuguese entry into the Indian Ocean in 1498 is often referred to as "the Vasco da Gama era," a euphemism for an era of European dominance.[17] For example, Paul Kennedy has argued that the Europeans dominated the world for "four centuries" prior to World War I.[18] However, recent scholarship has emphasized that the "old image" of this period as the Vasco da Gama era "of a succession of hegemonic European powers controlling the early modern Indian Ocean—first the Portuguese, then the Dutch, and finally the British—is now no longer acceptable."[19] The Portuguese entry into the Indian Ocean "was not the 'break with the past' that is sometimes described," as a "multicentered or polycentric equilibrium emerged in the Indian Ocean trade," after some readjustment.[20] Not only did the Portuguese become a "part of the structure of medieval Asian trade," but the Dutch "also carried on trade much as any Asian merchant" would have done, despite the growing role of armed trade and monopolies.[21]

This was largely because the commodities of European trade such as South and Southeast Asian spices "could not be produced in Europe at all, or could only be produced there with considerable difficulty."[22] More important, China and India remained the manufacturing powerhouses for centuries prior to the Industrial Revolution. Due to this "Sino-Indian Great Divergence," the European powers had to pay in bullion (mined from the Americas) for the silk and cotton textiles of China and India.[23] Therefore, Asian trading networks continued to remain resilient and even thrived in the centuries after 1498. According to Michael Pearson, the Europeans did not introduce "any qualitative change into the [Indian] ocean for the first three hundred years of their presence there."[24] This is of course not to deny the growing role of armed trade, but only to emphasize that the European powers were not hegemonic during these centuries.[25] It was only in the aftermath of the Industrial Revolution and the Napoleonic Wars that a European power became dominant in Asia.[26]

British Naval Power and Maritime Asia

Britain's defeat of France during the Napoleonic Wars and "the takeover of Dutch possessions (South Africa, Ceylon, Malacca)" are believed to have turned the Indian Ocean into a "British lake."[27] Others have argued that the Indian Ocean had become a "British lake" by the end of the Seven Years' War (1756–1763).[28] However, the French continued in Mauritius, and the Dutch remained ensconced in Java and the Moluccas until they were dislodged by the British—with the support of their Indian sepoys—during the Napoleonic Wars. Consequently, Derek McDougall has referred to the post-1815 Indian Ocean as "a 'British lake' centered on India."[29] While there is no doubt that Britain emerged as the leading naval power in the world after 1815, it is a matter of some debate whether British naval power was hegemonic and if this naval hegemony was necessary for the functioning of the maritime trading system.

According to Kenneth Pomeranz and Steven Topik, "the British navy was really enforcing a world more like premodern Asia, and Britain's illustrious forebears were close kin to those it now condemned as criminals [or pirates]."[30] In other words, a hegemonic British navy was perhaps not needed to keep the trade routes open in the Indian Ocean since such a navy did not exist in premodern Asia, as explained in Chapter 3. Therefore, for Sugata Bose, the Indian Ocean was "both ... a British lake and it was not," for in the zone stretching from Zanzibar to Singapore, Indian and Chinese "intermediary capitalists" built their "own lake."[31] Consequently, a layered order existed in the Indian Ocean in which local agency played a key role despite colonialism, and British power did not (and perhaps could not) stamp out "sectors or pockets of local dominance in Southeast Asia" of this "dependent seaborne commerce" of the Asians.[32] As such, even as Britain emerged as the leading naval power after 1815, the quest for such a navy can be explained by factors other than the need to make the trading system run.

Buzan and Little's framework of politico-military and politico-economic interactions underpinned by ideas that make and shape international orders, as discussed in Chapters 2 and 3, is useful here too. First, in terms of politico-military interactions, Britain lacked serious maritime security rivals after the Napoleonic Wars. Britain's naval primacy "depended far more on the persistent weakness of defeated European rivals," the absence of powerful indigenous naval actors in Asia, and the awareness that "any attempt to move from primacy to hegemony would be risky."[33] Second, in terms of politico-economic interactions, trade for Britain was survival-driven, and not just about wealth or political power. Given Britain's acute dependency on imported food as well as raw materials such as cotton for the Industrial Revolution, the British navy sought to rule the waves.[34]

Third, in an ideational sense, the British leadership also made "a conscious connection with the Roman imperium."[35] This is perhaps not that surprising because, as discussed in Chapter 2, Rome also did not have serious security rivals after the destruction of Carthage, and because of its reliance on maritime trade for food. Furthermore, in the realm of ideas, Britain remained mercantile, not liberal, at least in the early decades after 1815.[36] It was a combination of these factors, along with the need to defend Britain, an island state, which led Britain to emerge as the leading naval power. Even as its powerful navy might have served British interests, a hegemonic British navy was not required to make the Indian Ocean trading system run, for it upheld a world like premodern Asia that lacked such a naval power. It was the *local* conditions in the Indian Ocean that enabled Britain to exercise a particular kind of power.

As noted by Andrew Lambert, the British did not "so much impose" a trading order, but instead worked "to sustain it in the defense of their interests" by relying on "an effective sea-based deterrent."[37] However, this is only true for British interactions with the Western great powers. In the eastern Indian Ocean (and indeed in the world outside Europe), British naval power did play an important role in the making and shaping of British colonialism. Our argument is simply that naval hegemony was not needed to keep the sea lanes open, especially in the Indian Ocean.

In other words, the nature of British naval primacy was far more contingent than is commonly assumed in the international relations scholarship. Britain's naval dominance—to the degree that it existed—depended more upon "situational conditions."[38] Consequently, the Western great powers "did not experience British naval mastery as a yoke" due to "the peculiarly hollow character of naval hegemony."[39] The powerful British navy upheld British—not systemic—interests. Patrick O'Brien has even argued that Britain's rulers did not "contemplate or presume to occupy the [hegemonic] place retrospectively assigned to them by social science."[40] This raises serious doubts for the Anglo-American hegemonic "succession" paradigm of Gilpin, and for those like Ikenberry who trace the origins of the liberal order to Britain in the nineteenth century.[41]

American Naval Power and Maritime Asia

Even after the beginning of Britain's "free trade" regime in 1846 (albeit "free trade" linked with colonialism), the United States resorted to "economic nationalism" through "informal means" including "high tariff walls," and by establishing "a rival imperial trade bloc" in the Americas.[42] Notably, "US naval growth beginning in the 1880s was funded by revenues from the tariff."[43] However, not only did the United States face no rival in the 1890s with the termination of the Anglo-American military rivalry around that time, but "the United States was not a trading nation" as "less than 10 per cent of U.S. GDP came from foreign trade" in 1900.[44]

Consequently, the rise of America's naval power was not driven by politico-military interactions with rivals. At the same time, politico-economic interactions to help support the management of a liberal economic order were also not its motivations. Instead, it was the influence of Mahanian ideas and aspirations to the world leadership in the British (and Roman) mold that was decisive. The American naval strategist Alfred Thayer Mahan was of the opinion that the British path to global predominance through naval mastery was open to "any state that had the mind and the will to follow its example."[45] This Mahanian view had a definite influence on the emerging American approach to naval power around the beginning of the twentieth century.[46] According to Lambert, the "US neither needed nor wanted a global sea-control navy, but it was most anxious that Britain should not have one. ... In both World Wars US policymakers treated Britain as a strategic and economic rival to be defeated, even if it chose to do so with fiscal tools."[47] The tools employed by the Americans in their contest with the British were in the domains of finance, international communications, global transportation, and fossil fuels.

Not surprisingly, competition "rather than cooperation continued to characterize the [Anglo-American] relationship on key political-economic issues" well into the mid-twentieth century, and both the decline of British power and the rise of American power in the first half of the century have been overstated in the literature.[48] Given all these qualifications, O'Brien has referred to the Anglo-American "hegemonic succession paradigm" and "the representation of Pax Britannica as an antecedent or precedent for the hegemony of the United States" as "a myth" and a "theory without history."[49]

The United States did emerge as *primus inter pares* among the naval powers after the Second World War. According to Stephen Wertheim, America's elites consciously chose the policy of armed primacy after the fall of France in 1940. However, this was "not merely the material condition" of American preponderance, nor was it about "contain[ing] or defeat[ing] a particular rival. ... [Instead, primacy was] an axiom about America's role in the world, closer to the status of an identity than to that of a policy or strategy."[50] Importantly, after 1945 the Americans wanted an influence comparable to Britain's before the war, and therefore the acquisition of overseas military bases was an important American war aim.[51] The number of permanent American military bases increased from fourteen in the 1930s to over 1,000 by 1956.[52]

Notably, the U.S. navy faced an uncertain future immediately after 1945. The "defence of sea lanes and trade did not count," and it was the Korean War (1950–1953) that "saved the navy."[53] During its ensuing Cold War with the Soviet Union, the United States did not pursue the Mahanian strategy of sea control for commercial reasons. Instead, American strategy was about using its power, especially sea power, "to magnify the power of Western forces in general," and for the territorial defense of Western Europe and Japan.[54] In other words, *power projection* and containment of the Soviet Union, as opposed to *sea control* to make the trading system run, were the chief purposes of America's naval power during the Cold War.[55]

For its part, the Soviet navy was "powerless to contest U.S. supremacy," and the Soviet economy was only partially integrated with the world economy.[56] "[B]y far, the most important role of the Soviet Navy in the Cold War was its potential contribution to the defence of the [Soviet] homeland."[57] The Soviet navy "was not built to challenge the Western navies on the high seas for sea control."[58] The presence of nuclear weapons may have also played a role in ensuring that "neither side could afford to block the other's seaborne access."[59] Indeed, Cold War superpower competition "never led to a disruption of seaborne trade."[60]

While the United States was clearly the leading naval power during the Cold War, especially in the Atlantic and the Pacific Oceans, Britain continued to be the leading sea power in the Indian Ocean immediately after the Second World War.[61] This further complicates the narrative of successive Anglo-American hegemonies discussed above. In the 1950s and 1960s, "the US Navy remained under what it regarded as a British-administered regional security umbrella" in the Indian Ocean.[62] It was only after the British withdrawal from the "east of Suez" after 1971, and with America's growing naval presence in Diego Garcia (a British-held territory in the Indian Ocean taken from Mauritius), that America emerged as the leading naval power there.[63]

However, the 1970s and 1980s also saw the establishment of Soviet military bases (and/or the Soviet use of local military bases) in East Africa and Yemen as well as Cam Rahn Bay. Naval presence in Vietnam also gave the Soviets the ability to oversee the Strait of Malacca in the eastern Indian Ocean.[64] Soviet naval presence in the Indian Ocean meant that the region remained nonhegemonic even as the United States boasted the most powerful navy there. In any case, the superpowers did not obstruct seaborne commerce during the Cold War. "Since 1945 the defence of maritime trade has only rarely been an issue, with the Tanker War of the late 1980s and Somali piracy the high points of Western activity."[65]

The end of the Cold War and the Soviet withdrawal from the Indian Ocean made the United States the dominant power in the region. In the post–Cold War world, American naval power has been "presented as the key guarantor" of the " 'global commons' ... the idea that free movement by sea, particularly of trade, was a general good that was essential to the world system."[66] However, Carla Norrlof has argued that America's "primary consideration has been the protection of American business and political interests ... even though security provision in the form of military bases and naval patrols has been *a public good of sorts* from which other non-American firms may also have benefitted."[67] This implies that to the degree American naval dominance has provided these public goods "of sorts," they are the consequence of American power (perhaps even unintended), rather than the cause behind the establishment of such an American order in the first place.

Furthermore, others have noted that "offensive economic warfare has virtually disappeared from discussions of naval utility," thereby raising the question whether a hegemonic navy that keeps trade routes open for the functioning of a maritime trading system is needed at all.[68] The "shipping that delivers food, fuel, and raw materials is effectively unguarded, often beyond the control of national states" that "rely on a combination of international law and shared interest, rather than naval force, to ensure shipping moves without hindrance from other nations, or non-state actors."[69]

Even Barry Posen, who had earlier noted that American "military power underwrites world trade" by commanding the commons, has now argued that a "security hegemon" is "unnecessary to insure international trade," because "[m]utual deterrence" can protect the global trade routes.[70] Given that the rise of China is raising the possibility—at least the academic possibility—of naval blockades, and therefore of offensive economic warfare between the great powers, we need to understand the emerging order in the contemporary Indo-Pacific in the context of this larger theoretical and historical background.

Structure and Interactions in the Indo-Pacific
Politico-Military and Politico-Economic Interactions

Writing in the aftermath of 9/11, Kennedy believed that there was only one military superpower in the world. He argued that the "Pax Britannica was run on the cheap ... the Royal Navy was equal only to the next two navies," while "right now all the other navies in the world combined could not dent American maritime supremacy."[71] Indeed, for James Holmes and Toshi Yoshihara, "[t]hat America rules the waves is a virtual axiom of contemporary international politics," and the world had "taken for granted that the US Navy underwrites freedom of navigation."[72] However, as China emerged as the largest trading power in the world by 2013, Beijing undertook its concomitant naval buildup. According to Hu Bo, one of China's leading naval scholars, China was "very likely to overtake the United States to become the largest stakeholder of the world's sea lanes."[73]

The U.S.-China maritime contest is partially an outcome of the relative decline of America's naval supremacy and the rise of Chinese naval power. Given its dependency on imported energy from the Middle East to fuel its growing economy, China is interested in the safety of its sea lanes, which run from the China Seas into the Indian Ocean. The Indian Ocean is also crucial for China's international trade and for the Belt and Road Initiative (BRI).[74] Indeed, Southeast Asia's "gateway position between the Pacific and Indian Oceans, and its role as a global hub for maritime trade and transport" has made the eastern Indian Ocean a region of strategic significance for China.[75] Given the stakes, Friedberg is of the opinion that "if they are going to initiate hostilities in the Pacific, China's leaders will have strong incentives to do so simultaneously in the Indian Ocean."[76] Not surprisingly, America's leaders "no longer intend to treat China, India, or Southeast Asia as separate bilateral cases" when it comes to maritime issues.[77]

However, as explained above, a hegemonic navy is not needed to make the trading system run. For Lambert, the United States continues to remain a continental power, albeit one with the most powerful navy in the world. The United States is the "dominant sea power in strategic terms, but no one would argue that it is dependent upon the ocean for its existence."[78] This view is also echoed by Posen, for whom the United States has a large and diverse economy "producing manufactured goods, advanced technology, raw materials, energy, and foodstuffs," and connections "with Canada and Mexico further broaden the base. Though free trade is beneficial, the United States can go it alone if necessary."[79] For David Gompert, even as "sea power is an important aspect of American power now, it was the foundation of British power" in the nineteenth century, given its different strategic environment, including dependency on imported food and raw materials.[80] Therefore, "sea power does not have inordinate importance as it did in Britain when the Royal Navy was synonymous with greatness," because "the United States is the world's leading power in virtually *all* respects."[81]

Similarly, the reorientation of China's economy due to its commercial rivalry with the United States and the "dual circulation" strategy is likely to tilt it domestically even as international ties will remain important.[82] In any case, the U.S.-China economic rivalry centers on tariffs, standard settings, technology, finance, and infrastructure, and is therefore very different from the zero-sum trade contest between Rome and its classical rivals in the Mediterranean, or the contest between the mercantile European powers of the early modern period that influenced Mahan's thinking.[83] China is among America's top three trading partners (along with Canada and Mexico), while America remains China's leading trade partner despite some "decoupling."[84] More important, it seems like systemic/economic leadership transition is not in the offing in the U.S.-China rivalry, and that their economic contest is likely to center around the status of *primus inter pares* (or relative rank).[85]

Consequently, the U.S.-China contest seems primarily motivated neither by traditional security concerns nor by trade-related issues per se. Instead, it seems to be rooted in the ideational issues related to prestige and status at the apex of the international system.[86] For Wertheim, America's quest of armed primacy that began during the Second World War was "intended to outlive the circumstances of its origination and shape the distant, perhaps perpetual, future."[87] Similarly, Fritz Bartel has argued that the end of the Cold War in which America emerged victorious had affirmed the belief "that the United States should remain the most powerful country in the world."[88]

In turn, Wang Gungwu has argued that China is "really a continental power," and that it is "acquiring enough maritime power to protect itself against the maritime global world" led by the United States.[89] Importantly, China is aware of its relatively weak naval position, especially because China has "never really won a serious naval battle" in its entire history.[90] Therefore, Chinese leaders are now beginning to understand that it is important to be a maritime power in order to be a truly global power.[91] According to Singapore's Lee Kuan Yew, Chinese leaders want to "share this century as co-equals with the U.S."[92] It is these status/positional dynamics that are at play in the U.S.-China maritime contest in the eastern Indian Ocean.

Under President Donald Trump, the United States was determined "to maintain U.S. strategic primacy in the Indo-Pacific region" while preventing China "from establishing new, illiberal spheres of influence," as the United States feared that China aimed "to dissolve U.S. alliances and partnerships in the region."[93] The administration of President Joseph Biden has also reiterated America's determination "to strengthen our [America's] long-term *position* in and commitment to the Indo-Pacific," by building "a balance of influence that is maximally favorable to the United States" and its allies and partners, as the fear of China's pursuit of "a sphere of influence in the Indo-Pacific . . . [in order] to become the world's most influential power" continues.[94]

In fact, soon after the Cold War, the Pentagon was talking about "deterring potential competitors from *even aspiring* to a larger regional or global role," as it sought to preserve America's dominant position into the future.[95] Importantly, East Asia was identified as "a region whose resources would, under consolidated control, be sufficient to generate global power."[96] By 2001, the Pentagon had come to define the "east Asian littoral . . . as the region stretching from south of Japan through Australia and into the Bay of Bengal."[97]

In other words, the United States has been determined to maintain its primacy since the end of the Cold War, and the primary reason behind this quest has been the resolve to maintain America's *position* as the leading superpower while preventing the emergence of a regional (Asian) and global challenger. As such, this determination is not driven by the desire to keep the sea routes open for the functioning of the global economy, since such a hegemon is not needed in the first place, although America's position has often been justified in these terms.

Furthermore, the "expansion" of the definition of maritime East Asia to include Australia and the Bay of Bengal in 2001—even before the term "Indo-Pacific" became common—was to some degree a tacit acknowledgment of the fact that China's power was rapidly rising, and that a newer approach was needed to maintain American primacy.[98] By thus expanding the region, the United States was making it difficult for China to dominate its (now much larger) region, given its greater geographical scope and the addition of other powerful actors like Australia and India.[99] By the mid-2000s, the United States was already "pivoting" to Asia (even before formally articulating this strategy in 2011) with the aim of maintaining American primacy and preventing Chinese hegemony.[100]

However, it was also increasingly clear that "contested zones" where "the United States can probably pursue selective engagement but not . . . primacy," and where the United States "will not be able to establish command [of the commons/sea]," were fast becoming a reality.[101] China's military-technological transformation centered on anti-access and area denial (A2/AD) strategies, and long-range precision-guided munitions have transformed maritime East Asia into such a contested zone.[102] Indeed, the general prognosis is that China will be increasingly able to challenge the United States at greater distances from the Chinese coast.[103] Although there is no doubt that the United States remains the strongest naval power in the world, it is *primus inter pares* as opposed to one that maintains command of the maritime Asian commons.

The U.S.-China naval competition, then, centers on two interconnected politico-military and politico-economic facets. First, as leading economic powers, the United States and China are developing their navies "to protect and expand [their] trade" as they vie for the top *position* at the apex of the international system.[104] While the United States is clearly trying to preserve its *position* as the leading naval power, China is trying to prevent American hegemony (or command of the seas) in the Indo-Pacific given China's own reliance on the sea lanes. Consequently, China's "objective is to acquire an effective presence and maintain basic operational depth" in the Indo-Pacific, as opposed to "overthrowing the United States and India in the Pacific and Indian Oceans."[105] Even as China is rapidly rising, it is in a relatively disadvantageous geographical position when it comes to accessing the Indian Ocean given the long supply lines and the "gateway" position of the maritime Southeast Asian chokepoints noted above. Consequently, China is seeking secure access to the Indian Ocean as opposed to hegemony in the Indo-Pacific.[106]

As a result, the second dimension in their naval rivalry revolves around the geopolitics of access. The United States is determined to maintain continued access to regions around China given China's growing A2/AD capabilities. In the meantime, China faces the "Malacca dilemma" in accessing the Indian Ocean given the overall maritime superiority of the United States in the Indo-Pacific. Accessing the Indian Ocean is crucial for both China's energy security and its Belt and Road Initiative.[107] Consequently, the "rivalry between [the] major powers is likely to be played out in large part in terms of naval power projection and with new warships and related technologies."[108] However, naval power projection does not require command of the seas. As early as the 1970s, Hedley Bull was already expressing a "grave doubt as to whether the kind of sea power traditionally pursued by the Western powers," which was "directed towards the command of the seas in wartime and paramount political influence over distant coastal states in peacetime," could "continue to be exercised."[109]

These two dynamics—competition over relative position and the geopolitics of access—are shaping the American and Chinese strategic approaches to the Indo-Pacific. While the United States is seeking to prevent (and perhaps reverse) its relative naval decline in the Indo-Pacific, China seems more interested in protecting its sea lanes in the Indian Ocean in general instead of specifically controlling the sea lanes. China is also keen to prevent the emergence of American (or Indian) hegemony in the Indian Ocean. None of this means that China is on a path toward regional hegemony.

At the same time, Southeast Asia is not a passive region in this great power rivalry. Instead, the region is actively shaping great power engagement. The most important Southeast Asian ideational underpinning is the rejection of hegemonism, whether American, Chinese, or that of any other player.[110] Consequently, the cumulative American, Chinese, Indian, and Southeast Asian strategic approaches to the eastern Indian Ocean are in the process of creating a nonhegemonic and decentered regional order. The shared management entailed in the decentralized combination of the local agency of Southeast Asia and the efforts of the major powers is collectively providing the regional public good of the security of the sea lanes.

The United States' Approach and Politico-Military Interactions

There are three strands in America's emerging strategy. First, the United States is transforming its postwar hub-and-spokes pattern of alliances into various bilateral and minilateral alignments.[111] The United States is not only deepening some of its full-fledged alliances (with Japan and Australia, for example), but is also pursuing security relationships beyond such alliances with partners like Vietnam and India. Furthermore, America's various security partners are also forging defense and security relationships with each other instead of creating such links with the United States only. Scholars are referring to such relationships as "networks" and "patchworks."[112]

The Quad is perhaps the most prominent of such groupings in the Indo-Pacific. Japan's proactive diplomacy with its other three partners—in bilateral and trilateral settings—was crucial to the formation of the Quad. India has entered into military logistics agreements with all three of its Quad partners.[113] These agreements have provisions for reciprocal access to military facilities for supplies and fuels, thereby increasing the reach of their respective militaries.[114] Japan and Australia have also entered into a reciprocal access agreement that paves the way for their militaries "to work seamlessly with each other on defense and humanitarian issues," thus making Japan's strategic relationship with Australia its closest such partnership after its alliance with the United States.[115]

Notably, China perceives the Quad to be directed against it.[116] However, China is not unduly worried as the Quad falls short of a full-fledged alliance. Since India does not have an alliance with the United States (or with the other Quad members), Beijing thinks of the Quad as "an uneasy 3+1 rather than a monolithic quartet."[117] India's quest for strategic autonomy, along with the others' reluctance to fight alongside India against China in the Himalayas, means that such alliances are unlikely. In other words, there is recognition in China of the Quad as "a mechanism for the four countries concerned to coordinate their policies, rather than indicating a single, fixed strategy."[118]

Furthermore, China now possesses the largest navy in the world in terms of the number of vessels.[119] Between 2014 and 2018, China also launched vessels with a combined tonnage "greater than the tonnages of the entire French, German, Indian, Italian, South Korean, Spanish, or Taiwanese navies."[120] The United States nevertheless maintains the most technologically capable naval forces in the world and has advantages over China when it comes to carriers, submarines, and land-based air power in support of naval operations given America's regional and global network of military bases.[121] The United States' Quad partners also possess capable naval forces and are unlikely to be "pushovers," especially in certain geographic/local theaters.[122] Consequently, neither the United States (by itself or via the Quad) nor China is likely to emerge as hegemonic in the contested zones of the Indo-Pacific.

Second, the United States is promoting the rise of India. One of the "desired end states" of President Trump's Indo-Pacific strategy was to ensure that India "remains preeminent in South Asia and takes the leading role in maintaining Indian Ocean security, increases engagement with Southeast Asia, and expands its economic, defense, and diplomatic cooperation with other U.S. allies and partners in the region."[123] Similarly, one of President Biden's "action plans" in the Indo-Pacific includes America's "support" for "India's continued rise and regional leadership," including active connections with Southeast Asia.[124] The underlying logic behind this strategy is the belief that the rise of India will help balance China's power in the region, for India has reasons independent of the United States to do so as a consequence of the Sino-Indian rivalry. In other words, the simultaneous presence of Sino-American and Sino-Indian rivalries and the absence of such a strategic rivalry between the United States and India enable the United States to accommodate the slow rise of India.

Not surprisingly, China's leading scholars of India have noted that the United States is "promoting India from the periphery of the Asia-Pacific region to the core of the Indo-Pacific region."[125] While this is likely to exacerbate the Sino-Indian rivalry, China's primary concern is to prevent the emergence of a hegemonic power in the Indian Ocean that could deny access to China.[126] Given India's overall naval inferiority compared with China, there is little fear of India's ability to do so by itself. Furthermore, the absence of an alliance between the United States and India also implies that a joint bid by them to deny China access to the Indian Ocean is unlikely.

According to Gabriel Collins and William Murray, "China is not fundamentally vulnerable to a maritime energy blockade in circumstances other than a global war."[127] Even that would require blockading not just the Malacca Strait but also the Lombok and Sunda Straits, in addition to the routes around Australia. Furthermore, the "[s]ecurity of regional sea-borne trade and security of sea-borne trade with China are completely entangled," thereby creating more hurdles for any potential blockade, as it will also adversely affect America's East Asian allies and partners.[128] Not surprisingly, Cuiping Zhu has noted that "no country including India will have the ability to independently control the ocean in the future. The control over the Indian Ocean by the US is likely to be the final stage of control over the ocean by a single country since the Western world rules [sic] the Indian Ocean."[129] In other words, a hegemonic power controlling the sea routes and managing the trading system is unlikely to emerge even as major power competition is resulting in the pursuit of coercion and countercoercion strategies by the rival great powers. Instead of sea control, these powers seem to be building the capabilities to project their naval power.

The third component of the United States' strategic approach to the Indo-Pacific includes the involvement of extraregional partners and allies in regional affairs. Biden's Indo-Pacific strategy specifically calls for engaging with allies and partners from "outside of the region," especially the EU and NATO.[130] While NATO's engagement with the Indo-Pacific is in its early stages, individual European powers are already engaging with the region.

The United Kingdom has teamed up with the United States and Australia through the trilateral AUKUS security pact that aims to provide Australia with nuclear powered submarines.[131] The United Kingdom and Japan are also working on a reciprocal access agreement like the one between Australia and Japan noted above.[132] India and the United Kingdom are also in the process of negotiating a reciprocal logistics pact that will enhance the reach of their respective militaries.[133] Along with the Five Power Defence Arrangements (FPDA) among Singapore, Malaysia, Australia, New

Zealand, and the United Kingdom, these developments are likely to raise Britain's strategic profile in the Indo-Pacific.[134]

Similarly, France is also a resident power with island territories in the Indian Ocean and the South Pacific. India and France have already signed a mutual logistics agreement for their militaries, and France has also unveiled its Indo-Pacific strategy and is fostering closer links with Australia and Japan.[135] The engagement of these extraregional powers in the Indo-Pacific points toward an "open" regional order that is not restricted to the countries of the Indo-Pacific.

Consequently, America's three-pronged approach to the region centered on the Quad, India, and the involvement of the extraregional powers is in fact pointing toward multipolarity.[136] However, this is a more diffuse multipolarity, akin to what Evelyn Goh has referred to as a "patchwork."[137] After all, ranging from full-fledged alliances to security partnerships, there are different degrees of security alignments in the region. Furthermore, these states also have very different threat perceptions of China. While the United States and Japan are keen to slow (and perhaps reverse) their relative decline vis-à-vis China, India is approaching China as a rising power (albeit warily, due to the large power gap with China).[138]

Australian analysts also worry that "[g]rowing Indian naval power may not always reinforce Canberra's interests unless it can be coordinated with Australian or U.S. activity."[139] Unlike Australia, which is seeking to augment America's power and position in the Indo-Pacific, a rising India will probably use its power "to maximise India's influence, not America's."[140] This patchworked multipolarity of multiple powers with different strategic interests, with different relationships with China, and in multiple fora (from the Quad to AUKUS) that are the sites of cooperation in different functional areas, means that America's own approach to the Indo-Pacific is pointing toward a nonhegemonic multiplex region.

China's Approach: Mutually Reinforcing Politico-Economic and Politico-Military Interactions

As discussed in Chapter 3, historical Chinese empires approached the region stretching from the South China Sea into the Indian Ocean as a singular maritime space. In the contemporary context,

China's growing dependence on the Indian Ocean sea lanes, the
BRI (which includes the so-called Maritime Silk Road, or MSR),
and the United States' approach to the Indo-Pacific discussed
above mean that China continues to think of the Indian Ocean as
"[g]eo-strategically ... closely linked" to the South China Sea.[141]
Indeed, as mentioned above, the Chinese navy is officially striving
to emerge as a two-ocean navy. According to Garver, "[u]nless
China can secure its interests in the SA-IOR," or South Asia-
Indian Ocean Region, "China will remain a regional East Asian
power and fall short of its aspiration of being a global power."[142]

Consequently, some scholars have argued that China is building a Mahanian navy that seeks sea control. For Holmes and Yoshihara, Chinese strategists "seem especially attached to the more
bellicose dimensions of Mahan's work," and the "command of the
commons has assumed a central position in Chinese strategic
thinking and military strategy."[143] Similarly, Yves-Heng Lim has argued that China is seeking "sea control in the Indian Ocean" and
that this quest is "bound to create frictions, if not outright conflict"
with India and the United States.[144] However, this is hardly the
dominant view in the literature. According to Hu, China cannot
emerge as dominant in the Indian Ocean unless the United States
and India "make major strategic mistakes" or "suffer a sharp decline in their national power."[145] These developments are not very
likely, especially simultaneously.

Therefore, China is more interested in building "strategic buffer zones along China's long sea lanes of communication," as opposed to becoming a regional hegemon.[146] While this strategy may
involve "selective sea control in certain parts of the Indian Ocean,"
especially if China is able to establish a network of military bases
along its maritime routes, this offensive thrust is driven by China's
relatively weak position compared to the United States and geographical disadvantages in relation to India.[147] China seeks to maintain "operational depth" as it seeks access to the Indian Ocean, in
addition to developing the ability to pursue countercoercion if sub-
jected to coercion by its adversaries.[148]

"China is not yet building up a global network of bases to
massively project power abroad or to attack the United States," or
India for that matter.[149] Unlike the United States, which enjoys

access to military bases overseas at least partially due to its military alliances, China is unlikely to underwrite the security of the states where its military bases may emerge (except, perhaps, in select cases), as China has tended to avoid alliances.[150] As such, China is only likely to have a "restricted constituency of support" for its overseas military bases.[151]

China established its first overseas military base in Djibouti in the western Indian Ocean in 2017. However, the United States, Italy, France, and Japan also have military bases in that country.[152] Similarly, Singapore entered into a pact with China in 2019 "that allows Chinese warships to continue using its military facilities."[153] However, this is a politico-commercial agreement, and "a more persistent" Chinese presence in Singapore "seems highly unlikely given the city-state's close security links with the US."[154] Singapore and India also have a reciprocal logistics agreement that allows their respective navies to use the other side's facilities for resupplies and fuel. According to Ng Eng Hen, the Singaporean defense minister, this agreement will promote closer India–Singapore cooperation in Indian waters as well as the Strait of Malacca.[155] In other words, this race for bases and the geopolitics of access are not a zero-sum game. While China is certainly emerging as a major power in the Indian Ocean, it is hardly the only one.

Consequently, others have argued that China is not seeking maritime dominance. Although a Mahanian school of thought does exist in China (alongside other schools of thought on matters pertaining to sea power), China is in fact seeking "multiple ways to project its sea power."[156] Except perhaps in its near-seas coastal waters, "China has no interest in sea control beyond a certain degree of strategic depth, including a secure bastion area for ballistic missile submarines."[157] In other words, even this limited degree of sea control is largely driven by strategic reasons as opposed to those related to maritime trade. China's naval modernization is largely about the quest to cement its great power credentials and to ensure the security of its maritime routes.[158] Therefore, China is pursuing a three-pronged approach in pursuit of these interests, none of which implies sea control.

First, even as China is determined to emerge as a maritime power, it is not putting all its "eggs in the maritime basket."[159] China is seeking access to the Indian Ocean directly via maritime routes and indirectly via continental routes through Myanmar and Pakistan. "Strategically, Myanmar is China's link to the Indian Ocean."[160] A gas pipeline carrying supplies from the Bay of Bengal to southern China became operational in 2013, while a parallel pipeline started pumping oil in 2014.[161] Similarly, plans are also underway to connect western China with the Persian Gulf via Pakistan. Although these developments may imply a different vulnerability by implicating China in Pakistan's and Myanmar's domestic politics and internal security concerns, they have the potential to ameliorate China's "Malacca dilemma."

Chinese analysts are under no illusion that these pipelines will remove China's dependence on the Strait of Malacca. Nevertheless, these options are still being pursued as a "form of effective hedging in order to prevent other countries from blackmailing China" given its maritime vulnerabilities.[162] China's leading strategists are among the advocates of such "continental bridges" to the Indian Ocean.[163] China's search for these continental routes to the Indian Ocean also demonstrates that it is not pursuing (and perhaps cannot pursue) sea control in the eastern Indian Ocean.

Second, China's BRI also builds upon this land–sea complementarity. Although the BRI has been critiqued as a unilateral Chinese initiative that seeks to mimic the U.S. hub-and-spoke model in Asia, its overland component is also seen as a lifeline "in case of supply disruptions at sea or economic isolation."[164] It is also significant that many of these overland routes (like the one via Pakistan into the Persian Gulf) traverse way beyond the eastern Indian Ocean. Similarly, the maritime component of the BRI also aims to go beyond Southeast Asia via the "China + ASEAN + X" model into South Asia, East Africa, the Middle East, and beyond.[165] Not surprisingly, China's supply routes and the BRI—analogous to America's support for extraregional powers in the Indo-Pacific discussed above—are also pointing toward an "open" order in the eastern Indian Ocean.

Third and finally, China is pursuing its own minilateral initiatives. The Lancang–Mekong Cooperation (LMC) mechanism that held its first summit in 2016 is "the first Chinese-built Southeast Asian institution."[166] The LMC includes China and the countries of mainland Southeast Asia (Cambodia, Laos, Myanmar, Thailand, and Vietnam), and focuses on sustainable development, regional infrastructure, and nontraditional security issues.[167] However, it should not be seen in isolation, since this mechanism allows China to engage with several Southeast Asian countries collectively in a multilateral setting other than ASEAN.

Furthermore, China, Laos, Myanmar, and Thailand have been conducting joint patrols on the Lancang-Mekong River since 2011.[168] It has even been suggested that this so-called Mekong mode implies a security architecture "*dominated* by China and *supported* by other Mekong countries."[169] In turn, the United States has specifically raised the issue of "extraterritorial river patrols" as a new challenge in Southeast Asia that is undermining existing institutions.[170] These developments have the potential to divide continental and maritime Southeast Asia.[171]

In turn, the BRI has the potential to accelerate this trend. The Singapore–Kunming Rail Link (SKRL) may create an "alternative" route from southern China into the Bay of Bengal via "southern Thailand and the western Malay Peninsula," thereby contributing to reducing China's reliance on the maritime routes.[172] The East Coast Rail Link (ECRL) connecting the Thai-Malaysian border in the northeast to Malaysia's west coast is "also intended to provide ... a land link between the contested South China Sea and the busy Strait of Malacca shipping corridor."[173] As with Pakistan and Myanmar, the SKRL and ECRL may also entangle China with the domestic political issues of these countries. Nevertheless, given the continental-maritime contest between the United States and China, there is now an "intense interest in the potential unity of Southeast Asia as an independent region."[174] Whether or not the Sino-American rivalry reorders Southeast Asia along its continental and maritime axes, China does not seem to be pursuing sea control or naval hegemony, even as it attenuates America's post–Cold War regional predominance through its growing power projection capabilities.

The Flow of Ideas: Southeast Asian Agency and "the ASEAN Way" in the Indo-Pacific

The Southeast Asian states, whether individually or collectively, are not mere spectators in the U.S.-China contest in the Indo-Pacific. Southeast Asia is actively shaping great power engagement with the region.[175] More specifically, it is the regional norms embedded in the so-called ASEAN Way that are being projected into the Indo-Pacific. The ASEAN Way refers to the regional norms that emerged in Southeast Asia during the Cold War that sought conflict avoidance while preventing great power domination in the region.[176] Focusing on informality, consultation, and consensus, they emerged from the region's effort to stay strategically relevant in the context of great power rivalry. The ASEAN Way typically refers to four core features: the nonuse of force and pacific settlement of disputes; regional autonomy and "regional solutions to regional problems"; the doctrine of noninterference; and avoidance of military pacts and preference for bilateral defense cooperation.

After the Cold War, norms that emphasized cooperative security and "open" regionalism were promoted in the wider Asian region. The aim of this normative framework was to coengage all the major powers while promoting strategic restraint and responsible conduct. Some of these ideas spread through institution building in the form of soft regionalism such as the ARF. Others were embodied in ASEAN's Treaty of Amity and Cooperation (TAC), which has been signed by all the members of the EAS. While there is no need to overstate the amplification of these norms from Southeast Asia into the wider Indo-Pacific, they have come to constitute a regional "cognitive prior."[177]

The region rejects hegemonism and wants to avoid a zero-sum rivalry between the United States and China. The Unites States remains the region's largest cumulative foreign investor, even as China has emerged as its largest trade partner.[178] Given the United States' long-standing security links with the region and Southeast Asia's complex relationship with China, rooted in history and geography, the regional states have chosen "to work selectively with China and the United States, rather than siding entirely with one or the other."[179]

Southeast Asian states are "ambivalent about the United States" and the role it "should play in the region," as the United States often appears "distracted, arrogant, condescending, fickle, and self-preoccupied."[180] At the same time, the region's unity over China has also frayed, and on certain issues, such as the South China Sea, Beijing is seen as a bully. For example, China has "told

Southeast Asian states to not talk about the South China Sea among themselves prior to meeting as a group with China," and such high-handedness has meant a "surplus in [China's] repellent power" in parts of the region.[181] Southeast Asia has adopted a three-pronged approach to manage this rivalry that ultimately seeks to reject hegemony by keeping both China and the United States engaged in the region in addition to working with other external powers.

First, Southeast Asian states have been the initiators of many of the changes in the regional order, and "regional states have widened the composition of this order."[182] Importantly, Southeast Asian states are setting their own discourse on the Indo-Pacific.[183] Indonesia sees itself at the center of the Indo-Pacific region, a "Global Maritime Fulcrum" that connects the Indian and Pacific Oceans.[184] Furthermore, Indonesia's approach to the Indo-Pacific had a major influence on the AOIP. The AOIP emphasized its "open" and "inclusive" nature, and avoided the term "free" as used in the American articulation of it, as it was seen as directed toward China. Similarly, while no state in the region rejects China's BRI, they also keep their exposure to the BRI limited, as shown by the pushback from the second Mahathir government in Malaysia.[185] Additionally, latent ideas such as the Indonesian initiative for an "Indo-Pacific wide treaty" modeled on ASEAN's TAC also point toward the amplification of ASEAN's norms and ideas at the level of the Indo-Pacific in the future.[186]

As noted by Martin Stuart-Fox almost two decades ago, the Southeast Asian states "want the United States to remain a powerful presence [in the region] . . . but they do not want to be part of any balance-of-power coalition. At the same time, they also want to make room for China."[187] Southeast Asia is also wary of the Quad transforming into a collective defense organization (although there is little prospect of the Quad developing into a military alliance, as discussed above). As with its rejection of balance-of-power configurations, Southeast Asia is also against hegemonic regionalism given its simultaneous coengagement with the United States and China.

ASEAN-led institutions such as EAS, the ARF, and the ADMM-Plus are perhaps the only Indo-Pacific–wide regional institutions, and they include both the United States and China, in addition to other important powers, despite past and ongoing ri-valries among many of them. While sometimes disparagingly dis-missed as mere "talk-shops," such groupings are among the few venues where the "strategic rivals" can cooperate "towards the real-ization of functional goals," including regional capacity building for humanitarian and disaster relief (HADR) and other nontradi-tional dimensions of maritime security.[188] At the same time, it should be noted that the membership of some of these institutions, such as the ARF, extends beyond the Indo-Pacific. Along with the AOIP, which is concerned with "regional architecture in Southeast Asia *and the surrounding regions,*" ASEAN's initiatives, like those of the United States and China discussed above, also point toward an "open" regional order.[189]

Second, the Southeast Asian states are also establishing their own minilaterals that are not ASEAN-led. The Indonesia-Singa-pore Coordinated Patrols to counter piracy in the Singapore Strait, initiated in 1992, were followed by a series of other such bilateral initiatives in maritime Southeast Asia. By 2004, this was trans-formed into the Malacca Straits Sea Patrol with the addition of Malaysia, while Thailand joined this initiative in 2008, as these four states sought to coordinate their naval patrols in the Malacca and Singapore Straits. In fact, they are even allowed "hot pursuit rights of five nautical miles into the sovereign waters of the other members."[190] In the meantime, Malaysia, Singapore, and Indonesia had already started cooperative air patrols over the Straits of Ma-lacca and Singapore by 2005 through an initiative known as "Eyes in the Sky" Combined Maritime Air Patrols. This was followed by the creation of their Intelligence Exchange Group in 2006. The threefold endeavor of these four states (coordinated naval patrols, coordinated air patrols, and intelligence sharing) is now known as the Malacca Straits Patrol (MSP).[191]

It is noteworthy that the beginning of this minilateral in 2004 was prompted by the Lloyd's Joint War Risk Committee's classifi-cation of the Malacca Strait "as a war zone," thereby raising the in-surance premium for ships passing through that waterway.[192] In addition to these financial considerations, the littoral states were wary of any attempt by the external great powers to dominate the Malacca Strait. "For Singapore, Indonesia, and Malaysia, the key to preventing other powers from controlling access to the region is to find the resources to control it themselves," despite the many differences among the Southeast Asian states.[193] By 2006, Lloyd's had removed the Malacca Strait's designation as a war zone. This development further demonstrates that a hegemonic navy is not needed to make the trading system run as local initiative can perform such security functions by generating these public goods in specific locales of concern, including at important chokepoints such as the Malacca Strait.

Similarly, maritime attacks by the Abu Sayyaf Group led to the launch of the Sulu-Sulawesi Seas Patrols (SSSP) by Indonesia, Malaysia, and the Philippines in 2017. Notably, these patrols are modeled on the MSP and include coordinated naval and air patrols as well as intelligence sharing (but without hot pursuit rights).[194] In part, this initiative emerged as a result of concerns in Indonesia and Malaysia that China would send its ships to patrol these waters at the behest of the Philippines.[195] Nevertheless, China and other major powers like Japan and the United States have demonstrated their support for this initiative by helping the local states with capacity building for maritime security.[196] Importantly, this trilateral mechanism emerged even as Malaysia and the Philippines have maritime boundary issues related to the Sabah territorial dispute.[197] These problems notwithstanding, the MSP and the SSSP point toward local initiatives backed by the great powers that collectively produce regional public goods.

Third and finally, the Southeast Asian states are also actively engaging India in the eastern Indian Ocean. Singapore is perhaps one of the more enthusiastic supporters of India's engagement with the region. As early as 2005, Goh Chok Tong noted that "India's rise" would make it "less tenable to regard South and East Asia as distinct strategic theaters interacting only at the margins."[198] India is also a member of the EAS, ARF, and ADMM-Plus. Although India is not a member of the MSP, it does engage in bilateral coordinated patrols with all three of its maritime neighbors in the eastern Indian Ocean: Indonesia, Thailand, and Myanmar.[199] Furthermore, India also has a reciprocal naval logistics agreement with Vietnam in addition to the one with Singapore noted above.[200] Indian military facilities on the Andaman and Nicobar Islands allow

New Delhi to project its power not only into the Strait of Malacca, but also into the South China Sea.[201] According to Sam Bateman, "both India and China have claims to being Southeast Asian countries in their own right."[202] The Chinese military is aware of India's eastward ambitions and is concerned about "Japan's going southward [into the Indian Ocean] and India's advancing eastward ... intersect[ing] in the South China, forming dual arcs" directed at China.[203]

While India's engagement with the region may seem relatively new, it hearkens to the days of the "cosmopolitan Indian Ocean of time and memory," as discussed in Chapter 3.[204] In fact, Southeast Asia's orientation toward Northeast Asia only and the relative neglect of the Indian Ocean is a recent and short-lived phenomenon in the longer sweep of history. The region is gradually assuming its pivotal role at the nexus of India and China, and is actively connecting the Indian Ocean with the South China Sea.

Conclusion

In sum, the rise of China and the Sino-American rivalry do not portend a hegemonic, Thucydidean power transition. At the same time, great power rivalry and the increasingly "open" dimension of the regional order also make ASEAN-centrality suspect (except rhetorically). Crucially, local initiative is central to regional order making in the Indo-Pacific. As the United States and China compete for relative position and maritime access, Southeast Asia is co-engaging both the major powers while rejecting hegemony. Along with the ASEAN-led institutions and the regional norms embodied in the ASEAN Way, Southeast Asian states are beginning to provide regional public goods for the safe transit of trade. They are doing so both individually and collectively, partnering with each other and with all the consequential players in the region. Southeast Asia's active participation—along with others such as India, Japan, and Australia, in addition to the United States and China—in the making of the regional order has given it added depth and resilience as it has become "thick" with the participation of multiple actors. The passing of American dominance is not producing disorder or instability. In fact, a nonhegemonic order is in the making in the Indo-Pacific even in the absence of a grand design, although the process is being actively influenced by ASEAN's normative framework. As Southeast Asia actively assumes its pivotal position between China and India, an open, decentered, and multiplex Indo-Pacific is in the making with echoes of the classical Indian Ocean, where a nonhegemonic order prevailed despite power asymmetries among the various players. A hegemonic navy exercising sea control is not in the offing in the Indo-Pacific.

Conclusion

The Past as Prelude: An Emerging Indo-Pacific Multiplex

W E HAVE UNDERTAKEN LARGE-SCALE, cross-cultural, and trans-epochal comparisons between the Roman Mediterranean (~sixth century B.C.E.–third century C.E.) and the classical Indian Ocean (first–fifteenth centuries C.E.) in this book. Our analysis has implications for contemporary debates on the role of power and ideas in the making of world orders.[1] These debates often revolve around three key issues: (1) hegemony and power; (2) the power of ideas; and (3) the provision of public goods in the different international orders. In each of these areas, the Mediterranean and the Indian Ocean/Southeast Asian systems offer contrasting pictures. Simply put, the classical Indian Ocean provides a different paradigm of international order. The Indian Ocean/Southeast Asian system suggests a nonhegemonic, decentered, and ideationally driven pattern of interactions, whereas in the Mediterranean it was the materially powerful actors that played the leading role. Unlike the classical Indian Ocean, a coercive hegemonic order emerged in the Mediterranean, where even the ideational dynamics were dictated by the materially powerful actors.

We discuss these issues and their implications for the emerging world order in this concluding chapter, which is divided into two sections. First, we systematically compare the Roman Mediterranean and the Classical Indian Ocean around the three key themes mentioned above. Such a comparison broadens our understanding of power and agency in international relations theory. It calls for abandoning Eurocentrism and allowing diversity and pluralism in theory, thereby making a contribution to Global IR. Consequently, we pay particular attention to the classical Indian Ocean here, for this system is new to the international relations scholarship. This is also important for our findings related to nonhegemonic orders and may be more applicable to the emerging order in the contemporary Indo-Pacific. As we show in the second section, contemporary beliefs related to a hegemonic contest between the United States and China in the Indo-Pacific are ultimately based on universalizations that emerge from the Roman Mediterranean. By contrast, we argue that the contextualized generalizations that emerge from the classical Indian Ocean allow for other possibilities.

Before proceeding, we wish to emphasize that "[c]omparison itself is not synonymous with reification."[2] We are not arguing that there is something innate in the Mediterranean that makes Western orders materially and coercively driven while Asian orders are somehow intrinsically peaceful. Our argument is that IR theory as we understand it today universalizes from the historical experiences of the classical Mediterranean. However, the classical Mediterranean was connected through different processes than the classical Indian Ocean. Whereas war and coercion played a crucial role in generating the hegemonic Rome-centric order in the Mediterranean, trade and cultural integration were far more important in maritime Asia. In this way, we offer the international system-level analogue to the arguments on state formation by Jack Goldstone and John Haldon, who observe:

> In the Western tradition . . . ideological integration has been seen, until recently, at least, as a secondary aspect of state formation, a reflection, perhaps, of the dominance of military institutions and coercion in the political history of the western Eurasian world. . . . [However, the] persistence of ideological integration can allow states to survive even with considerable administrative decentralization.[3]

While Roman hegemonic power held the Mediterranean together, the decentralized classical Indian Ocean remained connected through cultural and commercial interactions. This does
not mean that war was absent from the classical Indian Ocean, as
we have shown in Chapter 3. Nevertheless, the patterns set in mo-
tion by the politico-military, politico-economic, and ideational interactions discussed in earlier chapters generated very different
types of orders in these two systems. Therefore, the generalizations
that emerge from the classical Indian Ocean—that orders can be
nonhegemonic and decentered—are just as valid as those that have
emerged from the Roman Mediterranean and have dominated international relations theoretical scholarship with their emphasis on
coercion and hegemony. It is the context of these generalizations
that gives them their full meaning and analytical weight.

Therefore, macrohistorical comparisons are crucial, and even
Fernand Braudel noted that the "comparative history of the world"
is "the only scale on which our problems can be solved or at any
rate correctly posed."[4] Without engaging in comparative macrohistorical exercises of understudied international systems like the classical Indian Ocean undertaken here, we risk remaining stuck in
Eurocentric modes of thinking while ignoring large-scale decentered patterns through which humans may have organized their international systems and societies for long stretches of time (and
may do so yet again, albeit with suitable variation to account for
the changed context). Since a decentered global order may indeed
be the future of our international system,[5] this emphasis on maritime Asia is apt, and we argue that the classical Indian Ocean
represents the paradigmatic case of such a nonhegemonic and decentered order. After all, that system thrived for centuries without
a system-wide hegemon. By contrast, the better-known Roman
Mediterranean has generally been approached as the paradigmatic
case of a hegemonic (core–periphery) international order.

Such large-scale historical comparisons advance knowledge by
making three types of contributions. First, they produce context-specific
generalizations, and consequently advance IR theory. Our comparison
of the classical Mediterranean and the classical eastern Indian Ocean
tells us that maritime trading orders do not need hegemonic navies to
manage the system. Commercial and cultural integration can hold such

systems together depending upon the patterns of interpolity interactions. Consequently, the public goods of trade and security can emerge from the decentralized practices of multiple actors, large and small, through shared management of the system. Second, and relatedly, these findings can also help us understand real-world transformations—such as those underway in the contemporary Indo-Pacific—in a new light instead of remaining stuck in old ways of thinking.

Before turning to these features in the following two sections of this chapter, it should be noted that the third and final contribution of such comparisons is to force us to rethink international history. Consequently, IR theorization can also contribute to newer understandings of the past instead of simply using history to develop theory. Our comparative exercise makes three such contributions to our understanding of the past. First, as we have shown, it is important to approach Southeast Asia as an "open" region. Southeast Asia was deeply interconnected with the eastern Indian Ocean as well as the South China Sea. Consequently, we cannot approach historical Southeast Asia as a closed region by focusing only on intra–Southeast Asian dynamics, or by treating it as a part of a larger East Asian space by neglecting its Indian Ocean orientation. Second, and relatedly, this perspective enables us to see the so-called Chinese tributary system as embedded within a larger, decentered maritime Asian world, instead of making essentialized claims about China's timeless centrality.

Third, and finally, our macrohistorical analysis also allows us to challenge the dominant historical narratives of the hegemonic order theories, whether liberal or otherwise, because our account highlights the coercion and violence entailed in those processes that have otherwise been glossed over in mainstream interpretations. As noted in the Introduction, the liberal hegemony argument of G. John Ikenberry (and his collaborators) ignores the violence of British imperialism after emphasizing "willing" collaboration. However, it is also surprising that even realist accounts of hegemonic stability like that of Robert Gilpin refer to *Pax Britannica* as "generally liberal" instead of coercive and imperial, even as Gilpin acknowledged in a footnote that "[t]he possession of India was a critical factor in England's global political and economic position."[6]

This elision of violence, coercion, and warfare in the hegemonic *Pax Romana*, *Pax Britannica*, and *Pax Americana* is at least partially an outcome of the relative neglect of maritime trading systems in IR theorization. However, by "sink[ing] a huge anchor in [historical] details" in our comparative and extrapolative chapters that explicitly focus on maritime worlds, we challenge the traditional hegemonic accounts while simultaneously showing other—nonhegemonic—possibilities.[7] Consequently, we argue for more engagement with (Asian) history for IR theorization, and agree with Evelyn Goh that "the assertion that there is no need for new theories or approaches because the existing ones explain the world quite well is simply wrong."[8] Our theorization has important implications for the debates around power and ideas in the making and shaping of international orders.

Power and Ideas in the Roman Mediterranean and the Classical Indian Ocean
Hegemony and Power

Roman hegemony in the Mediterranean represented Rome's "authoritative power."[9] After all, the Romans understood the exercise of their power as a relationship of command and obedience that was backed by military coercion.[10] Hegemonic ordering emerged "structurally" through a top-down process in the Mediterranean, in which the identities and positions of the "center" and the "provinces" were established that enabled the flow of economic resources from the periphery to the core.[11] Roman hegemony was not created to constrain the hegemon through a legitimized set of rules.[12] This hegemonic power purposively tried to coopt the provincial elite through Hellenization/Romanization, and allowed them to partake in the material and social benefits of this trading system.[13] While the Mediterranean may have eventually enjoyed an imperial peace for two centuries after 31 B.C.E., this peace emerged out of system-wide conquest and was maintained under the watchful eye of the permanent Roman navy.

In contrast to Rome's structural hegemony, China's loose primacy in the eastern Indian Ocean was not established through military means, nor was it simply emergent due to China's much larger economy. This maritime system was forged from the combination of the "productive power"[14] of several actors with different social and material capacities that nevertheless allowed them to generate collective action through the interaction of their decentralized choices. Unlike the Roman Mediterranean, where the structural identities of the center and the periphery emerged out of coercive interactions, the eastern Indian Ocean was characterized by the relationships between "pre-constituted social actors,"[15] both Sinic and Indic. Therefore, Chinese primacy was not imposed top-down. Instead, it was both top-down and bottom-up, as China and the Southeast Asian polities sought to manage the material power asymmetry between them to meet their different material and social needs.

The "mode of power" constitutes the material and ideational relations "that are generative of both actors and the way in which power is exercised."[16] Unlike Rome, where coercion played an important role in power relations, attraction played a key role in the eastern Indian Ocean. The ideology of Sinocentrism as well as the ideas that underpinned the *mandala* polities emphasized attracting and wooing subordinates while downplaying coercion.[17] However, Southeast Asian polities were not attracted to China due to Sinic ideas of "relational affection and obligation."[18] The cognitive mode underpinning the *mandala* ideas was Indic (not Sinic). Since *mandala* polities have both superordinate and subordinate actors, as explained in Chapter 3, Southeast Asian actors emphasized "power sharing" to manage their social and material interactions.[19]

Consequently, the social distance between the Indianized and Sinicized worlds could be bridged through the ritual practices of the tributary system. In other words, Southeast Asia was not bandwagoning with China for material advantages, and their different ideational worlds did not make social interactions incommensurable. The social praxis of their different ideational systems made coexistence despite cultural diversity possible.[20] Not surprisingly, Roman hegemony disappeared with the waning of Roman power. By contrast, China's loose primacy in the diverse eastern Indian Ocean world was durable and survived for centuries even in the absence of a system-wide hegemonic navy, despite the rise and fall of several Chinese dynasties and multitudes of Southeast Asian polities.

Chinese primacy in Southeast Asia had another important characteristic. China "did not seek to control the foreign policies of the tributary states other than towards itself."[21] Southeast Asian polities engaged with polities in India "independent[ly]" of their relations with the Chinese empires.[22] Furthermore, diplomatic relations between Indian and Southeast Asian polities did not represent a relationship of paramountcy and subordination given the convergent development of polities on both sides of the Bay of Bengal, even as the Southeast Asian polities actively localized Indic ideas. Despite their "acceptance of the Chinese world order, Southeast Asian kingdoms never saw themselves as committed to that order alone. . . . India was always an alternative pole of [sociological] attraction (and status). . . . Their foreign relations cultures, while hierarchical, recognised several potentially competing centres of power, and made allowance for shifting power relationships."[23] In such a fluid world, where no power ruled the seas, order emerged out of the dynamic interactions of multiple local actors, where Southeast Asian agency made all the difference. Therefore, maritime Asia, a decentered realm, is representative of an alternative paradigm of order making and order shaping, in contrast to the hegemonic logic of the core–periphery Mediterranean system.

The Power of Ideas

Although the Hellenization of the classical Mediterranean was associated with the processes of *colonization, hegemonic socialization,* and imperial *appropriation,* the Indianization of Southeast Asia was almost entirely pacific. The most important known examples of Indian military campaigns in Southeast Asia were the attacks carried out by the Cholas in the eleventh century, possibly as a punitive action against Sriwijayan interference in Chola trade with Song China. But this was far from the normal pattern of relations between Indic and Southeast Asian polities. While the Cholas may have exercised some form of geopolitical influence around the northern edges of the Strait of Melaka after these attacks, it is noteworthy that they occurred centuries after the *localization* entailed in the spread of Indic culture had begun. Although violence was certainly not absent in maritime Asia, it was far from being the primary vehicle for the spread of Indian culture. (It is noteworthy that the list of history's 100 deadliest events compiled by *National Geographic* does not feature any wars across the Indian Ocean in the periods under consideration here, but does include wars in the classical Mediterranean such as the First and Second Punic Wars, as well as the Ming conquest and occupation of northern Vietnam.)[24]

A second major difference between Hellenization and Indianization has to do with local initiative and agency. While local agency has been emphasized in the process of the Hellenization of the Mediterranean in the archaic age, it appears to have been greater in the case of Indianization. For example, the local population of Sicily did not call upon Greek culture to legitimize Greek rule. In fact, the Sikels faced the threat of extinction from the Greeks. By contrast, the Southeast Asians deliberately borrowed Indic ideas after having been familiar with them for centuries. While the Khmers Indianized while remaining Khmer, as discussed in Chapter 3, the Hellenization of Sicily left very little trace of the preexisting culture and identity of the local population. In the words of a narrative found in the exhibits of the Syracuse Museum:

> From the 7th century onwards, the indigenous cultures are
> to be transformed by the contact with the Greeks, and the
> process of assimilation and acculturation will go on until
> the absorption of Greek culture by the natives, so that from
> 5th century B.C. differences will be only economic rather
> than cultural.[25]

This was in marked contrast to the spread of Indian culture in Southeast Asia. As we have seen, not only did the elements of the preexisting local culture remain fairly visible, but the Southeast Asians also modified or localized the foreign elements in accordance with indigenous cultures and practices. Notwithstanding the fact that the design of Southeast Asian Hindu temples is based on the sacred Mount Meru and is undergirded by Indic conceptions of state and kingship, one finds, as many commentators have noted, that there is no Angkor Wat, Bayon, or Borobudur in India.

Finally, in both the Roman Mediterranean and Southeast Asia, the more powerful political actors, Rome and China, did not turn out to wield the most powerful ideational influence. After all, Romanization was informed by Hellenization, and Rome *appropriated* the local ideas of the subjugated Greek people to assert and maintain its imperial power. By contrast, in Southeast Asia it was the *ideas of power* that served local political, economic, and cultural needs, which were localized in the absence of imperialism. These ideas were based upon Indic politico-cultural models that were perceived as universal. Outside of northern Vietnam, where Sinicization was based on *hegemonic socialization* and *imperialism*, it was Indic ideas that prevailed. Additionally, northern Vietnam Indianized to some degree even in the absence of the hegemony of subcontinental polities.

Although the "exchanges across the Bay of Bengal were made on the basis of equality," the Chinese "always demanded that the 'southern barbarians' acknowledge Chinese suzerainty by the regular sending of tribute."[26] While the Vietnamese transformed through *hegemonic socialization*, they cleverly used Sinic ideas in the long run "to defend" their own "independent status in the face of Chinese imperial pretensions."[27] By contrast, Pollock has pointed out that the same cannot be said "in the case of the Khmer's use of Sanskrit," which spread in the absence of subcontinental hegemony/imperialism.[28] However, it would be erroneous to conclude that the rest of Southeast Asia turned toward Indian culture to escape from China's strategic domination.

Monica Smith has argued that the adoption of the Chinese model would have "implied or invited Chinese control," and therefore the Southeast Asians looked toward India, as "Indian political entities were too weak for physical expansion."[29] However, such an instrumentalist reading of the spread of Indic ideas in Southeast Asia is not tenable, and certainly not beyond the examples of Linyi and Funan in the late third century that Smith used. As late as the tenth century, there were large Southeast Asian polities like Pagan on the mainland of which the Chinese "knew nothing."[30] Furthermore, as argued in Chapter 3, prior to the conquest of Yunnan by the Yuan, and in the absence of a viable navy until the Song, most of continental Southeast Asia and almost all of maritime Southeast Asia was beyond the strategic reach of the Chinese empires.

In fact, the main difference between Indianization and Sinicization appears to be ideational. As Yuri Pines has pointed out, the

> alternative to submission—and the only act that meant real independence [in the Sinic world]—would be to proclaim oneself as an emperor, a new "Son of Heaven," second to none. This, however, implied that a local leader sought the unification of All-under-Heaven under his aegis, which meant that he could neither coexist with other self-proclaimed emperors nor tolerate autonomous kingdoms, at least in the long-term.[31]

Not only was state formation in the Sinic world "accomplished using Chinese forms and titles," it was also paradoxically "dependent on formal recognition from the Chinese empire."[32] By contrast, state formation in the Indianized world of Southeast Asia did not depend upon formal recognition from any subcontinental polity. All that an ambitious ruler had to do was to replicate the ideal Indic polity in his realm and attract subordinates of his own. The creation of these idealized realms entailed self-legitimizing processes, and allowed all such kings to claim universal titles—like the *cakravartin* ruler—for themselves even as the actual extent of their *mandala* polities remained limited in practice. As explained above, coexistence and mutually beneficial commercial interactions between the self-proclaimed Chinese Son of Heaven and the universal *cakravartin* rulers of the *mandala* polities were nevertheless possible despite their different ideational underpinnings.

The Provision of Public Goods in the Two World Orders

In the Mediterranean, it was Rome, the hegemonic power, which supplied the public goods to make the trading system run. These public goods included protection (involving the implicit threat of violence), the suppression of piracy, and *sea control* exercised by the hegemonic Roman navy to keep the sea routes open. This generated a core–periphery economic system in the Mediterranean that ensured the flow of material resources (both revenue and human resources/slaves) into the Roman/Italian center. In other words, the Roman hegemon established a "tributary" system that enriched Rome. Although a general peace or *Pax Romana* did exist in the Mediterranean, it emerged only after Rome's Mediterranean-wide imperial conquest. Even as the tribute from the subordinate polities then transformed into formal taxation from the provinces, it continued to flow from the Mediterranean periphery into the Roman center. Rome and Italy remained exempt from land taxes for centuries.

By contrast, maritime Asia was configured differently. First, there was no *Pax Sinica* in the classical eastern Indian Ocean, even though the various (large) Chinese empires were the most powerful political actors of that system. China's promotion of security and the management of interpolity conflict in the region were occasional and selective. For example, conflict between China's tributaries like Champa and Dai Viet, or between those in the Java Sea and the Strait of Malacca, was not uncommon despite occasional Chinese attempts to mediate between them.

This is especially true for the period prior to the twelfth century, when China did not have a navy that sailed beyond northern Vietnam.[33] Later, under the Yuan and the early Ming, it was the Chinese empires that were the sources of large-scale regional warfare. Similarly, China's suppression of piracy was also irregular and episodic, even under the Ming. As discussed in Chapter 3, China tried to tackle piracy through the practices of the tributary system— by refusing to accept tribute from piratical subordinates—instead of systemically eradicating maritime piracy.[34] In other words, Chinese power was not associated with regional peace in maritime Asia, where conflict remained endemic.

Second, there was no hegemonic Chinese navy exercising sea control in maritime Asia. The public good of the security of the sea lanes emerged from the accretion of local and decentralized initiatives: the Southeast Asian *mandala* polities only sought to control their local waters, while the Chinese empires resorted to political manipulation via the tributary system (but only at the Chinese end of the system). In other words, unlike the Roman Mediterranean, where the Roman hegemon ensured sea control via hegemonic (or great power) management, the public good of the security of the sea lanes in maritime Asia emerged from *shared management* of the

trading system. Even as the polities of maritime Asia competed vigorously for trade, the eastern Indian Ocean lacked a hegemonic
naval power that dominated entire trade routes, as happened in the
Mediterranean. Importantly, the local agency of the Southeast
Asians played a crucial role in the creation and maintenance of this
system.

This made maritime Asia into a truly decentered realm. It was
the Southeast Asians, especially those from the Austronesian
groups, who pioneered the sea routes to China and India, and continued to play the key role in connecting that system. Furthermore,
they did so on ships built with local techniques and sailed using
local navigational ideas. While the Indians certainly joined the
Southeast Asians on these voyages from an early date, the Chinese
role was initially passive for several centuries. Later, when active
Chinese participation started under the Song, they continued to remain just one among several actors sailing these waters. After
China started manufacturing oceangoing vessels under the Song,
the Chinese built upon the shipping techniques of the Southeast
Asians.

These "hybrid" ships then continued to coexist with the "indigenous traditions" of both China and Southeast Asia.[35] As spectacular as the Yuan and Ming fleets were, they simply sailed across
routes that had been used by the Southeast Asians (and others) for
centuries. According to Hedley Bull, "sea power" is also determined
by the "merchant marine" and by the polity's "maritime outlook
and tradition," and does not depend upon naval (military) power
alone.[36] Sea power remained dispersed in this decentered world.
Maritime trade in Asian waters was not dominated by China or the
ethnic Chinese, and it remained in the hands of the region's pluralistic trading communities.

Nevertheless, there was a loose form of Chinese primacy in
maritime Asia displayed in the practices of the so-called tributary
system. However, there were important differences with the
Roman Mediterranean. While tribute in the Roman world consisted of revenue and resources that flowed into the Roman center
at the expense of the periphery, tribute in maritime Asia simply
meant gifts, as explained in Chapter 3. Although Roman tribute
consisted of taxes and rent, "tribute transactions" in maritime Asia

represented a relationship of "selling and purchasing" in the guise of "tribute goods and 'gifts.' . . . In fact, it is quite legitimate to view tribute exchange [in maritime Asia] as a commercial transaction."[37] Not surprisingly, Rome became rich through its Mediterranean tribute. However, China had to pay large sums of money for maritime Asian products. As explained earlier, some Chinese empires even became "poorer" as a consequence. In other words, in contrast to the Roman tributary system that generated a core–periphery order by enriching Rome, maritime Asia was a decentered realm, and the tributary system was just one part of this larger decentered world where the economic benefits were more evenly distributed.

Therefore, even as the Southeast Asian polities accepted a form of asymmetry in their relations with China through the rituals of the tributary system, they were hardly the peripheries of a Chinese center. After all, tribute in Southeast Asia was understood very differently from that at the Chinese end of this system. While China accepted tribute as gifts that confirmed its civilizational superiority, Southeast Asian rulers thought of it as "the polite exchange of gifts as a form of formality that went with mutually beneficial trade" and believed that the rituals of this system in China "established status hierarchy, not vassalage."[38] The *cakravartin* rulers of the polities like the Angkor *mandala*, with their large capital city (which was perhaps the largest pre-industrial city in the world) and monumental temple architecture, were hardly China's civilizational inferiors. In fact, there were times when the Chinese themselves went to Southeast Asian centers for cultural attainment. For example, the Chinese Buddhist monk Yijing went to study Sanskrit in Sriwijaya in the seventh century after sailing there on Sriwijayan ships.[39]

Just like the fluid and dynamic hierarchy among the rulers of the Southeast Asian *mandalas* (both within these *mandalas* and between them), the relationship between the Southeast Asian *mandalas* and China was also "impermanent."[40] Therefore, Chinese hierarchy was accepted "without discredit," and it had to be constantly created and recreated through the rituals of the tributary system.[41] After all, they were self-proclaimed *cakravartin* rulers in dialogue with the self-proclaimed Son of Heaven. The *shared management* of the practices of this world are perhaps best understood through the example of the Song emperor Taizu accepting the tribute of a rhinoceros horn "with a pattern resembling a dragon and the Chinese character for 'Song' " from Sriwijaya "as evidence that he had received the mandate of heaven."[42] A gift from this cultural center with long-distance navigation technologies and skills that "became a prominent symbol of the Song dynasty's legitimacy" hardly made Sriwijaya an inferior, except in the official rhetoric of the Sinocentric elite.[43]

Chinese primacy, to the degree that it existed, was therefore loose and fluid. Outside of Sinic Dai Viet, Chinese investiture was not the pathway to political legitimacy in the Indianized world of the Southeast Asia. In this *mandala* realm, it was the creation of an idealized polity of Sanskrit political texts (and monumental temple architecture and Indic names) that played such a role. It is noteworthy that Southeast Asian court chronicles "say next to nothing about China ... because to have done so would neither have enhanced the king's glory, nor reinforced the Southeast Asian (Hindu/Buddhist) worldview."[44] Unlike the Roman emperor, who ruled Egypt as a pharaoh, the Chinese emperor did not preside over the Southeast Asian *mandala* polities as a Buddhist *cakravartin*. China's loose primacy was, then, a dynamic attribute of this system, and Southeast Asian agency played an active role in producing it, both materially and ideationally. Maritime Asia was held together by these decentralized and diverse cultural and trading practices even in the absence of a hegemonic navy exercising sea control.

A Decentered or Multiplex Order in the Emerging Indo-Pacific

This book has provided a comparative study of the Mediterranean and Indian Ocean, with lessons for the contemporary Indo-Pacific region, which subsumes the historic Indian Ocean region. Hence our final section offers some conclusions concerning the shape of the emerging Indo-Pacific international order, which we characterize as a multiplex international order, as opposed to a hegemonic or multipolar one.

We start by recapping some of the key theoretical arguments and backdrop of our book. Since the international relations theoretical scholarship has largely emerged from the universalization of Western historical experiences, analogies are often drawn from the Roman Mediterranean, or generalizations that emerge thereof are universalized, while nonhegemonic and decentered historical orders of the type that existed in Asia are ignored. For example, Gilpin drew an analogue with the Roman Empire and argued that "Pax Britannica and Pax Americana, like the Pax Romana, ensured an international system of relative peace and security."[45] This Roman analogy was also invoked by Paul Kennedy, for whom Britain "reproduce[d] afloat something like the political and economic dominance of the Roman Empire" as "seaborne trade" was "dominated by [Roman/British] naval power."[46] Consequently, these scholars have interpreted the history of the post-1498 Indian Ocean as the "the Vasco da Gama era" or a "succession" of European naval hegemonies, as explained in Chapter 4.

Given this reliance on Mediterranean history, international relations scholarship sees naval hegemony and sea control as necessary for the making and shaping of maritime trading systems. For Kennedy, "[a]s soon as man had recognized the suitability of the sea as a medium through which to dispatch troops or to exchange wares, he turned his attention to constructing a weapon which would enable him to achieve and retain *command of the sea*—the ship of war."[47] Therefore, he argued that "the need to secure command of the maritime trade-routes" is one of the "central axioms of the doctrine of sea power."[48] According to Gilpin's notion of hegemonic stability, "British sea command" provided the framework for the economic order in the nineteenth century, and the United States did so in the twentieth century as the "successive" hegemonic power.[49] Joseph Nye's liberal hegemonic argument also shares this view of successive British and American hegemonies. Nye has argued that "the United States, like the United Kingdom in the nineteenth century, has an interest in keeping international commons, such as the oceans, open to all."[50] According to a recent Council on Foreign Relations "backgrounder," the U.S. Navy "has a command of the sea" analogous to "the British Navy more than a century before it," and it "protects seaborne commerce" and "generally maintains order at sea."[51] As per this view, an important public good provided by these hegemonic powers was their command of the sea to make the trading system work.

Such views are in fact echoed in the works of many scholars. According to Ken Booth, the difference between "balance of power systems on land and at sea" is that "the former [have] usually been based on an equilibrium of power, [while] the latter [have] been based on preponderance. Over the last century-and-a-half, the high level of order and freedom at sea was the result of *pax Britannica* followed by *pax Americana*," as they were both "preponderant naval powers."[52] For Geoffrey Gresh, "Europe dominated much of East Asia's maritime space" for "centuries," and the United States "has ruled the waves and the international order that came with it" since the end of the Cold War.[53]

Geoffrey Till has explicitly noted that the "canon of sea power thinking and analysis is heavily dominated by Western, rather than Asian, Arabic, African, or South American thought."[54] Furthermore, "the great masters of Western thought, Alfred Thayer Mahan and Sir Julian Corbett," were especially concerned with "the ways in which sea control might be secured, maintained, and exploited" despite their many differences.[55] Mahanian thought, with its emphasis on the "control" of "mercantile trade and routes," is particularly evident in Kennedy's work and in his emphasis on British "naval mastery."[56] Mahan's thinking also influenced American thought at the beginning of the twentieth century, as noted in Chapter 4. According to Andrew Lambert, this " 'New' American Navy" was "Roman" as it was "serving the interests of a continental great power."[57] Importantly, this "Mahanian doctrine of sea power" has "continued to dominate US military thinking" ever since.[58]

Michael Mastanduno has referred to the navy as a lynchpin of American hegemony as it "controlled and protected global trade routes."[59] For Michael Mandelbaum, even as the U.S. Navy patrolled the world's oceans to keep the sea lanes open "in case of war," it provided protection to commercial shipping as "a by-product."[60] In a similar vein, David Shambaugh has argued that the United States has been providing maritime Asia with the "public good" of "keeping open the sea lanes and commons throughout," although many regional militaries, especially those in Southeast Asia, were "free riding" on the United States.[61]

In other words, these ideas and practices drawn from the Mediterranean, European, and American milieux are taken as universal and axiomatic—and applicable to all times and all places. However, by ignoring the coercion entailed in the Roman path to Mediterranean supremacy, this view also mischaracterizes British and American naval predominance by downplaying the role of colonialism in the case of the former, and the pathway of the global wars and rivalries of the twentieth century for the latter. On that understanding, it does not take much to view American naval power (or British naval power in the past) as being oriented toward the status quo, while presenting any challenge to it as revisionism.

In fact, the looming Sino-American Thucydidean hegemonic transition discussed in Chapter 4 is at least partly informed by this perspective. According to Graham Allison, China, as a "rising power," is endeavoring to hasten America's "retreat" from maritime Asia. (For Allison, the United States is the "ruling power.")[62] Others also argue along these lines. For Bruce Jones, for example, naval power is "the handmaiden to American hegemony" and "the US Navy was securing the trade of its allies."[63] Furthermore, China was in the process of making "a bid for counter-hegemony" and was "fast becoming a fuller maritime power than the United States."[64]

However, as argued in this book, the classical Indian Ocean trading system centered on modern Southeast Asia was developed and sustained for centuries in the absence of a hegemonic naval power. With its "porous" eastern borders that flow "imperceptibly into the South China Sea and the Pacific Ocean," the Indian Ocean "has a fundamentally different history" from that of the Mediterranean Sea.[65] For the Indian Ocean world—"the world's first 'global economy' "—"economic and cultural integration proved more efficient than force."[66] More important, "[n]one of the Indian Ocean states seriously attempted to control or regulate trade."[67] This is not to argue that the Indian Ocean trading world was uniquely peaceful, for naval violence and piracy were certainly features of the region's maritime history.[68] However, despite evidence for some naval and maritime conflict, "nothing suggests that they took place on a similar scale as, for example, in Mediterranean history."[69]

Although historians have known that the classical Indian Ocean was organized differently from the Mediterranean, it has heretofore been ignored by international relations scholars and foreign policy analysts. Therefore, instead of the hegemonic succession implied in the power shift from the United States to China, we argue for a paradigm shift in thinking related to the making and shaping of maritime trading systems.[70] Our analysis of the geopolitical dynamics in the contemporary eastern Indian Ocean makes the case for a nonhegemonic international order with echoes of the classical eastern Indian Ocean, where such a hegemonic navy did not exist. Instead of a hegemonic navy exercising sea control, as in the Roman Mediterranean, we think that *shared management* that accrues from the decentralized decisions of several great and lesser powers will collectively provide the public good of the security of the sea lanes in the Indo-Pacific. Not only is Southeast Asia not free-riding, but Southeast Asian agency is also crucial to the making and shaping of the emerging regional order. Furthermore, the norms embodied in the ASEAN Way are actively shaping the region's politico-military and politico-economic interactions.

In other words, the rise of China as an Indo-Pacific naval power does not imply a Chinese counterhegemonic bid to displace the United States. A nonhegemonic international order is in the making in the eastern Indian Ocean. Not only is Sinocentrism unlikely, but the United States is also not likely to reestablish the primacy that it enjoyed after the Cold War. While the rise of China has diminished American predominance, neither of these powers is likely to emerge as hegemonic. China and the United States are competing over relative position in the region and aim to secure their access to the regional maritime commons. In other words, their competition revolves around naval power projection, not sea control. Moreover, they are not the only major powers in the region, as others such as India, Japan, Australia, France, and the United Kingdom also form a part of the emerging regional dynamics.

Furthermore, our analysis shows that local—Southeast Asian—initiative matters. Southeast Asian states are individually and collectively coengaging all the major powers while rejecting the hegemony of any single great power. The Southeast Asian states are also trying to limit great power rivalry by giving all of them access to the region. Southeast Asia's vision of the Indo-Pacific is not that of a hermetically sealed region. Instead, it points toward an "open" order as Southeast Asia resumes its historical role as the pivot connecting the Indian Ocean and the South China Sea.

ASEAN-led institutions are engaging all the great powers. Furthermore, Southeast Asian minilaterals like the Malacca Straits Patrol (MSP) and the Sulu-Sulawesi Sea Patrols (SSSP) can provide regional public goods for the security of the trade routes at select locales, as argued in Chapter 4. These initiatives are also supported by the major powers through various mechanisms including capacity building (by the United States, China, and Japan) and coordinated patrols (with India).

In turn, the United States is approaching the Indo-Pacific through minilaterals like the Quad and AUKUS, while promoting the rise of India and supporting the engagement of extraregional (especially European) powers with the region. Meanwhile, China is building continental bridges to the Indian Ocean and pursuing the BRI (which points toward a different kind of openness in the form of China + ASEAN + X). China is also pursuing its own minilaterals, such as the Lancang-Mekong Cooperation mechanism and the Mekong River Patrols. As such, China is not trying to dominate the maritime passageway even as it is seeking access to it and is developing the capabilities to project its military power.

Therefore, the waning of America's post–Cold War leadership does not mean that "turbulent seas [lie] ahead," as argued by some.[71] The "plausible alternative" to the American "role as the functional equivalent of the world's government"—a view reminiscent of hegemonic stability—is not "less" governance and "less … pleasant" consequences, as argued by others.[72] Nor should we implicitly believe that to "wish for a multipolar international order" instead of a dominant power that provides "the infrastructure of law and order necessary to keep the trade routes open" is "the height of folly."[73]

Generalizations that emerge from the Roman precedent are not universal, they are context-dependent. Nevertheless, the strong association between hegemony and order in mainstream accounts of international relations also distorts prescriptions for American foreign policy. More specifically, proponents of liberal hegemony posit a binary choice between America's full engagement, which is believed to promote order, and "pull[ing] back" by the United States, which is viewed as a challenge for "protecting the global economic commons" such as the sea lanes and commercial shipping corridors.[74] However, this is a false binary because the United

States can remain fully engaged without being hegemonic. Based on the precedent of the classical eastern Indian Ocean, ongoing developments in the contemporary Indo-Pacific—where the United States continues to remain engaged but is no longer hegemonic— show that the accretion of the decentralized choices of multiple powers can collectively produce the public goods of trade and security in maritime systems. In fact, the shared management of the system by multiple actors adds depth and resilience to the international order, as it is no longer dependent upon the material power of any one single actor. Therefore, contra G. John Ikenberry, Charles Krauthammer, and Richard Haass, who were quoted in the opening section of the Introduction, the passing of U.S. hegemony is not producing a "less desirable" world with insecure sea lanes, or, worse, disorder.

To restate our main findings, including those with both academic and policy relevance, a multiplex international order is in the making in the Indo-Pacific. Our reasons for this assertion, using the conceptualization of multiplex order in Chapter 1, and the discussion of the empirical chapters, are as follows.

First, it is far from likely that the Indo-Pacific, of which the Indian Ocean is a part, will develop into a hegemonic order. In the past (after World War II), one could speak of U.S. hegemony in East Asia, one that was far from complete anyway. But U.S. hegemony was far less complete in the Indian Ocean part of the Indo-Pacific. Today, with U.S. global hegemony seriously eroding, it is even more difficult to apply that label to U.S. power and influence over the wider Indo-Pacific region, notwithstanding India's increasing strategic alignment with the United States. It is even less likely that China will emerge as a hegemonic power—even as a regional hegemon—in the Indo-Pacific. Some of the barriers to this have been discussed in Chapter 4, and are otherwise familiar— among them, the limits of China's naval power-projection capability in the Indian Ocean segment of the Indo-Pacific. In addition, China's economic clout, though substantial, is undercut by a pushback against the BRI from many countries in the region. The economic rise of India also offsets Chinese economic dominance to some degree. And China suffers from limited soft power, or a "trust deficit," especially in Southeast Asia.[75] The Indo-Pacific is primarily a maritime arena, and hence control of the sea is critical to turning it into a maritime hegemony by a single power. But the United States is likely to be the last naval superpower to command the seas.[76] Sea control, whether by the United States, China, or India, is not in the offing in the Indo-Pacific.

Second, we argue that multipolarity does not adequately describe the international order of the Indo-Pacific. As noted in Chapter 1, multipolarity is about the distribution of material power, with little recognition of the role of other actors, including regional and middle powers, or institutions, which are subsumed under the big power poles. But in reality, some regional powers and regional groupings play a significant role in shaping an international order—providing predictability and stability, and sometimes economic well-being through regional integration. Multipolarity pays scant attention to ideas, norms, and nonstrategic interaction capacity, which were quite important in the Indian Ocean international order in the past and will remain so into the future. In other words, we hold that while the distribution of material power in the Indo-Pacific may be shaped by multiple great powers, including the United States, China, India, and to a lesser degree the EU, Russia, and Japan, it is a far cry from a classic multipolar system.

Middle powers such as Australia, and regional powers such as Indonesia and Vietnam, play a significant role in shaping Indo-Pacific international order, and they are not, especially the regional powers, beholden to U.S. or Chinese power and purpose. For example, Indonesia has steadfastly refused to take sides in the U.S.-China competition. ASEAN as a group also remains reluctant to choose between the United States and China in shaping its security and economic direction. Further into the Gulf region, Saudi Arabia, a country with much financial clout in the Indo-Pacific, is signaling a shift away from its close alignment with the United States, while in the southern tip of the African segment of the Indo-Pacific, South Africa is turning against the United States. Yet neither of them is embracing a Chinese hegemonic sphere. Similarly, Iran is an adversary of the United States without being a Chinese ally.

In other words, while multiple great powers are present in the region, they are promoting overlapping and layered forms of governance even as they may individually be pursuing their own self-interest. In the Indo-Pacific, great power dominance in general is substantially tempered by institutions like the EAS, ARF, and ADMM-Plus, and initiatives that exist at the subregional level in maritime Southeast Asia (such as the MSP and the SSSP, as discussed in Chapter 4). While some forms of cooperation involve the great powers (the China-led BRI and Lancang-Mekong Cooperation mechanism, or the U.S.-led Quad), they are hardly harbingers of regional hegemonism. As noted above, the important role of larger groupings like the ARF and EAS, which include not only most nations of the Asian region but also all the great powers of the world at the present time (the EU is part of the ARF but not the EAS), adds to the cross-cutting nature of regional interactions, which prevents the hegemony of a single power or the collective dominance of a group of powers (multipolarity). This pattern is further sustained not least by the principle of "ASEAN-centrality," which, while eroding somewhat, remains the only acceptable convening formula for Asia-Pacific and Indo-Pacific regionalism.

One implication of the foregoing analysis is that a key feature of the emerging Indo-Pacific international order is the central role of Asian countries, including great powers, rising powers, regional powers, and their economic and security connections in formative roles in the making and shaping of the international order. At the same time, the active agency of the non-great powers is also integral to this order, as ASEAN is playing a pivotal, constitutive, and especially normative role in this decentered, nonhegemonic, and open order in the Indo-Pacific.

Third, as discussed in Chapter 4, patterns of economic interactions and interdependence linkages in the Indo-Pacific remain diverse and cross-cutting. Despite attempts at decoupling, trade and investment ties between China and the United States, and between China and U.S. allies such as Japan, South Korea, the Philippines, and Thailand, remain substantial. In fact, China has become the main bilateral trading partner of the vast majority of Indo-Pacific nations, including those mentioned above, which look to the United States for security. This situation is reinforced by the generally inclusive or "open" nature of Asia-Pacific regional groupings (keeping in mind that Asia-Pacific, not Indo-Pacific, remains the most common organizing framework for regional bodies in the area). The

RCEP economic grouping, which the United States is not a part of, binds China with major Asian economies except India. The Asia-Pacific Economic Cooperation (APEC) grouping, of which both China and the United States are members, does not include India.

Finally, cultural diversity and ideological pluralism remain the hallmarks of the Indo-Pacific international order. Unlike Western Europe or the transatlantic region, there is, and never will be, in the Indo-Pacific the predominance of a single cultural or civilizational framework, nor will this doom it to experience a Huntingtonian "clash of civilizations." Unlike the predominance of Christianity in Europe and the transatlantic arena, the religious and civilizational landscape of the Indo-Pacific has been and will remain shaped by Buddhism, Hinduism, and Confucianism, as well as Islam and Christianity, which have made their way into the region in more recent centuries. This makes it impossible for the region to embrace not only a Western model of domestic or regional governance, but also Chinese or Indian or Islamic cultural dominance or modes of governance. Ideologically, too, unlike Western Europe and the north Atlantic regions, the Indo-Pacific will remain very pluralistic, with democracies, quasi democracies, authoritarian regimes, military dictatorships, and communitarian societies interacting and mostly coexisting. While such ideological pluralism may seem conducive to disunity or conflict, it has not prevented regional cooperation, including within ASEAN, in a part of the world that is a veritable mosaic of cultures, religions, and political systems.

All these features of the emerging Indo-Pacific ensure its fit within a multiplex international order framework, rather than a hegemonic or even a multipolar one (the latter except in the narrow sense of distribution of material power). But this is also not the vision of the Indo-Pacific as represented in the Quad or the strategic vision pushed by the United States, which excludes China. Rather, it is the classical decentered Indian Ocean–style multiplex order—a nonhegemonic, open, inclusive, and dynamic order—as distinct from the hegemonic classical Mediterranean, that is likely to come closer to defining the emerging and future Indo-Pacific region. Academics and policymakers will be well advised to take note of this if they want to develop a more viable and durable Indo-Pacific construct.

Acknowledgments

THIS BOOK HAS BEEN in the making for some time. Some of the initial research and conceptualization behind the book was done by Acharya in Sicily in 2011, and was presented by him in a lecture to the *CdLM Storia e cultura dei paesi mediterranei* at the University of Catania, Sicily, in January 2011. Subsequent versions were presented in a keynote speech by Acharya to the Asian Political and International Studies Association (APISA) Congress in Ankara in October 2012; at the 54th International Studies Association Annual Convention in San Francisco in April 2013; and in his ongoing course lectures at American University in Washington, DC. In 2017, Pardesi joined Acharya in the project, leading to an expansion of its scope. He has presented some of the core arguments of the book, most recently at a LUCIR Seminar at Leiden University in April 2023; at the GIGA Institute for Asian Studies in Hamburg in April 2023; in an online webinar organized by the Graduate Research and Development Network on Asian Security (GRADNAS) in May 2023; and at a Political Science and International Relations Seminar at Victoria University of Wellington, New Zealand, in August 2023. Our sincere thanks to all the participants at these events for their valuable comments and suggestions.

Thanks are also due to the Research Trust of Victoria University of Wellington for two small grants to cover the costs of the maps of the classical Mediterranean and classical Southeast Asia (the eastern Indian Ocean), and the index.

We would also like to express our gratitude to Jaya Aninda Chatterjee, our editor at Yale University Press, for her interest, patience, and continuous encouragement for this book over the years. Finally, thanks are due to Harry Haskell, our copyeditor, whose hard work ensured that we were able to clearly express our ideas.

Notes

Introduction

1. Gideon Rose, ed., *What Was the Liberal Order? The World We May Be Losing* (New York: Foreign Affairs, 2017); "Out of Order? The Future of the International System," *Foreign Affairs*, vol. 96, no. 1 (January/February 2017); Andrew Browne, "The End of America's World Order," *Bloomberg*, November 19, 2019, https://www.bloomberg.com/news/newsletters/2019-11-19/the-end-of-america-s-world-order? (accessed 2/22/2024); Alfred McCoy, "The End of Our World Order Is Imminent," *The Nation*, February 28, 2019, https://www.thenation.com/article/archive/end-of-world-order-empire-climate-change/ (accessed 6/16/2021).
2. G. John Ikenberry, *Liberal Leviathan: The Origins, Crisis, and Transformation of the American World Order* (Princeton: Princeton University Press, 2011).
3. Anne-Marie Slaughter, "The Return of Anarchy?," in "The Next World Order," special 70th anniversary issue, *Journal of International Affairs* (2017): 11–16; Robert Blackwill and Thomas Wright, *The End of World Order and American Foreign Policy* (New York: Council on Foreign Relations, May 2020), https://www.cfr.org/report/end-world-order-and-american-foreign-policy (accessed 2/22/2024).
4. Ikenberry, *Liberal Leviathan*, 32.
5. Charles Krauthammer, "The Unipolar Moment," *Foreign Affairs*, vol. 70, no. 1 (1990/1991): 27.
6. Richard N. Haass, "The Unraveling: How to Respond to a Disordered World," *Foreign Affairs*, vol. 93, no. 6 (November/December 2014): 70–74, 75–79.
7. Barry Buzan and Ole Wæver, *Regions and Powers: The Structure of International Security* (Cambridge: Cambridge University Press, 2003). Some elements of Buzan and Wæver's theory of "regional security complexes"

are helpful in conceptualizing nonhegemonic international orders (NHIOs). Some regional security complexes are nonhegemonic: for example, those regional security complexes which are "centered" by an institution (e.g., EU-Europe), rather than by a great power (East Asia or North America). A "standard" regional security complex, marked by the absence of a global level power in them, can be a NHIO, provided it does not have a regional hegemon (bear in mind that Buzan and Wæver allow such regional security complexes to have regional hegemons, which is contrary to the idea of NHIOs). While some such linkages and comparisons can be made and are helpful, the concept of NHIOs is an entirely distinct theoretical construct, and should not be viewed as an adjunct to the theory of regional security complexes. Its focus is not on how regions are organized, but on exploring and analyzing patterns of international relations which have emerged without a hegemon or by taming any single or collective hegemony.

8. Theda Skocpol, "Doubly Engaged Social Science: The Promises of Comparative Historical Analysis," in James Mahoney and Dietrich Rueschemeyer, eds., *Comparative Historical Analysis in the Social Sciences* (New York: Cambridge University Press, 2003), 409.

9. Skocpol, "Doubly Engaged Social Science," 411.

10. Wang Gungwu, "The Universal and the Historical: My Faith in History," in *New Thinking on Peace: Essays on Peace and Human Security, Civilizational Dialogue, History, Education, Global Citizenship and University of the 21st Century*, compiled lectures of Wang Gungwu et al. (Singapore: Singapore Soka Association, 2006), 23–40, quote on p. 27.

11. Louis Gernet, quoted in Fernand Braudel, *The Mediterranean in the Ancient World* (London: Penguin, 2001), 258.

12. Iver B. Neumann, "Entry into International Society Reconceptualized: The Case of Russia," *Review of International Studies*, vol. 37, no. 2 (2011): 471.

13. Raymond Cohen and Raymond Westbrook, *Amarna Diplomacy: The Beginnings of International Relations* (Baltimore: Johns Hopkins University Press, 1992), 5.

14. Kurt A. Raaflaub, "Series Editor's Preface—The Ancient World: Comparative Histories," in Kurt A. Raaflaub, ed., *War and Peace in the Ancient World* (Malden: Blackwell Publishing, 2007), vii.

15. Wang Gungwu, "The Universal and the Historical: My Faith in History," Fourth Daisaku Ikeda Annual Lecture (Singapore: Singapore Soka Association, 2005), 6.

16. Daniel H. Deudney, *Bounding Power: Republican Security Theory from the Polis to the Global Village* (Princeton: Princeton University Press, 2007), 91.

17. Deudney, *Bounding Power*, 91. Although Deudney stresses republican and not imperial Rome, he does discuss the Punic Wars, the turning point in Rome's rise to imperial hegemony.

18. Neville Morley, *The Roman Empire: The Roots of Imperialism* (London: The Pluto Press, 2010), 2.

19. "Rome gave the Mediterranean world its own code of law and left as a legacy to Western civilization the first law of nations." See Robert Gilpin, *War & Change in World Politics* (New York: Cambridge University Press, 1981), 36 and 192.

20. Gilpin classifies the Punic Wars between Rome and Carthage as an example of a hegemonic war. See Gilpin, *War & Change in World Politics*, 200. Copeland looks at the Peloponnesian War and the Punic Wars to review Thucydides' account and the debate over whether war is caused by domestic or international factors. See Dale C. Copeland, *The Origins of Major War* (Ithaca: Cornell University Press, 2000), 210–13. Mearsheimer cites the Roman Empire as an example of his thesis that great powers can achieve regional hegemony, although he does not discuss this in great detail. He also mentions the Mughal and Qing empires as regional hegemonies. John J. Mearsheimer, *The Tragedy of Great Power Politics*, rev. ed. (New York: W. W. Norton, 2014), 272.

21. Richard Ned Lebow, "Thucydides the Constructivist," *American Political Science Review*, vol 1, no. 3 (2001): 547–60; Richard Ned Lebow, *The Cultural Theory of International Relations* (Cambridge: Cambridge University Press, 2008); and Christian Reus-Smit, *The Moral Purpose of the State: Culture, Social Identity, and Institutional Rationality in International Relations* (Princeton: Princeton University Press, 2001).

22. Deudney, *Bounding Power*.

23. Andrew Bacevich, *American Empire: The Realities and Consequences of U.S. Diplomacy* (Cambridge: Harvard University Press, 2004). Also see J. Rufus Fears, "The Lessons of the Roman Empire for America Today," Heritage Lecture #917, December 19, 2005, https://www.heritage.org/political-process/report/the-lessons-the-roman-empire-america-today (accessed 2/22/2024). For a study of how the founding American leaders were influenced by Mediterranean thought, see Carl J. Richard, *The Founders and the Classics: Greece, Rome, and the American Enlightenment* (Cambridge: Harvard University Press, 1994).

24. Barry Buzan and Richard Little, "The Idea of 'International System': Theory Meets History," *International Political Science Review / Revue internationale de science politique*, vol. 15, no. 3 (July 1994): 235. Following Morley, *The Roman Empire*, we would argue that these were to some extent constructed or imagined antecedents, especially during the Renaissance, which reflected the search for a usable past on which to base the European revival.

25. George Modelski and William R. Thompson, *Seapower in Global Politics, 1494–1993* (London: Macmillan, 1988), 4.

26. Benjamin de Carvalho and Halvard Leira, "Introduction: Staring at the Sea," in Benjamin de Carvalho and Halvard Leira, eds., *The Sea and International Relations* (Manchester: Manchester University Press, 2022), 1.

27. Modelski and Thompson, *Seapower in Global Politics*, 6.
28. Carla Norrlof, "The Waning of Pax Americana?," *Great Discussions* (2018): 12–13. Norrlof also mentions two other *Pax* regimes. She notes that *Pax Ottomana* secured caravan routes (or overland routes), while *Pax Mongolica* used force to secure "sea lanes and trade routes." However, as argued later in this book, there was no *Pax Mongolica* in the eastern Indian Ocean under the Yuan dynasty.
29. Ali Parchami, *Hegemonic Peace and Empire: The Pax Romana, Britannica, and Americana* (London: Routledge, 2009), 61.
30. Parchami, *Hegemonic Peace and Empire*, 154.
31. Joseph Grieco, G. John Ikenberry, and Michael Mastanduno, *Introduction to International Relations: Enduring Questions & Contemporary Perspective* (London: Palgrave, 2015), 176.
32. Grieco, Ikenberry, and Mastanduno, *Introduction to International Relations*, 364.
33. Grieco, Ikenberry, and Mastanduno, *Introduction to International Relations*, 177.
34. Andrew Lambert, *Seapower States: Maritime Culture, Continental Empires, and the Conflict that Made the Modern World* (New Haven: Yale University Press, 2018), 317.
35. Kurt A. Raaflaub, "Series Editor's Preface," vii.
36. An exception here is the English School. See Adam Watson, *The Evolution of International Society: A Comparative Historical Analysis* (London: Routledge, 1992); Barry Buzan and Richard Little, *International Systems in World History* (New York: Oxford University Press, 2000). Also see Stuart J. Kaufman, Richard Little, and William C. Wohlforth, eds., *The Balance of Power in World History* (New York: Palgrave, 2007); and Cohen and Westbrook, *Amarna Diplomacy*.
37. Buzan and Little, "The Idea of 'International System,' " 231.
38. Buzan and Little, *International Systems in World History*, 3.
39. Michael Cox, Tim Dunne, and Ken Booth, "Empires, Systems and States: Great Transformations in International Politics," *Review of International Studies*, vol. 27 (December 2001): 15.
40. Buzan and Little, *International Systems in World History*, 11. The work of Immanuel Wallerstein is of course especially important in exploring the economic dimensions of international systems. See Immanuel Wallerstein, *The Modern World System*, 4 vols. (Berkeley: University of California Press, 2011).
41. This is the least developed element of the revised conception of international systems, and hence one of the key contributions of this book. Kauffman, Little, and Wohlforth do incorporate normative aspects of balance of power systems, while in the same volume and his other works David Kang brings out important ideational elements in his study of the East Asian international system before the Western colonial era. See Kaufman, Little, and Wohlforth, *The Balance of Power in World History*.

42. This is consistent with one of constructivism's central claims. See Alexander Wendt, "Collective Identity Formation and the International State," *American Political Science Review*, vol. 88, no. 2 (June 1994): 384–96. See also Buzan and Little, *International Systems in World History*, 12.

43. G. John Ikenberry and Charles A. Kupchan, "Socialization and Hegemonic Power," *International Organization*, vol. 44, no. 3 (Summer 1990): 283–315.

44. Barry Buzan and Richard Little, "The Idea of 'International System,' " 239.

45. New archaeological evidence would put the beginnings of the Southeast Asian/Indian Ocean system to the 1st–4th centuries C.E. See Amitav Acharya, *Civilizations in Embrace: The Flow of Ideas and the Transformation of Power* (Singapore: Institute of Southeast Asian Studies, 2012).

46. Persia and Carthage are the other major players in the classical Mediterranean, which featured prominently in the early balance of power dynamics of the Mediterranean system. But Persia ceased to be a major player after Alexander's defeat of Darius, when a key strand of Hellenization occurred through the establishment of the Hellenistic kingdoms. Subsequently, Roman expansion obliterated Carthage and the Hellenistic kingdoms. Although Carthage was an expansionist power, especially in Sicily and Spain, Hannibal's conquests were in response to Roman expansion. The source of the Carthaginian civilization was, of course, the Phoenicians from the Levant coast, whose expansion was motivated by commerce rather than conquest (hence with some parallels to Indian influence in Southeast Asia). But the influence of those two powers deserves more recognition than is found in traditional discussions of Mediterranean civilization and international order, although this is beyond the scope of this book.

47. J. M. Roberts and Odd Arne Westad, *The Penguin History of the World*, 6th ed. (Penguin: London, 2013), Kindle Loc. 4524.

48. Fernand Braudel, *The Mediterranean and the Mediterranean World in the Age of Philip II*, 2 vols. (Berkeley: University of California Press, 1995).

49. The Mediterranean analogy and its limits have been used to study the Indian Ocean, East Asia, and Southeast Asia (and combinations thereof). As explained in Chapter 3, we focus on Southeast Asia, stretching from the eastern Indian Ocean into the South China Sea. Notable works influenced by this Mediterranean analogy include K. N. Chaudhuri, *Trade and Civilization in the Indian Ocean: An Economic History from the Rise of Islam to 1750* (New York: Cambridge University Press, 1985); K. N. Chaudhuri, *Asia before Europe: Economy and Civilization of the Indian Ocean from the Rise of Islam to 1750* (Cambridge: Cambridge University Press, 1990); Heather Sutherland, "Southeast Asian History and the Mediterranean Analogy," *Journal of Southeast Asian Studies*, vol. 34, no. 1 (2003): 1–20; and Angela Schottenhammer, ed., *The East Asian Mediterranean: Maritime Crossroads of Culture, Commerce and Human Migration* (Wiesbaden: Harrassowitz Verlag, 2008).

50. Philip E. Steinberg, *The Social Construction of the Ocean* (Cambridge: Cambridge University Press, 2001), 39–67. Additionally, Steinberg considered

Micronesia as a third type of such ocean-space construction, along with the Indian Ocean and the Mediterranean.

51. Theda Skocpol and Margaret Somers, "The Uses of Comparative History in Macrosocial Inquiry," *Comparative Studies in Society and History*, vol. 22, no. 2 (1980): 178.

52. Kenneth Pomeranz, *The Great Divergence: China, Europe, and the Making of the Modern World Economy* (Princeton: Princeton University Press, 2000), 8.

53. Jack A. Goldstone, *Revolution and Rebellion in the Early Modern World*, 25th Anniversary Edition (New York: Routledge, 2016), 54, 61.

54. Patrick O'Brien, "Historiographical Traditions and Modern Imperatives for the Restoration of Global History," *Journal of Global History*, vol. 1, no.1 (2006): 5–7.

55. For examples of such extrapolative works, see chapter 7 in Peter J. Katzenstein, *A World of Regions: Asia and Europe in the American Imperium* (Ithaca: Cornell University Press, 2005); and chapter 6 in Amitav Acharya, *Whose Ideas Matter? Agency and Power in Asian Regionalism* (Ithaca: Cornell University Press, 2009).

56. Francis Fukuyama, *The Origins of Political Order: From Prehuman Times to the French Revolution* (New York: Farrar, Straus and Giroux, 2011); Henry Kissinger, *World Order* (New York: Penguin Press, 2014); Niall Ferguson, *Civilization: The West and the Rest* (London: Allen Lane, 2011); and John M. Hobson, *The Eastern Origins of Western Civilization* (Cambridge: Cambridge University Press, 2004).

57. Judith Goldstein and Robert O. Keohane, "Ideas and Foreign Policy: An Analytic Framework," in Judith Goldstein and Robert O. Keohane, eds., *Ideas and Foreign Policy: Beliefs, Institutions, and Political Change* (Ithaca: Cornell University Press, 1993), 9.

58. Stuart J. Kaufman, Richard Little, and William C. Wohlforth, "Conclusion: Theoretical Insights from the Study of World History," in Kaufman, Little and Wohlforth, *The Balance of Power in World History*, 246.

59. Kaufman, Little and Wohlforth, "Conclusion," 244.

60. Kaufman, Little and Wohlforth, "Conclusion," 244.

Chapter One. Power, Ideas, and International Systems/Orders

1. Fareed Zakaria, *The Post-American World* (New York: W. W. Norton, 2008), 242.

2. Robert O. Keohane, *After Hegemony: Cooperation and Discord in the World Political Economy* (Princeton: Princeton University Press, 1984), 46.

3. F. S. Northedge, *The International Political System* (London: Faber and Faber, 1976).

4. Hedley Bull and Adam Watson, "Introduction," in Hedley Bull and Adam Watson, eds., *The Expansion of International Society* (Oxford: Clarendon Press, 1984), 1.

5. Importantly, some scholars "draw no distinction between international society and system, historically or theoretically," and "treat international society as a particular kind of social structural formation, preceded by, and embedded within, wider networks of global social and political interaction." Christian Reus-Smit and Tim Dunne, "The Globalization of International Society," in Tim Dunne and Christian Reus-Smit, eds., *The Globalization of International Society* (New York: Oxford University Press, 2017), 33.

6. Barry Buzan and Richard Little, *International Systems in World History* (New York: Oxford University Press, 2000).

7. Buzan and Little, *International Systems in World History*, 12.

8. Buzan and Little, *International Systems in World History*, 90–96.

9. Buzan and Little, *International Systems in World History*, 12.

10. Hedley Bull, *The Anarchical Society*, 3rd ed. (Basingstoke: Macmillan, 2002), 4.

11. Bull, *The Anarchical Society*, 16–19.

12. Bull, *The Anarchical Society*, 19.

13. John K. Fairbank, ed., *The Chinese World Order: Traditional China's Foreign Relations* (Cambridge: Harvard University Press, 1968). For more recent work that applies the term *world order* to major civilizations, see Henry Kissinger, *World Order* (New York: Penguin, 2014); Barry Buzan and Amitav Acharya, *Reimagining International Relations: World Orders in the Thought and Practice of Indian, Chinese and Islamic Civilizations* (Cambridge: Cambridge University Press, 2022).

14. Andrew Hurrell, *On Global Order: Power, Values, and the Constitution of International Society* (Oxford: Oxford University Press, 2007), 3.

15. Amitav Acharya, *The End of American World Order* (Cambridge: Polity, 2014).

16. Kissinger, *World Order*, 2.

17. Amitav Acharya, *Constructing Global Order: Agency and Change in World Politics* (Cambridge: Cambridge University Press, 2018).

18. Amitav Acharya, "Global South Reacts to Western Call for Unity Against Russia," *Responsible Statecraft*, 20 March 2022, https://responsiblestatecraft.org/2022/03/29/global-south-reacts-to-western-call-for-unity-against-russia/ (accessed 2/24/2024).

19. Patrick Morgan, "Regional Security Complexes and Regional Orders" and David A. Lake and Patrick M. Morgan, "The New Regionalism in Security Affairs," in David A. Lake and Patrick M. Morgan, eds., *Regional Orders: Building Security in a New World* (University Park: Pennsylvania State University Press, 1997), 32 and 3–19.

20. "World Order," *Oxford English Dictionary*, September 2023, https://doi.org/10.1093/OED/8231727668 (accessed 12/11/2023).

21. Mohammed Ayoob, "Regional Security and the Third World," in Mohammed Ayoob, ed., *Regional Security in the Third World* (London: Croom Helm, 1986), 4.

22. "World Order," *Macmillan English Dictionary: For Advanced Learners of American English* (Oxford: Macmillan Education, 2005), 1686.

23. For details, see Acharya, *Constructing Global Order,* 4–5.

24. Karl W. Deutsch and David J. Singer, "Multiple Power Systems and International Stability," *World Politics,* vol. 16, no. 3 (1964): 390–406.

25. Muthiah Alagappa, "The Study of International Order," in Muthiah Alagappa, ed., *Asian Security Order: Instrumental and Normative Features* (Stanford: Stanford University Press, 2003), 39.

26. Acharya, *Constructing Global Order.*

27. Buzan and Little, *International Systems in World History.*

28. "The ancient Greek and modern societies of states exhibit a basic similarity: both have been organized according to the principle of sovereignty." Christian Reus-Smit, "The Constitutional Structure of International Society and the Nature of Fundamental Institutions," *International Organization,* vol. 51, no. 4 (Autumn 1997): 570.

29. "Hegemony," Merriam-Webster.com, https://www.merriam-webster.com/dictionary/hegemony (accessed 12/9/2023).

30. John J. Mearsheimer, *The Tragedy of Great Power Politics,* rev. ed. (New York: W. W. Norton, 2014), 68.

31. Robert W. Cox, *Production, Power and World Order: Social Forces in the Making of History* (New York: Columbia University Press, 1987), 7.

32. Robert W. Cox, "Gramsci, Hegemony and International Relations: An Essay in Method," *Millennium,* vol. 12, no. 2 (1983): 162–75.

33. Robert W. Cox, *Approaches to World Order* (Cambridge: Cambridge University Press, 1996), 136.

34. Robert Cox, "Robert Cox on World Orders, Historical Change, and the Purpose of Theory in International Relations," 37, http://www.theory talks.org/2010/03/theory-talk-37.html (accessed 12/29/2022); Cox, *Approaches to World Order,* 85–143.

35. Teresa L. Thompson, "Ideological Hegemony," in Teresa L. Thompson, ed., *Encyclopedia of Health Communication* (Thousand Oaks: Sage, 2014), 688–89, https://doi.org/10.4135/9781483346427 (accessed 2/22/2024).

36. For discussion of empires—their sources of order and variation—see Michael Doyle, *Empires* (Ithaca: Cornell University Press, 1986); Alexander Motyl, *Revolutions, Nations, Empires: Conceptual Limits and Theoretical Possibilities* (New York: Columbia University Press, 1999); S. N. Eisenstadt, *The Political Systems of Empires: The Rise and Fall of the Historical Bureaucratic Societies* (New York: Free Press, 1969); Karen Dawisha and Bruce Parrott, *The Disintegration and Reconstruction of Empires* (Armonk: M. E. Sharpe, 1966). For a discussion of European empire and reactions to it, see Philip D. Curtin, *The World and the West: The European Challenge and the Overseas Response in the Age of Empire* (New York: Cambridge University Press, 2000); Tarak Barkawi and Mark Laffey, "Retrieving the Imperial: Empire and International Relations," *Millennium,* vol. 31 (2002): 109–27.

37. Doyle, *Empires*, 40. Watson also made a similar distinction. See Adam Watson, *The Evolution of International Society: A Comparative Historical Analysis* (London: Routledge, 1992), 15.

38. Barkawi and Laffey, "Retrieving the Imperial."

39. Kenneth N. Waltz, "Political Structures," in Robert O. Keohane, ed., *Neorealism and Its Critics* (New York: Columbia University Press, 1986), 73.

40. Buzan and Little, *International Systems in World History*, 440.

41. David A. Lake, "Beyond Anarchy: The Importance of Security Institutions," *International Security*, vol. 26, no. 1 (Summer 2001): 129–60.

42. Also see Ayşe Zarakol, *Hierarchies in World Politics* (Cambridge: Cambridge University Press, 2017).

43. David C. Kang, "Hierarchy and Stability in Asian International Relations," in G. John Ikenberry and Michael Mastanduno, eds., *International Relations Theory and the Asia-Pacific* (New York: Columbia University Press, 2003), 166–67.

44. "Suzerainty," *Cambridge Dictionary*, https://dictionary.cambridge.org/us/dictionary/english/suzerainty (accessed 12/9/2023).

45. "Suzerainty is a vaguer concept." See Watson, *The Evolution of International Society*, 15.

46. Fairbank, *The Chinese World Order*. This earlier notion of a Chinese world order emphasizing Confucian virtues such as the emperor's impartiality and benevolence toward tributary states has been challenged by a new body of work which emphasizes Chinese realpolitik. Alastair Iain Johnston, *Cultural Realism: Strategic Culture and Grand Strategy in Chinese History* (Princeton: Princeton University Press, 1998).

47. John K. Fairbank, "Introduction," in Denis Twitchett and John K. Fairbank, eds., *The Cambridge History of China*, vol. 10: *Late Ch'ing, 1800–1911*, part 1 (Cambridge: Cambridge University Press, 1978), 30.

48. Manjeet S. Pardesi, "Decentering Hegemony and 'Open' Orders: Fifteenth-Century Melaka in a World of Orders," *Global Studies Quarterly*, vol. 2, no. 4 (2022).

49. John K. Fairbank, "A Preliminary Framework," in *The Chinese World Order*, 9.

50. Amitav Acharya, "Will Asia's Past Be Its Future?," *International Security*, vol. 28, no. 3 (Winter 2003/2004): 149–64; Wang Gungwu, "China's Overseas World," in Wang Gungwu, *To Act Is to Know: Chinese Dilemmas* (Singapore: Eastern Universities Press, 2003), 306; Wang Gungwu, "Early Ming Relations with Southeast Asia," in Fairbank, *The Chinese World Order*, 50.

51. Acharya, "Will Asia's Past Be Its Future?," 154. Also see James Millward, "We Need a New Approach to Teaching Modern Chinese History," *Medium*, October 9, 2020, https://jimmillward.medium.com/we-need-a -new-approach-to-teaching-modern-chinese-history-we-have-lazily-re peated-false-d24983bd7ef2 (accessed 2/24/2024).

52. Wang, "China's Overseas World," 302.

53. Wang, "China's Overseas World," 303. Also see Chapter 3.

54. Andrew J. Nathan and Robert S. Ross, *The Great Wall and Empty Fortress: China's Search for Security* (New York: W. W. Norton, 1997), 21.

55. Barry R. Posen, "Command of the Commons: The Military Foundation of U.S. Hegemony," *International Security*, vol. 28, no. 1 (2003): 5.

56. Christopher Layne, "The Unipolar Illusion Revisited: The Coming End of the United States' Unipolar Moment," *International Security*, vol. 31, no. 2 (2006): 12.

57. Joseph S. Nye, "American Hegemony or American Primacy?," Project Syndicate, March 9, 2015, https://www.project-syndicate.org/commen tary/american-hegemony-military-superiority-by-joseph-s—nye-2015 -03 (accessed 2/24/2024).

58. Mark Beeson, "Hegemony," *Oxford Bibliographies*, https://www.oxfordbib liographies.com/display/document/obo-9780199756223/obo-978 0199756223–0101.xml (accessed 12/9/2023).

59. Ian Clark, *Hegemony in International Society* (Oxford: Oxford University Press, 2011), 16.

60. A. F. K. Organski, *World Politics* (New York: Knopf, 1958), 322.

61. Organski, *World Politics*, 292.

62. Charles P. Kindleberger, *The World in Depression: 1929–1939* (Berkeley: University of California Press, 1973; rev. ed. 1986).

63. But in making this argument—and this is often forgotten—Kindleberger argued that the condition of a single nation having a globally dominant economy could only occur under very special (and unlikely) circumstances. He presented this option merely as a heuristic and not a condition that one should expect in empirical reality. Kindleberger's objective was to point out the empirical impossibility of hegemonic stability and to promote the understanding of cooperation needed to build a well-functioning world order. HST is thus the incorrect application of this heuristic to the field of international relations.

64. Isabelle Grunberg, "Exploring the 'Myth' of Hegemonic Stability," *International Organization*, vol. 44, no. 4 (Autumn 1990): 431.

65. Grunberg, "Exploring the 'Myth' of Hegemonic Stability," 432.

66. Robert Gilpin (with Jean Gilpin), *The Political Economy of International Relations* (Princeton: Princeton University Press, 1987); Stephen Krasner, "State Power and the Structure of International Trade," *World Politics*, vol. 28, no. 3 (1976): 317–43. See also Joshua S. Goldstein and Jon C. Pevehouse, *International Relations, Brief Edition, 2012–2013 Update* (Harlow: Pearson, 2014), 56, 80, and 125.

67. Grunberg, "Exploring the 'Myth' of Hegemonic Stability," 432.

68. Grunberg, "Exploring the 'Myth' of Hegemonic Stability," 433. Also see David P. Calleo, *Beyond American Hegemony: The Future of the Western Alliance* (New York: Basic Books, 1987), 218 and 220; David P. Calleo and

Benjamin Rowland, *America and the World Political Economy: Atlantic Dreams and National Reality* (Bloomington: Indiana University Press, 1975), 17; both cited in Grunberg, "Exploring the 'Myth' of Hegemonic Stability," 432.

69. Ruggie asserts that while multilateralism was not a postwar American invention, "[l]ooking more closely at the post–World War II situation . . . it was less the fact of American *hegemony*, that accounts for the explosion of multilateral arrangements than of *American* hegemony." John Gerard Ruggie, "Multilateralism: The Anatomy of an Institution," in John Gerard Ruggie, ed., *Multilateralism Matters: The Theory and Praxis of an Institutional Form* (New York: Columbia University Press, 1993), 8.

70. For a critique of the ethnocentric bias of the hegemonic stability theory, such as Gilpin's contention that free trade is imposed by a "superior society," see Grunberg, "Exploring the 'Myth' of Hegemonic Stability," 444–48. The reference is to Robert Gilpin, *War and Change in World Politics* (Cambridge University Press, 1981), 129.

71. Duncan Snidal, "The Limits of Hegemonic Stability Theory," *International Organization*, vol. 39, no. 4 (Autumn 1985): 614.

72. One example of the denial of non-Western agency or contributions to international orders would be found in the very idea of "reciprocity" as implied in Bull's formulation of the lack of "capacity of Asian and African powers to enter into relationships on a reciprocal basis with European states." Absence of such reciprocity is a key rationale for the "standard of civilisation" thesis, used by European theorists and leaders to justify colonization and exclude and marginalize non-Western societies. The European standard of civilization and the concept of reciprocity are based on the ability "to provide domestic law and order, administrative integrity, protection of the rights of foreign citizens, or the fulfilment of contracts," and to play the game of balance of power. Hedley Bull and Adam Watson, "Conclusion," in Bull and Watson, *The Expansion of International Society*, 427. This was in reality intended to secure for themselves economic opportunities and privileges (everything else, including spreading the gospel, was secondary), which had been gained sometimes voluntarily, but on many occasions through use of force or coercion. Not only were the benefits to non-Western states in these arrangements unclear, but non-Western states might have recognized that they would be entering into one-sided relationships that would heavily favor the Europeans. The demand for reciprocity in this sense could be construed as an excuse for exploitation. By viewing the expansion of European international society as a matter of Europeans seeking reciprocity, the early English School proponents obscured the fact that colonialism was a fundamentally nonreciprocal institution. *The Expansion* remained ambiguous about the "standard of civilisation" criteria employed by the Europeans. Bull and Watson acknowledge that standard of civilization reflected European arrogance and

was highly self-serving, but still stress the standard as being based on the realities of international life. Bull and Watson, "Conclusion," 427.

73. Though providing the clearest and most influential articulation of the concept, Ikenberry followed other liberal thinkers. On his part, Keohane mentioned "liberal international arrangements" and "liberal international political economy," rather than "liberal international order." Keohane was borrowing from Gilpin's observation about the role played by Britain and the United States in creating and enforcing "the rules of a liberal international economic order." See Robert O. Keohane, *After Hegemony: Cooperation and Discord in the World Political Economy* (Princeton: Princeton University Press, 1984), 8, 31, and 54. It was after the Cold War that the liberal order, strengthened by the defeat of communism and the advance of democracy and capitalism under internationalist U.S. leadership, acquired its broadest meaning: encompassing economic interdependence (free trade), multilateral rules and institutions, democratic political systems, and values and norms (especially universal human rights).

74. G. John Ikenberry, *Liberal Leviathan: The Origins, Crisis, and Transformation of the American World Order* (Princeton: Princeton University Press, 2011), 224. In this book, Ikenberry uses a variety of expressions to denote the same: "liberal hegemonic order" (xi, 224), "American-led liberal world order" (xii), "American-led liberal hegemony" (224), "free world, the American system, the West, the Atlantic world, Pax Democratica, Pax Americana, the Philadelphia system" (35). See p. 7 for a brief description of these descriptions of U.S.-led order.

75. Ikenberry, *Liberal Leviathan*, xii, 18, and 224.

76. Ikenberry, *Liberal Leviathan*, 7.

77. Ikenberry, *Liberal Leviathan*, xiii.

78. Ikenberry, *Liberal Leviathan*, 6.

79. Ikenberry, *Liberal Leviathan*, 9.

80. In understanding this debate, on which there is a vast literature, it is useful to separate works of those who focus on the decline of the United States and the decline of the international order it built, keeping in mind that the latter does not always refer specifically to the LIO, but also to other referents, such as unipolarity, or simply to the U.S.-led world order or U.S. hegemony. In this book, we use the terms "LIO," "liberal world order," "Liberal Hegemony," and "U.S.-led liberal hegemonic order" interchangeably. Those who argue that U.S. power is declining include Paul Kennedy, *The Rise and Fall of the Great Powers* (New York: Vintage, 1989); Fareed Zakaria, *The Post-American World* (New York: W. W. Norton, 2009); Parag Khanna, *The Second World: How Emerging Powers Are Redefining Global Competition in the Twenty-First Century* (New York: Random House, 2009); National Intelligence Council, *Global Trends 2025: A Transformed World* (Washington, DC: Government Printing Office, 2008); and Ian Bremmer, *Every Nation for Itself: Winners and Losers in a G-Zero World* (New York:

Penguin, 2012). Those who refute the decline of U.S. power include Michael Beckley, "China's Century? Why America's Edge Will Endure," *International Security*, vol. 36, no. 3 (Winter 2011/12): 41–78; Michael Beckley, *Unrivaled: Why America Will Remain the World's Sole Superpower* (Ithaca: Cornell University Press, 2018); Stephen G. Brooks and William C. Wohlforth, *World Out of Balance: International Relations and the Challenge of American Primacy* (Princeton: Princeton University Press, 2008); Stephen G. Brooks and William C. Wohlforth, "Assessing the Balance," *Cambridge Review of International Affairs*, vol. 20, no. 2 (June 2011): 201–19; Robert J. Lieber, *Power and Willpower in the American Future: Why the United States Is Not Destined to Decline* (Cambridge: Cambridge University Press, 2012); Robert Kagan, *The World America Made* (New York: Vintage, 2012); Josef Joffe, *The Myth of America's Decline: Politics, Economics, and a Half Century of False Prophecies* (New York: Liveright, 2014). But the polarity debate does not tell us about changes to order. For writings of those who argue that the U.S.-led international order is in decline, see Christopher Layne, "This Time It's Real: The End of Unipolarity and the Pax Americana," *International Studies Quarterly*, vol. 56, no. 1 (March 2012): 203–13; Barry R. Posen, "From Unipolarity to Multipolarity: Transition in Sight?," in G. John Ikenberry, Michael Mastanduno, and William C. Wohlforth, eds., *International Relations Theory and the Consequences of Unipolarity* (New York: Cambridge University Press, 2012), 317–41; and Amitav Acharya, *The End of American World Order* (New York: Polity, 2014). Acharya was the first to distinguish between the decline of U.S. power and the decline specifically of the LIO, arguing that the former may happen whether the United States itself is declining or not. Now there is a growing literature on LIO's crisis and decline, including by those who believe that the LIO was a "myth" and will not survive. See Naazneen Barma, Ely Ratner, and Steven Weber, "The Mythical Liberal Order," *National Interest* (March/April 2013): 56–67, https://nationalinterest.org/article/the-mythical-liberal-order-8146 (accessed 2/22/2024); John J. Mearsheimer, "Bound to Fail: The Rise and Fall of the Liberal International Order," *International Security*, vol. 43, no. 4 (Spring 2019): 7–50; John J. Mearsheimer, *The Great Delusion: Liberal Dreams and International Realities* (New Haven: Yale University Press, 2018); Charles L. Glaser, "A Flawed Framework: Why the Liberal International Order Concept Is Misguided," *International Security*, vol. 43, no. 4 (Spring 2019): 51–87; Patrick Porter, "A World Imagined: Nostalgia and Liberal Order," Policy Analysis No. 843 (Washington, DC: CATO Institute, June 5, 2018), https://www.cato.org/policy-analysis/world-imagined-nostalgia-liberal-order (accessed 2/22/2024); Bentley B. Allan, Srdjan Vucetic, and Ted Hopf, "The Distribution of Identity and the Future of International Order: China's Hegemonic Prospects," *International Organization*, vol. 72, no. 4 (Fall 2018): 839–69; and Stacie E. Goddard, "Embedded Revisionism: Networks, Institutions, and Challenges to

World Order," *International Organization*, vol. 72, no. 4 (Fall 2018): 763–97. Among the defenders of the LIO's resilience and ability to survive, see G. John Ikenberry, "Liberal Internationalism 3.0: America and the Dilemmas of Liberal World Order," *Perspectives on Politics*, vol. 7, no. 1 (March 2009): 71–87; Joseph S. Nye, "Will the Liberal Order Survive? The History of an Idea," *Foreign Affairs*, vol. 96, no. 1 (January/February 2017): 10–16; and Daniel Deudney and G. John Ikenberry, "Liberal World: The Resilient Order," *Foreign Affairs*, vol. 97, no. 4 (July/August 2018): 16–24.

81. Amitav Acharya, *The End of American World Order* (Cambridge: Polity, 2014).

82. Acharya, *The End of American World Order*, 15.

83. Alexander Cooley and Daniel Nexon, *Exit from Hegemony: The Unraveling of the American Global Order* (New York: Oxford University Press, 2020).

84. Duncan Snidal, "The Limits of Hegemonic Stability Theory," *International Organization*, vol. 39, no. 4 (1985): 579–614.

85. Young identified three types of leadership: structural, entrepreneurial, and intellectual: "The structural leader translates power resources into bargaining leverage in an effort to bring pressure to bear on others to assent to the terms of proposed constitutional contracts. The entrepreneurial leader makes use of negotiating skill to frame the issues at stake, devise mutually acceptable formulas, and broker the interests of key players in building support for these formulas. The intellectual leader, by contrast, relies on the power of ideas to shape the thinking of the principles in processes of institutional bargaining." Oran R. Young, "Political Leadership and Regime Formation: On the Development of Institutions in International Society," *International Organization*, vol. 45, no. 3 (Summer 1991): 307.

86. David Rapkin, "Leadership and Cooperative Institutions," in Andrew Mack and John Ravenhill, eds., *Pacific Cooperation: Building Economic and Security Regimes in the Asia-Pacific Region* (St. Leonards: Allen and Unwin, 1994), 109.

87. Andrew F. Cooper, Richard A. Higgott, and Kim R. Nossal, *Relocating Middle Powers: Australia and Canada in a Changing World Order* (Vancouver: University of British Columbia Press, 1993), 12.

88. Cooper, Higgott, and Nossal, *Relocating Middle Powers*, 13.

89. Rapkin, "Leadership and Cooperative Institutions," 118.

90. Stephen G. Brooks and William C. Wohlforth, "The Rise and Fall of the Great Powers in the Twenty-first Century," *International Security*, vol. 40, no. 3 (2016): 8.

91. Brooks and Wohlforth, "The Rise and Fall of the Great Powers in the Twenty-first Century," 8.

92. Barry R. Posen, "Emerging Multipolarity: Why Should We Care?," *Current History*, vol. 108, no. 721 (November 2009): 350.

93. Zaki Laidi, "What Multipolarity Really Means," http://www.laidi.com/sitedp/sites/default/files/Week%201.pdf (accessed 4/15/2020).

94. The terms "Multiplex" and "G-Plus" are coined by Acharya, to distinguish multipolarity from the emerging world order. Acharya, *The End of American World Order*; Amitav Acharya, "After Liberal Hegemony: The Advent of a Multiplex World," *Ethics and International Affairs*, vol. 31, no. 3 (Fall 2017): 271–85. The word *multiplex* derives from Latin "multi- + plicāre to fold." See "Multiplex," *Dictionary.com*, https://www.dictionary.com/browse/multiplexing (accessed 12/9/2023). The word was first used in mid-sixteenth-century mathematics. In its original sense, it meant "having many folds; many times as great in number; of many parts." See "Multiplex," *Online Etymology Dictionary*, https://www.etymonline.com/word/multiplex (accessed 12/9/2023).

As an adjective, multiplex conveys the sense of "having many parts or aspects"—such as "the multiplex problem of drug abuse." It can also mean "manifold" and "multiple," as in "the multiplex opportunities in high technology." See "Multiplex," *Dictionary.com*, https://www.dictionary.com/browse/multiplexing (accessed 12/9/2023). Perhaps the most common form of usage refers to a multiplex cinema or theater: "a group of two or more motion-picture theatres on the same site or in the same building, esp. a cluster of adjoining theaters." See "Multiplex," *Collins English Dictionary*, https://www.collinsdictionary.com/dictionary/english/multiplex (accessed 12/9/2023). Yet another meaning associated with multiplex is "multidimensional," specifically three-dimensional mapmaking, or mapmaking in a "stereoscopic device that makes it possible to view pairs of aerial photographs in three dimensions." See "Multiplex," https://www.collinsdictionary.com/dictionary/english/multiplex (accessed 12/9/2023). In the telecommunications field, the meaning of multiplex or multiplexing can be understood by contrasting it with the term "mirroring." Mirroring "takes one data file and copies it to many devices," whereas multiplexing "writes the data files to many places simultaneously" without having a single point of origin. See "Multiplexing," *Free On-Line Dictionary of Computing*, https://foldoc.org/multiplex (accessed 12/9/2023). All these meanings speak to a connected multiplicity in structure and interactions in creating a common product or public good and service.

95. "A Worrying New World Order," *The Economist*, September 11, 2008, https://www.economist.com/europe/2008/09/11/a-worrying-new-world-order (accessed 2/22/2024); Richard N. Haass, "The Age of Nonpolarity: What Will Follow U.S. Dominance?," *Foreign Affairs*, vol. 87, no. 3 (May/June 2008): 44–56.

96. For an earlier attempt to distinguish among different types of leadership, see Young, "Political Leadership and Regime Formation."

97. Other concepts have been suggested as alternatives to "LHO" or "multipolarity," such as "multi-ordered" and "multinodal." The idea of a multi-ordered world has similarities with the emphasis on regions or localities in the multiplex concept, but it does not suggest how or to what extent

the orders are connected. See Trine Flockhart, "A Multi-Ordered World," *RSA Journal*, vol. 164, no. 3 (2018): 26–31. The multinodal world is rather similar to the multiplex world. Brantly Womack presents the multimodal world "as a stable pattern of states, each the locus of one end of a radiating bundle of bilateral relationships. Given their vast differences of size and assets, most relationships between states are asymmetric." Brantly Womack, "China's Future in a Multinodal World Order," *Pacific Affairs*, vol. 87, no. 2 (2014). This harks back to the notion of hierarchy, and lays too much stress on bilateralism or a "hub-and-spoke" configuration, thereby understating the importance of multilateral relationships.

98. For historical examples of such decentered systems, see Pardesi, "Decentering Hegemony and 'Open' Orders"; Manjeet S. Pardesi, "International Order in Ancient India," in Amitav Acharya, Daniel A. Bell, Rajeev Bhargava, and Yan Xuetong, eds., *Bridging Two Worlds: Comparing Classical Political Thought and Statecraft in India and China* (Oakland: University of California Press, 2021), 284–310.

Chapter Two. The International Order of the Roman Mediterranean (~Sixth Century B.C.E.–Third Century C.E.)

1. Greg Woolf, *Rome: An Empire's Story*, 2nd ed. (New York: Oxford University Press, 2022), 209; Kurt A. Raaflaub, "From City-State to Empire: Rome in Comparative Perspective," in Johann P. Arnason and Kurt A. Raaflaub, eds., *The Roman Empire in Context: Historical and Comparative Perspectives* (Malden: Wiley-Blackwell, 2011), 52.

2. Peter Fibiger Bang, *The Roman Bazaar: A Comparative Study of Trade and Markets in a Tributary Empire* (Cambridge: Cambridge University Press, 2008). This transepochal study compares the Roman Empire with the Mughal empire (and to a lesser degree with the Ottoman and Ming/Qing empires).

3. Greg Woolf, "Rome and Imperialism," in Immanuel Ness and Zak Cope, eds., *The Palgrave Encyclopedia of Imperialism and Anti-Imperialism*, 2nd ed. (Cham: Palgrave Macmillan, 2021), 2333.

4. James Tan, "The Roman Republic," in Andrew Monson and Walter Scheidel, eds., *Fiscal Regimes and the Political Economy of Premodern States* (Cambridge: Cambridge University Press, 2015), 224; Michael Mann, *The Sources of Social Power*, vol. 1 (Cambridge: Cambridge University Press, 1986), 268; Tan, "The Roman Republic," 225.

5. Walter Scheidel, "The Early Roman Monarchy," in Monson and Scheidel, *Fiscal Regimes and the Political Economy of Premodern States*, 229–57 (especially 240).

6. Peter Fibiger Bang, "Lord of All the World—The State, Heterogeneous Power and Hegemony in the Roman and Mughal Empires," in Peter Fibiger Bang and C. A. Bayly, eds., *Tributary Empires in Global History* (Basingstoke: Palgrave Macmillan, 2011), 181, 185.

7. Mann, *The Sources of Social Power*, 250.

8. Greg Woolf, "Inventing Empire in Ancient Rome," in Susan E. Alcock, Terence N. D'Altroy, Kathleen D. Morrison, and Carla M. Sinopoli, eds., *Empires: Perspectives from Archaeology and History* (Cambridge: Cambridge University Press, 2001), 312.

9. Woolf, "Rome and Imperialism," 2342.

10. Johann P. Arnason, "The Roman Phenomenon: State, Empire, and Civilization," in Arnason and Raaflaub, *The Roman Empire in Context*, 357.

11. Mann, *The Sources of Social Power*, 269.

12. Andrew Wallace-Hadrill, *Rome's Cultural Revolution* (Cambridge: Cambridge University Press, 2008), 26; Robin Waterfield, *Taken at the Flood: The Roman Conquest of Greece* (New York: Oxford University Press, 2014), 212.

13. Waterfield, *Taken at the Flood*, 212.

14. Woolf, "Inventing Empire in Ancient Rome," 314.

15. Mann, *The Sources of Social Power*, 271.

16. Geoffrey Rickman, "The Creation of *Mare Nostrum:* 300 BC–500 AD," in David Abulafia, ed., *The Mediterranean in History* (London: Thames & Hudson, 2003), 132.

17. David Abulafia, *The Great Sea: A Human History of the Mediterranean* (Oxford: Oxford University Press, 2011), 199.

18. Abulafia, *The Great Sea*, 199.

19. Scheidel, "The Early Roman Monarchy," 252.

20. Wallace-Hadrill, *Rome's Cultural Revolution*, 26.

21. Peregrine Horden and Nicholas Purcell, *The Corrupting Sea: A Study of Mediterranean History* (Malden: Blackwell, 2000), 24–25.

22. J. G. Manning, *The Open Sea: The Economic Life of the Ancient Mediterranean World from the Iron Age to the Rise of Rome* (Princeton: Princeton University Press, 2018), 237.

23. Horden and Purcell, *The Corrupting Sea*, 25.

24. Matthew P. Loar, Carolyn MacDonald, and Dan-el Padilla Peralta, "Introduction," in Matthew P. Loar, Carolyn MacDonald, and Dan-el Padilla Peralta, eds., *Rome, Empire of Plunder: The Dynamics of Cultural Appropriation* (Cambridge: Cambridge University Press, 2018), 3.

25. Erich S. Gruen, *The Hellenistic World and the Coming of Rome*, vol. 1 (Berkeley: University of California Press, 1984), 260.

26. W. V. Harris, *Roman Power: A Thousand Years of Empire* (Cambridge: Cambridge University Press, 2016); Woolf, *Rome*.

27. Robert Morstein-Marx and Nathan Rosenstein, "The Transformation of the Republic," in Nathan Rosenstein and Robert Morstein-Marx, eds., *A Companion to the Roman Republic* (Malden: Blackwell, 2006), 625.

28. Manning, *The Open Sea*, 238.

29. Angelos Chaniotis, *Age of Conquests: The Greek World from Alexander to Hadrian* (Cambridge, MA: Harvard University Press, 2018), 3–7.

30. Kostas Vlassopoulos, *Greeks and Barbarians* (New York: Cambridge University Press, 2013), 280. According to Vlassopoulos, the interactions between the Greeks and others in the Mediterranean were shaped by networks of connectivity (mobility of people, ideas, and technologies); colonization (through the creation of *apoikiai*); Panhellenic festivals, institutions, and ideas; and through the impact of empires.

31. Arnold J. Toynbee, *A Study of History: Abridgement of Volumes VII–X*, ed. D. C. Somervell (New York: Oxford University Press, 1987), 4.

32. Adam Watson, *The Evolution of International Society: A Comparative Historical Analysis* (London: Routledge, 1992), 94–106.

33. Daniel Deudney, " 'A Republic for Expansion': The Roman Constitution and Empire and Balance-of-Power Politics," in Stuart J. Kaufman, Richard Little, and William C. Wohlforth, eds., *The Balance of Power in World History* (New York: Palgrave, 2007), 149; Michael W. Doyle, *Empires* (Ithaca: Cornell University Press, 1986), 83.

34. Arthur M. Eckstein, *Mediterranean Anarchy, Interstate War, and the Rise of Rome* (Berkeley: University of California Press, 2006), 2.

35. Eckstein, *Mediterranean Anarchy*, 5; Deudney, " 'A Republic for Expansion,' " 155.

36. Barry Buzan and Richard Little, *International Systems in World History* (New York: Oxford University Press, 2000), 92.

37. Horden and Purcell, *The Corrupting Sea*, 25.

38. Mario Torelli, "The Battle for the Sea Routes: 1000–300 BC," in Abulafia, *The Mediterranean in History*, 99–121.

39. According to Lambert, the Mediterranean had emerged as "a single economic system" between 800 and 500 B.C.E. See Andrew Lambert, *Seapower States: Maritime Culture, Continental Empires and the Conflict That Made the Modern World* (New Haven: Yale University Press, 2018), 34.

40. Bang, "Lord of All the World," 179, 181.

41. P. F. Bang, "Rome and the Comparative Study of Tributary Empires," *The Medieval History Journal*, vol. 6, no. 2 (2003): 209.

42. Woolf, "Rome and Imperialism," 2340–41.

43. Bang, *The Roman Bazaar*, 82.

44. Mann, *The Sources of Social Power*, 274.

45. Peter Fibiger Bang, "The King of Kings: Universal Hegemony, Imperial Power, and a New Comparative History of Rome," in Arnason and Raaflaub, *The Roman Empire in Context*, 339.

46. Mann, *The Sources of Social Power*, 269.

47. Although citizenship was extended to the Italian allies after the Social War (91–87 B.C.E.), a period long after the emergence of Rome's effective hegemony, it had served as "punishment for defeated communities" until the second century B.C.E. See Clifford Ando, "Making Romans: Citizens, Subjects, and Subjectivity in Republican Empire," in Myles Lavan, Richard E. Payne, and John Weisweiler, eds., *Cosmopolitanism and Empire:*

Universal Rulers, Local Elites, and Cultural Integration in the Ancient Near East and Mediterranean (New York: Oxford University Press, 2016), 169.

48. Peter F. Bang, "Tributary Empires and the New Fiscal Sociology: Some Comparative Reflections," in Monson and Scheidel, *Fiscal Regimes and the Political Economy of Premodern States*, 542.

49. Scheidel, "The Early Roman Monarchy," 249; Keith Hopkins, "The Political Economy of the Roman Empire," in Ian Morris and Walter Scheidel, eds., *The Dynamics of Ancient Empires: State Power from Assyria to Byzantium* (New York: Oxford University Press, 2009), 184.

50. Fernand Braudel, *Civilization and Capitalism, 15th–18th Century*, vol. 3: *The Perspective of the World*, trans. Siân Reynolds (London: Collins, 1984), 33.

51. Perry Anderson, *The H-Word: The Peripeteia of Hegemony* (Verso: London, 2017), 3. Watson's "pendulum" analogy also sees continuity across the notional spectrum from multiple independent political units to empires via the intermediate categories of hegemony and dominion. Watson, *The Evolution of International Society*, 13–18.

52. Krishan Kumar, *Visions of Empire: How Five Imperial Regimes Shaped the World* (Princeton: Princeton University Press, 2017), 42–43.

53. Paul W. Blank, "The Pacific: A Mediterranean in the Making?," *Geographical Review*, vol. 89, no. 2 (1999): 266.

54. Blank, "The Pacific," 269–70.

55. Given Watson's notional pendulum mentioned above (note 51), hegemony itself can be conceptualized along a spectrum from "loose" to "tight." Relatedly, others have characterized imperial control along such a spectrum. For example, Runciman conceptualized empires as both "loosely controlled" and "tightly controlled." Similarly, empires may be either "formal or informal" for Doyle too. See W. G. Runciman, "Empire as a Topic in Comparative Sociology," in Bang, *Tributary Empires in Global History*, 99; and Doyle, *Empires*, 30.

56. Ronald Findlay and Kevin H. O'Rourke, *Power and Plenty: Trade, War, and the World Economy in the Second Millennium* (Princeton: Princeton University Press, 2007), xxv. Also see Robert Gilpin, *War & Change in World Politics* (New York: Cambridge University Press, 1981); George Modelski and William R. Thompson, *Seapower in Global Politics, 1494–1993* (Seattle: University of Washington Press, 1987); and George Modelski and William R. Thompson, *Leading Sectors and World Powers: The Coevolution of Global Economics and Politics* (Columbia: University of South Carolina Press, 1996).

57. Philippe Beaujard, "The Indian Ocean in Eurasian and African World-Systems before the Sixteenth Century," *Journal of World History*, vol. 16, no. 4 (2005): 415. Also see Philippe Beaujard, *The Worlds of the Indian Ocean: A Global History*, vols. 1 and 2, translation edited by Tamara Loring, Francis Meadows, and Andromeda Tait (Cambridge: Cambridge University Press, 2019).

58. Jack A. Goldstone and John F. Haldon, "Ancient States, Empires, and Exploitation: Problems and Perspectives," in Scheidel, *The Dynamics of Ancient Empires*, 3.
59. Douglas A. Irwin and Kevin H. O'Rourke, "Coping with Shocks and Shifts: The Multilateral Trading System in Historical Perspective," in Robert C. Feenstra and Alan M. Taylor, eds., *Globalization in an Age of Crisis: Multilateral Economic Cooperation in the Twenty-First Century* (Chicago: The University of Chicago Press, 2014), 17.
60. Barry Buzan and George Lawson, *The Global Transformation: History, Modernity, and the Making of International Relations* (Cambridge: Cambridge University Press, 2015), 1. Buzan and Lawson refer to this interactive process as "mode of power."
61. In general, liberals emphasize "interdependence" among trading states while realists emphasize "control" over vital overseas supplies. See Hendrik Spruyt, "War, Trade, and State Formation," in Carles Boix and Susan C. Stokes, eds., *The Oxford Handbook of Comparative Politics* (New York: Oxford University Press, 2007), 211–35.
62. Neal G. Jesse, Steven E. Lobell, Galia Press-Barnathan, and Kristen P. Williams, "The Leader Can't Lead When the Followers Won't Follow: The Limitations of Hegemony," in Kristen P. Williams, Steven E. Lobell, and Neal G. Jesse, eds., *Beyond Great Powers and Hegemons: Why Secondary States Support, Follow, or Challenge* (Stanford: Stanford University Press, 2012), 4. Also see Charles Bright and Michael Geyer, "Regimes of World Order: Global Integration and Production of Difference in Twentieth-Century World History," in Jerry H. Bentley, Renate Bridenthal, and Anand A. Yang, eds., *Interactions: Transregional Perspectives on World History* (Honolulu: University of Hawai'i Press, 2005), 205. Hierarchy can take multiple forms in practice. For a noteworthy recent contribution on this, see Ayşe Zarakol, ed., *Hierarchies in World Politics* (Cambridge: Cambridge University Press, 2017).
63. David Abulafia, "Mediterraneans," in W. V. Harris, ed., *Rethinking the Mediterranean* (New York: Oxford University Press, 2005), 64.
64. See Kaufman, Little, and Wohlforth, *The Balance of Power in World History*, especially the introductory and concluding chapters.
65. Woolf, *Rome*, 117–18.
66. William C. Wohlforth, Stuart J. Kaufman, and Richard Little, "Introduction: Balance and Hierarchy in International Systems," in Kaufman, Little, and Wohlforth, *The Balance of Power in World History*, 16–17.
67. Rickman, "The Creation of *Mare Nostrum*," 133.
68. Wolfgang Spickermann, "The Roman Empire," in Yuri Pines, Michal Biran, and Jörg Rüpke, eds., *The Limits of Universal Rule: Eurasian Empires Compared* (Cambridge: Cambridge University Press, 2021), 115.
69. Harris, *Roman Power*, 15.
70. Eckstein, *Mediterranean Anarchy*, 159; Rickman, "The Creation of *Mare Nostrum*," 128.

71. Harris, *Roman Power*, 26, 32; Lincoln Paine, *The Sea & Civilization: A Maritime History of the World* (New York: Alfred A. Knopf, 2013), Kindle Loc. 2559.

72. Harris, *Roman Power*, 30–31.

73. Harris, *Roman Power*, 33.

74. Spickermann, "The Roman Empire," 117.

75. Daniel J. Gargola, "The Mediterranean Empire (264–134 BCE)," in Rosenstein and Morstein-Marx, *A Companion to the Roman Republic*, 147.

76. Arthur M. Eckstein, "Rome Dominates the Mediterranean," in Andrew S. Erickson, Lyle J. Goldstein, and Carnes Lord, eds., *China Goes to Sea: Maritime Transformation in Comparative Historical Perspective* (Annapolis: Naval Institute Press, 2012), 69.

77. Gargola, "The Mediterranean Empire," 149.

78. Spickermann, "The Roman Empire," 118.

79. Harris, *Roman Power*, 26.

80. Spickermann, "The Roman Empire," 118.

81. Gargola, "The Mediterranean Empire," 153.

82. Nathan Rosenstein, "War, State Formation, and the Evolution of Military Institutions in Ancient China and Rome," in Walter Scheidel, ed., *Rome and China: Comparative Perspectives on Ancient World Empires* (New York: Oxford University Press, 2009), 29.

83. Deudney, " 'A Republic for Expansion,' " 155.

84. William V. Harris, "Power," in Alessandro Barchiesi and Walter Scheidel, eds., *The Oxford Handbook of Roman Studies*, 2010, https://doi.org/10.1093/oxfordhb/9780199211524.013.0036 (accessed 11/4/2022).

85. Woolf, "Rome and Imperialism," 2337. In particular, see William V. Harris, *War and Imperialism in Republican Rome, 327–70 B.C.* (Oxford: Clarendon Press, 1979).

86. Woolf, "Rome and Imperialism," 2334.

87. Harris, *Roman Power*, 33.

88. Woolf, *Rome*, 78.

89. Michael Pitassi, *The Roman Navy: Ships, Men & Warfare, 350 BC–AD 475* (Barnsley: Seaforth Publishing, 2012), 359.

90. Woolf, *Rome*, 78.

91. Deudney, " 'A Republic for Expansion,' " 158.

92. Deudney, " 'A Republic for Expansion,' " 161.

93. Eckstein, *Mediterranean Anarchy*, 309.

94. Chester G. Starr, *The Roman Imperial Navy, 31 B.C.–A.D. 324* (Ithaca: Cornell University Press, 1941).

95. D. B. Saddington, "*Classes:* The Evolution of the Roman Imperial Fleets," in Paul Erdkamp, ed., *A Companion to the Roman Army* (Malden: Blackwell, 2007), 201; Eckstein, "Rome Dominates the Mediterranean," 65.

96. Harris, *Roman Power*, 34.

97. Eckstein, "Rome Dominates the Mediterranean," 65.

98. Pitassi, *The Roman Navy*, 44; Catherine M. Gilliver, "Battle," in Philip Sabin, Hans van Wees, and Michael Whitby, eds., *The Cambridge History of Greek and Roman Warfare*, vol. 2: *Rome from the Late Republic to the Late Empire* (Cambridge: Cambridge University Press, 2007), 143.

99. Spickermann, "The Roman Empire," 116.

100. Bang, "Trade and Empire," 42.

101. Andrew Wilson, "Machines, Power and Ancient Economy," *The Journal of Roman Studies*, vol. 92 (2002): 1–32.

102. Matthew P. Fitzpatrick, "Provincializing Rome: The Indian Ocean Trade Network and Roman Imperialism," *Journal of World History*, vol. 22, no. 1 (2011): 27–54. Notably, they conquered parts of Arabia and reached the Persian Gulf, and some Roman emperors even harbored the ambition of conquering India.

103. Ron Harris, "The Organization of India-to-Rome Trade: Loans and Agents in the Muziris Papyrus," in Giuseppe Dari-Mattiacci and Dennis P. Kehoe, eds., *Roman Law and Economics*, vol. 1: *Institutions and Organizations* (New York: Oxford University Press, 2020), 163–96.

104. Carlos Noreña, "Imperial Integration on Rome's Atlantic Rim," in Harriet I. Flower, ed., *Empire and Religion in the Roman World* (New York: Cambridge University Press, 2021), 35–70; Eckstein, "Rome Dominates the Mediterranean," 63.

105. Rolf Strootman, "Introduction: Maritime Empires in World History," in Rolf Strootman, Floris van den Eijnde, and Roy van Wijk, eds., *Empires of the Sea: Maritime Power Networks in World History* (Leiden: Brill, 2019), 13.

106. Abulafia, *The Great Sea*, 174; Rickman, "The Creation of *Mare Nostrum*," 131.

107. Eckstein, *Mediterranean Anarchy*, 234.

108. Doyle, *Empires*, 88.

109. Torelli, "The Battle for the Sea Routes," 104.

110. Rickman, "The Creation of *Mare Nostrum*," 131.

111. Abulafia, *The Great Sea*, 189.

112. Rosenstein, "War, State Formation, and the Evolution of Military Institutions in Ancient China and Rome," 31.

113. Peter Fibiger Bang, "Predation," in Walter Scheidel, ed., *The Cambridge Companion to the Roman Economy* (New York: Cambridge University Press, 2012), 201.

114. Nicholas Purcell, "The Ancient Mediterranean," in Peregrine Horden and Sharon Kinoshita, eds., *A Companion to Mediterranean History* (Chichester: Wiley Blackwell, 2014), 66.

115. Purcell, "The Ancient Mediterranean," 67.

116. Starr, *The Roman Imperial Navy*, 176.

117. Philip de Souza, "War at Sea," in Brian Campbell and Lawrence A. Tritle, eds., *The Oxford Handbook of Warfare in the Classical World* (New York: Oxford University Press, 2013), Kindle Loc. 8494.

118. Boris Rankov, "Fleets of the Early Roman Empire, 31 BC–AD 324," in Robert Gardiner, ed., *The Age of the Galley: Mediterranean Oared Vessels since Pre-Classical Times* (London: Conway Maritime Press, 1995), 78.

119. Adrian Goldsworthy, "War," in Sabin, van Wees, and Whitby, *The Cambridge History of Greek and Roman Warfare*, vol. 2, 105.

120. Eckstein, "Rome Dominates the Mediterranean," 72.

121. David J. Bederman, "The Sea," in Bardo Fassbender and Anne Peters, eds., *The Oxford Handbook of the History of International Law* (Oxford: Oxford University Press, 2012), 359–80.

122. Georgia L. Irby, *Using and Conquering the Watery World in Greco-Roman Antiquity* (London: Bloomsbury, 2021), 203; Kaius Tuori, "The Savage Sea and the Civilizing Law: The Roman Law Tradition and the Rule of Sea," in Hans Kopp and Christian Wendt, eds., *Thalassokratographie: Rezeption und Transformation antiker Seeherrschaft* (Berlin: de Gruyter, 2018), 210.

123. Starr, *The Roman Imperial Navy*, 179.

124. Pitassi, *The Roman Navy*, 368–78.

125. John Haldon, "The Political Economy of Empire: 'Imperial Capital' and the Formation of Central and Regional Elites," in Peter Fibiger Bang, C. A. Bayly, and Walter Scheidel, eds., *The Oxford World History of Empires*, vol. 1: *The Imperial Experience* (New York: Oxford University Press, 2021), 195.

126. Norms can have constitutive and regulative effects. Peter J. Katzenstein, "Introduction: Alternative Perspectives on National Security," in Peter J. Katzenstein, ed., *The Culture of National Security* (New York: Columbia University Press, 1996); Yuen Foong Khong, "East Asia and the Strategic 'Deep Rules' of International/Regional Society," in Barry Buzan and Yongjin Zhang, eds., *Contesting International Society in East Asia* (Cambridge: Cambridge University Press, 2014), 144–66; Goldstone and Haldon, "Ancient States, Empires, and Exploitation: Problems and Perspectives," 12.

127. Martha Finnemore, "Legitimacy, Hypocrisy, and the Social Structure of Unipolarity: Why Being a Unipole Isn't All It's Cracked Up to Be," *World Politics*, vol. 61, no. 1 (2009): 59.

128. David Abulafia, "Thalassocracies," in Horden and Kinoshita, *A Companion to Mediterranean History*, 142.

129. Torelli, "The Battle for the Sea Routes," 99.

130. Abulafia, *The Great Sea*, 184; Peter Fibiger Bang, "Trade and Empire: In Search of Organizing Concepts for the Roman Economy," *Past and Present*, vol. 195 (May 2007): 42.

131. Andrew Wilson, "A Forum on Trade," in Scheidel, *The Cambridge Companion to the Roman Economy*, 287.

132. Hopkins, "The Political Economy of the Roman Empire," 179–80. Only 11 percent of the population of Egypt was recorded as enslaved, compared to 35 percent for Italy.

133. Bang, "Trade and Empire," 40.
134. Neville Morley, "Slavery Under the Principate," in Keith Bradley and Paul Cartledge, eds., *The Cambridge World History of Slavery*, vol. 1: *The Ancient Mediterranean World* (Cambridge: Cambridge University Press, 2011), 265, 267, 274.
135. Harris, *Roman Power*, 21.
136. Keith Bradley, "Slavery in the Roman Republic," in Bradley and Cartledge, *The Cambridge World History of Slavery*, 244.
137. Harris, *Roman Power*, 86.
138. Harriet I. Flower, "The Imperial Republic," in Barchiesi and Scheidel, *The Oxford Handbook of Roman Studies*, https://doi.org/10.1093/ox fordhb/9780199211524.013.0033 (accessed 11/4/2022).
139. Bang, "Predation," 200.
140. Philip Kay, *Rome's Economic Revolution* (Oxford: Oxford University Press, 2014), 37–38.
141. James Lacey, *Rome: Strategy of Empire* (New York: Oxford University Press, 2022), 41.
142. Nicholas Sekunda and Philip de Souza, "Military Forces," in Philip Sabin, Hans van Wees, and Michael Whitby, eds., *The Cambridge History of Greek and Roman Warfare*, vol 1: *Greece, the Hellenistic World and the Rise of Rome* (Cambridge: Cambridge University Press, 2007), 352.
143. Bang, "Predation," 203, 208, 213.
144. Hopkins, "The Political Economy of the Roman Empire," 184.
145. Armin Eich and Peter Eich, "War and State-Building in Roman Republican Times," *Scripta Classica Israelica*, vol. 24 (2005): 25.
146. Kay, *Rome's Economic Revolution*, 1.
147. Kay, *Rome's Economic Revolution*, 58.
148. Kay, *Rome's Economic Revolution*, 57.
149. Kay, *Rome's Economic Revolution*, 2.
150. Abulafia, *The Great Sea*, 200.
151. Rickman, "The Creation of *Mare Nostrum*," 132.
152. Hopkins, "The Political Economy of the Roman Empire," 191.
153. Paul Erdkamp, "The Grain Trade in the Roman World," in Scheidel, *The Cambridge Companion to the Roman Economy*, 308.
154. Ronald Rogowski, *Commerce and Coalitions: How Trade Affects Domestic Political Alignments* (Princeton: Princeton University Press, 1989), 146.
155. Harris, "Power."
156. Wallace-Hadrill, *Rome's Cultural Revolution*, 23.
157. William E. Dunstan, *Ancient Rome* (Lanham: Rowman & Littlefield, 2011), 113–35.
158. Nicholas Ostler, *Empires of the Word: A Language History of the World* (London: Harper, 2005), Kindle Loc. 5272.
159. Gruen, *The Hellenistic World and the Coming of Rome*, 249.
160. Gruen, *The Hellenistic World and the Coming of Rome*, 251.

161. Rachel Mairs, "Hellenization," in Roger S. Bagnall, Kai Brodersen, Craige B. Champion, Andrew Erskine, and Sabine R. Huebner, eds., *The Encyclopedia of Ancient History* (Malden: Wiley-Blackwell, 2012), https://doi.org/10.1002/9781444338386.wbeah22144 (accessed 11/5/2022).

162. Simon Hornblower, "Hellenism, Hellenization," *Oxford Classical Dictionary*, December 22, 2015, https://doi.org/10.1093/acrefore/9780199381135.013.2994 (accessed 11/5/2022).

163. Thomas N. Habinek, *The Politics of Latin Literature: Writing, Identity, and Empire in Ancient Rome* (Princeton: Princeton University Press, 1998), 34.

164. Nicholas Purcell, "On the significance of East and West in today's 'Hellenistic' history: reflections on symmetrical worlds, reflecting through world symmetries," in Jonathan R. W. Prag and Crawley Quinn, eds., *The Hellenistic West: Rethinking the Ancient Mediterranean* (Cambridge: Cambridge University Press, 2013), 390.

165. Christoph Ulf, "Models of Culture Contact and Cultural Change: Moving Beyond National and Linguistic Traditions," in Franco de Angelis, ed., *A Companion to Greeks Across the Ancient World* (Hoboken: Wiley-Blackwell, 2020), 126.

166. On hegemonic socialization, see Amitav Acharya, *Constructing Global Order: Agency and Change in World Politics* (Cambridge: Cambridge University Press, 2018), 36–38.

167. Mogens Herman Hansen, "Colonies and Indigenous Hellenized Communities," in Mogens Herman Hansen and Thomas Heine Nielsen, eds., *An Inventory of Archaic and Classical Poleis* (New York: Oxford University Press, 2004), 152.

168. Franco de Angelis, "Colonies and Colonization," in George Boys-Stones, Barbara Graziosi, and Phiroze Vasunia, eds., *The Oxford Handbook of Hellenic Studies* (New York: Oxford University Press, 2009), 49.

169. Quoted in Roderick Beaton, *The Greeks: A Global History* (New York: Basic Books, 2021), 88.

170. Gocha R. Tsetskhladze, "Revisiting Ancient Greek Colonisation," in Gocha R. Tsetskhladze, ed., *Greek Colonisation—An Account of Greek Colonies and Other Overseas Settlements*, vol. 1 (Leiden: Brill, 2006), xxviii.

171. Hansen, "Colonies and Indigenous Hellenized Communities," 150–53.

172. Craig Benjamin and Merry E. Wiesner-Hanks, "The Mediterranean," in Craig Benjamin, ed., *The Cambridge World History*, vol. 4 (Cambridge: Cambridge University Press, 2015), Kindle Loc. 9077; Ostler, *Empires of the Word*, Kindle Loc. 5069.

173. Tamar Hodos, *Local Responses to Colonization in the Iron Age Mediterranean* (London: Routledge, 2006). However, they did not compete in the Black Sea, where the Greeks established colonies but not the Phoenicians, or in Sardinia, where the Phoenicians established colonies but not the Greeks.

174. Ian Morris and Alex R. Knodell, "Greek Cities in the First Millennium BCE," in Norman Yoffee, ed., *The Cambridge World History*, vol. 3 (Cambridge: Cambridge University Press, 2015), 360.

175. Mogen Herman Hansen, *Polis: An Introduction to the Ancient Greek City-State* (New York: Oxford University Press, 2006), 34.

176. Tsetskhladze, "Revisiting Ancient Greek Colonisation," xlviii.

177. Hansen, *Polis*, 34, 45.

178. Beaton, *The Greeks*, 85; Hansen, "Colonies and Indigenous Hellenized Communities," 150.

179. Tsetskhladze, "Revisiting Ancient Greek Colonisation," xlvii.

180. Mogens Herman Hansen, "The Lifespan of the Hellenic *Polis*," in Hansen and Nielsen, *An Inventory of Archaic and Classical Poleis*, 19.

181. Tsetskhladze, "Revisiting Ancient Greek Colonisation," lxv.

182. Hodos, *Local Responses to Colonization in the Iron Age Mediterranean*, 10.

183. Tsetskhladze, "Revisiting Ancient Greek Colonisation," xxix.

184. Robin Osborne, "Early Greek Colonization? The Nature of Greek Settlement in the West," in Nick Fisher and Hans van Wees, eds., *Archaic Greece: New Approaches and New Evidence* (London: Duckworth, 1998), 262.

185. Hansen, "Colonies and Indigenous Hellenized Communities," 151. On strategic interaction, see Acharya, *Constructing Global Order*, 33–36.

186. Beaton, *The Greeks*, 90.

187. D. W. R. Ridgway, "Colonization, Greek," in Simon Hornblower and Antony Spawforth, eds., *The Oxford Companion to Classical Civilization*, 2nd ed. (New York: Oxford University Press, 2014), 191; Vlassopoulos, *Greeks and Barbarians*, 15.

188. John Boardman, *The Greeks Overseas: Their Early Colonies and Trade* (London: Thames & Hudson, 1980), 190.

189. Hodos, *Local Responses to Colonization in the Iron Age Mediterranean*, 11.

190. Sara Owen, "Analogy, Archaeology and Archaic Greek Colonization," in Henry Hurst and Sara Owen, eds., *Ancient Colonizations: Analogy, Similarity and Difference* (London: Bloomsbury, 2005), 13.

191. Tsetskhladze, "Revisiting Ancient Greek Colonisation," lvi–lix.

192. Hodos, *Local Responses to Colonization in the Iron Age Mediterranean*, 152.

193. Owen, "Analogy, Archaeology and Archaic Greek Colonization," 20.

194. Hansen, *Polis*, 44.

195. Christoph Ulf, "Rethinking Cultural Contacts," in Robert Rollinger and Kordula Schnegg, eds., *Kulturkontakte in Antiken Welten: Vom Denkmodell zum Fallbeispiel* (Leuven: Peeters, 2014), 527.

196. Nicholas Purcell, "Colonization and Mediterranean History," in Hurst and Owen, *Ancient Colonizations*, 117, 120, 129.

197. Tsetskhladze, "Revisiting Ancient Greek Colonisation," xxix.

198. Tsetskhladze, "Revisiting Ancient Greek Colonisation," liii.

199. Hodos, *Local Responses to Colonization in the Iron Age Mediterranean*, 20.

200. Arnason, "The Roman Phenomenon," 373.
201. Tsetskhladze, "Revisiting Ancient Greek Colonisation," xlix.
202. Hansen, *Polis*, 33.
203. Hansen, *Polis*, 35–36.
204. Ulf, "Rethinking Cultural Contacts," 526.
205. Tsetskhladze, "Revisiting Ancient Greek Colonisation," lxv.
206. Tsetskhladze, "Revisiting Ancient Greek Colonisation," lxiv.
207. M. B. Hatzopoulos, "Macedonia and Macedonians," in Robin J. Lane Fox, ed., *Brill's Companion to Ancient Macedon: Studies in the Archaeology and History of Macedon, 650 BC–300 AD* (Leiden: Brill, 2011), 43–44.
208. Beaton, *The Greeks*, 175.
209. Simon Hornblower, *The Greek World, 479–323 BC*, 4th ed. (London: Routledge, 2011), 99.
210. Chaniotis, *Age of Conquests*, 391.
211. Beaton, *The Greeks*, 201.
212. Pierre Briant, "Colonization, Hellenistic," in Hornblower and Spawforth, *The Oxford Companion to Classical Civilization*, 191.
213. Vlassopoulos, *Greeks and Barbarians*, 280.
214. Vlassopoulos, *Greeks and Barbarians*, 280; Ostler, *Empires of the Word*, Kindle Loc. 5194.
215. Vlassopoulos, *Greeks and Barbarians*, 285–86.
216. Beaton, *The Greeks*, 205–10.
217. Anthony Pagden, *Worlds at War: The 2,500-Year Struggle between East and West* (New York: Random House, 2008), 94.
218. Vlassopoulos, *Greeks and Barbarians*, 285, 300.
219. Tim Whitmarsh, "Hellenism," in Barchiesi and Scheidel, *The Oxford Handbook of Roman Studies*, https://doi.org/10.1093/oxfordhb/9780199211524.013.0047 (accessed 11/5/2022).
220. Benjamin and Wiesner-Hanks, "The Mediterranean," Kindle Loc. 9443.
221. Quoted in Susan E. Alcock, *Graecia Capta: The Landscapes of Roman Greece* (Cambridge: Cambridge University Press, 1993), 1.
222. Andrew Wallace-Hadrill, "The Creation and Expression of Identity: The Roman World," in Susan E. Alcock and Robin Osborne, eds., *Classical Archaeology*, 2nd ed. (Chichester: Blackwell Publishing, 2012), 375; Whitmarsh, "Hellenism."
223. Erich S. Gruen, "Rome and the Greek World," in Harriet I. Flower, ed., *The Roman Republic*, 2nd ed. (New York: Cambridge University Press, 2014), 282.
224. Keith Branigan, "Hellenistic Influence on the Roman World," in John Wacher, ed., *The Roman World*, vol. 1 (London: Routledge, 1987), 41.
225. Branigan, "Hellenistic Influence on the Roman World," 45.
226. Mario Torelli, "The Topography and Archaeology of Republican Rome," in Rosenstein and Morstein-Marx, *A Companion to the Roman Republic*, 94.

227. Whitmarsh, "Hellenism."
228. Peter Fibiger Bang, "Imperial Ecumene and Polyethnicity," in Barchiesi and Scheidel, *The Oxford Handbook of Roman Studies*, https://doi.org/10.1093/oxfordhb/9780199211524.013.0043 (accessed 11/5/2022).
229. Whitmarsh, "Hellenism."
230. Whitmarsh, "Hellenism."
231. Waterfield, *Taken at the Flood*, 210.
232. Waterfield, *Taken at the Flood*, 210; Torelli, "The Topography and Archaeology of Republican Rome," 95.
233. Alessandro Barchiesi, "Roman Perspectives on the Greeks," in Boys-Stones, Graziosi, and Phiroze Vasunia, *The Oxford Handbook of Hellenic Studies*, 106.
234. Whitmarsh, "Hellenism" (emphasis original).
235. Wallace-Hadrill, *Rome's Cultural Revolution*, 24.
236. Waterfield, *Taken at the Flood*, 210.
237. Whitmarsh, "Hellenism."
238. Tim Whitmarsh, "Greece and Rome," in Boys-Stones, Graziosi, and Phiroze Vasunia, *The Oxford Handbook of Hellenic Studies*, 123.
239. Whitmarsh, "Greece and Rome," 121.
240. Whitmarsh, "Hellenism."
241. Wallace-Hadrill, "The Creation and Expression of Identity," 372.
242. Ostler, *Empires of the Word*, Kindle Loc. 5042.
243. Branigan, "Hellenistic Influence on the Roman World," 45.
244. Wallace-Hadrill, "The Creation and Expression of Identity," 384.
245. Beaton, *The Greeks*, 231.
246. Wallace-Hadrill, *Rome's Cultural Revolution*, 23–24.
247. Erich S. Gruen, *Rethinking the Other in Antiquity* (Princeton: Princeton University Press, 2011), 344–45.
248. Gruen, *Rethinking the Other in Antiquity*, 349.
249. Waterfield, *Taken at the Flood*, 213.
250. Bang, "Imperial Ecumene and Polyethnicity."
251. Torelli, "The Topography and Archaeology of Republican Rome," 96–97.
252. Ostler, *Empires of the Word*, Kindle Loc. 5272.
253. Wallace-Hadrill, *Rome's Cultural Revolution*, 26.
254. Mairs, "Hellenization."
255. Arnason, "The Roman Phenomenon," 368.
256. However, Greek culture was also changed as it responded to the Roman Empire. See Tim Whitmarsh, *Greek Literature and the Roman Empire: The Politics of Imitation* (New York: Oxford University Press, 2001).
257. Whitmarsh, "Hellenism."
258. Erich Gruen, "Rome and Others," in Rosenstein and Morstein-Marx, *A Companion to the Roman Republic*, 469.
259. William W. Batstone, "Literature," in Rosenstein and Morstein-Marx, *A Companion to the Roman Republic*, 561.

260. In 10 B.C.E., the historian Dionysius of Halicarnassus asserted that Rome was a Greek city and that the "Romans were Greek in origin." See Craige B. Champion, ed., *Roman Imperialism: Readings and Sources* (Malden: Blackwell, 2004), 268; and Woolf, *Rome*, 174. In 155 C.E., the Anatolian sophist Aelius Aristides also praised the Roman "world empire founded on military might" as "an inflated version of a Greek *polis.*" See Beaton, *The Greeks*, 251.

261. Waterfield, *Taken at the Flood*, 235.

262. Woolf, *Rome*, 221.

263. Peter Fibiger Bang, "The Roman Empire," in Peter Fibiger Bang, C. A. Bayly, and Walter Scheidel, eds., *The Oxford World History of Empire*, vol. 2: *The History of Empires* (New York: Oxford University Press, 2021), 264.

264. Harris, *Roman Power*, 30.

265. Pagden, *Worlds at War*, 105–6.

266. Lacey, *Rome*, 44.

267. Woolf, *Rome*, 86.

268. Kay, *Rome's Economic Revolution*, 189.

269. Woolf, *Rome*, 46.

270. Harris, *Roman Power*, 31.

271. Eckstein, "Rome Dominates the Mediterranean," 65, 74.

272. Rickman, "The Creation of *Mare Nostrum*," 135–36.

273. Bang, "The Roman Empire II," 22.

274. Abulafia, *The Great Sea*, 209.

275. Bang, "Imperial Ecumene and Polyethnicity." Roman coinage was also introduced in the subjugated polities (or their own local coins were stamped with the image of the Roman emperor).

276. Hopkins, "The Political Economy of the Roman Empire," 185; Goldstone and Haldon, "Ancient States," 24.

277. Bang, "Lord of All the World," 180.

278. Harris, *Roman Power*, 7.

279. Spickermann, "The Roman Empire," 113.

280. Nathan Rosenstein, "War and Peace, Fear and Reconciliation at Rome," in Kurt A. Raaflaub, ed., *War and Peace in the Ancient World* (Malden: Blackwell, 2007), 227.

281. Gargola, "The Mediterranean Empire," 150.

282. Harris, *Roman Power*, 34.

283. Andrew Erskine, "Polybius among the Romans: Life in the Cyclops' Cave," in Christopher Smith and Liv Mariah Yarrow, eds., *Imperialism, Cultural Politics, and Polybius* (New York: Oxford University Press, 2012), 17–32.

284. Hannah Cornwell, *"Pax" and the Politics of Peace: Republic to Principate* (New York: Oxford University Press, 2017), 34.

285. Erich S. Gruen, "Material Rewards and the Drive for Empire," in Champion, *Roman Imperialism*, 33.

286. Pompey's campaigns involved 500 warships, 120,000 infantry, and 5,000 cavalry. Goldsworthy, "War," 104; Woolf, *Rome*, 103.

287. The antipirate campaigns of Marcus Antonius in 102 B.C.E. marked the "first" Roman attempt to deal with this issue. Woolf, *Rome*, 156.

288. Simon Hornblower, "Sea Power, Greek and Roman," *Oxford Classical Dictionary*, March 7, 2016, https://doi.org/10.1093/acrefore/9780199938 1135.013.5775 (accessed 11/6/2022). Also see David Braund, "Piracy Under the Principate and the Ideology of Imperial Eradication," in John Rich and Graham Shipley, eds., *War and Society in the Roman World* (London: Routledge, 1993), 195–212; and Pitassi, *The Roman Navy*, 375.

289. Cornwell, *"Pax" and the Politics of Peace*, 197.

290. Cornwell, *"Pax" and the Politics of Peace*, 197.

291. Peter Fibiger Bang, "Between Aśoka and Antiochus: An Essay in World History on Universal Kingship and Cosmopolitan Culture in the Hellenistic Ecumene," in Peter Fibiger Bang and Dariusz Kołodziejczyk, eds., *Universal Empire: A Comparative Approach to Imperial Culture and Representation in Eurasian History* (Cambridge: Cambridge University Press, 2012), 68.

292. Arnaldo Momigliano, " 'Terra Marique,' " *The Journal of Roman Studies*, vol. 32, parts 1 and 2 (1942): 53–64.

Chapter Three. The International Order of the Classical Indian Ocean (~First–Fifteenth Centuries C.E.)

1. On this "Sino-Indian Great Divergence" until 1800, when China and India were the world's most productive regions, see James Belich, John Darwin, and Chris Wickham, "Introduction: The Prospect of Global History," in James Belich, John Darwin, Margret Frenz, and Chris Wickham, eds., *The Prospect of Global History* (New York: Oxford University Press, 2016), 7–8.

2. Philippe Beaujard, *The Worlds of the Indian Ocean: A Global History*, 2 vols. (Cambridge: Cambridge University Press, 2019). Also see Janel L. Abu-Lughod, *Before European Hegemony: The World System A.D. 1250–1350* (New York: Oxford University Press, 1989).

3. Craig Lockard, *Southeast Asia in World History* (New York: Oxford University Press, 2009), 15.

4. John K. Fairbank, "A Preliminary Framework," in John King Fairbank, ed., *The Chinese World Order: Traditional China's Foreign Relations* (Cambridge: Harvard University Press, 1968), 7.

5. Pierre-Yves Manguin, "Early States of Insular Southeast Asia," in Charles F. W. Higham and Nam C. Kim, eds., *The Oxford Handbook of Early Southeast Asia* (New York: Oxford University Press, 2022), https://doi.org/10.1093/oxfordhb/9780199355358.013.36 (accessed 12/4/2022).

6. James R. Rush, *Southeast Asia: A Very Short Introduction* (New York: Oxford University Press, 2018), https://doi.org/10.1093/actrade/97801902 48765.003.0002 (accessed 12/3/2022).

7. Victor Lieberman, *Strange Parallels: Southeast Asia in Global Context, c. 800–1830*, vol. 2 (Cambridge: Cambridge University Press, 2009), 15. While the societies of the historical Philippines are normally left out of the Indianization paradigm, recent scholarship has shown that Indic political ideas had an impact even there. See Joefe B. Santarita, "Panyupayana: The Emergence of Hindu Polities in the Pre-Islamic Philippines," in Shyam Saran, ed., *Cultural and Civilisational Links between India and Southeast Asia: Historical and Contemporary Dynamics* (Singapore: Palgrave Macmillan, 2018), 93–105.

8. Hermann Kulke and Dietmar Rothermund, *A History of India*, 4th ed. (New York: Routledge, 2004), 153.

9. O. W. Wolters, *Early Southeast Asia: Selected Essays*, ed. Craig J. Reynolds (Ithaca: Cornell University Southeast Asia Program, 2008), 67.

10. Lockard, *Southeast Asia in World History*, 6–7.

11. Engseng Ho, "Foreigners and Mediators in the Constitution of Malay Sovereignty," *Indonesia and the Malay World*, vol. 41, no. 120 (2013): 151.

12. David Singh Grewal, *Network Power: The Social Dynamics of Globalization* (New Haven: Yale University Press, 2008), 6.

13. Shared management is obviously distinct from the more familiar "great power management" of international relations theory. See Amitav Acharya, "Power Shift or Paradigm Shift? China's Rise and Asia's Emerging Security Order," *International Studies Quarterly*, vol. 58, no. 1 (2014): 160.

14. Bérénice Bellina, "Southeast Asia and the Early Maritime Silk Road," in John Guy, ed., *Lost Kingdoms: Hindu-Buddhist Sculpture of Early Southeast Asia* (New York: The Metropolitan Museum of Art, 2014), 21.

15. O. W. Wolters, *History, Culture, and Region in Southeast Asian Perspectives*, rev. ed. (Singapore: Institute of Southeast Asian Studies, 1999), 45.

16. Rush, *Southeast Asia*, https://doi.org/10.1093/actrade/9780190248765. 003.0002 (accessed 12/4/2022). On localization, see Wolters, *History, Culture, and Region in Southeast Asian Perspectives*; and Amitav Acharya, *Constructing Global Order: Agency and Change in World Politics* (Cambridge: Cambridge University Press, 2018), 33–67.

17. Charles F. W. Higham, "Social Change in Southeast Asia during the Iron Age" and Pierre-Yves Manguin, "Early States of Insular Southeast Asia," in Higham and Kim, *The Oxford Handbook of Early Southeast Asia*, https://doi.org/10.1093/oxfordhb/9780199355358.013.26 and https://doi.org/10.1093/oxfordhb/9780199355358.013.36 (accessed 12/4/2022).

18. Sheldon Pollock, *The Language of the Gods in the World of Men: Sanskrit, Culture, and Power in Premodern India* (Berkeley: University of California Press, 2006), 271.

19. Barbara Watson Andaya, "Imagination, Memory and History: Narrating India–Malay Intersections in the Early Modern Period," in Radhika Seshan,

ed., *Narratives, Routes and Intersections in Pre-Modern Asia* (London: Routledge, 2017), 11.

20. Quoted in Pollock, *The Language of the Gods in the World of Men*, 234.

21. Theodore G. T. Pigeaud, ed. and trans., *Java in the Fourteenth Century: A Study in Cultural History: The Nagara-Kertagama by "Rakawi" Prapanca of Majapahit, 1365 A.D.*, vol. 3 (The Hague: Martinus Nijhoff, 1960), 97.

22. Hermann Kulke, "State Formation and Social Integration in Pre-Islamic South and Southeast Asia," in Karashima Noboru and Hirosue Masashi, eds., *State Formation and Social Integration in Pre-modern South and Southeast Asia* (Tokyo: The Toyo Bunko, 2017), 317–20.

23. Wolters, *History, Culture, and Region in Southeast Asian Perspectives*, 28, 34. Also see S. J. Tambiah, *World Conqueror & World Renouncer* (Cambridge: Cambridge University Press, 1976).

24. Rush, *Southeast Asia*, https://doi.org/10.1093/actrade/97801902 48765.003.0002 (accessed 12/5/2022).

25. Hendrik Spruyt, *The World Imagined: Collective Beliefs and Political Order in the Sinocentric, Islamic and Southeast Asian International Societies* (Cambridge: Cambridge University Press, 2020), 259.

26. Andrew J. Coe and Scott Wolford, "East Asian History and International Relations," in Stephan Haggard and David C. Kang, eds., *East Asia in the World: Twelve Events that Shaped the Modern International Order* (Cambridge: Cambridge University Press, 2020), 278.

27. David C. Kang and Kenneth W. Swope, "East Asian International Relations over the *Longue Durée*," in Haggard and Kang, *East Asia in the World*, 23.

28. On open and closed systems/regions, see Barry Buzan and Richard Little, *International Systems in World History* (New York: Oxford University Press, 2000).

29. Rush, *Southeast Asia*, https://doi.org/10.1093/actrade/9780190248765. 003.0002 (accessed 12/3/2022).

30. Lockard, *Southeast Asia in World History*, 15.

31. Leonard Andaya, "A History of Trade in the Sea of Melayu," *Itinerario*, vol. 24, no. 1 (2000): 88.

32. John N. Miksic and Geok Tian Goh, *Ancient Southeast Asia* (New York: Routledge, 2017), 44.

33. Tom Hoogervorst, "Commercial Networks Connecting Southeast Asia with the Indian Ocean," *Asian History*, Oxford Research Encyclopedias, December 22, 2021, https://doi.org/10.1093/acrefore/9780190277727. 013.541 (accessed 12/4/2022).

34. Beaujard, *The Worlds of the Indian Ocean*, vol. 2, 86.

35. Tansen Sen, "The Military Campaigns of Rajendra Chola and the Chola-Srivijaya-China Triangle," in Hermann Kulke, K. Kesavapany, and Vijay Sakhuja, eds., *Nagapattinam to Suvarnadwipa: Reflections on the Chola Naval Expeditions to Southeast Asia* (Singapore: ISEAS, 2009), 61–75.

36. Rila Mukherjee, "The Indian Ocean World of Srivijaya," in Kenneth R. Hall, Suchandra Ghosh, Kaushik Gangopadhyay, and Rila Mukherjee, eds., *Cross-Cultural Networking in the Eastern Indian Ocean Realm, c. 100–1800* (New Delhi: Primus Books, 2019), 178. Tambralingga may have attacked Sri Lanka again in 1262.

37. Kenneth R. Hall and John K. Whitmore, "Southeast Asian Trade and the Isthmian Struggle, 1000–1200," in Kenneth R. Hall and John K. Whitmore, eds., *Explorations in Early Southeast Asian History* (Ann Arbor: The University of Michigan Center for South and Southeast Asian Studies, 1976), 303–40.

38. Rila Mukherjee, "Introduction: Bengal and the Northern Bay of Bengal," in Rila Mukherjee, ed., *Pelagic Passageways: The Northern Bay of Bengal Before Colonialism* (Delhi: Primus, 2011), 13.

39. Gang Deng, *Chinese Maritime Activities and Socioeconomic Development, c. 2100 B.C.–1900 A.D.* (Westport: Greenwood Press, 1997), 9.

40. Deng, *Chinese Maritime Activities and Socioeconomic Development*, 69.

41. Michael Flecker, "The Bakau Wreck: An Early Example of Chinese Shipping in Southeast Asia," *The International Journal of Nautical Archeology*, vol. 30, no. 2 (2001): 221.

42. Beaujard, *The Worlds of the Indian Ocean*, vol. 1, 317.

43. Beaujard, *The Worlds of the Indian Ocean*, vol. 1, 505.

44. Paul Wheatley, *The Golden Khersonese: Studies in the Historical Geography of the Malay Peninsula before A.D. 1500* (Kuala Lumpur: University of Malaya Press, 1961), 14.

45. Fabrizia Baldissera, "The Mobility of People and Ideas on the Seas of Ancient India," in Philip de Souza and Pascal Arnaud, eds., *The Sea in History: The Ancient World* (Woodbridge: The Boydell Press, 2017), 558.

46. Pierre-Yves Manguin, "Dialogues between Southeast Asia and India: A Necessary Reappraisal," in Anna L. Dallapiccola and Anila Verghese, eds., *India and Southeast Asia: Cultural Discourses* (Mumbai: The K. R. Cama Oriental Institute, 2017), 24–25.

47. Pollock, *The Language of the Gods in the World of Men*, 127, 130.

48. Pollock, *The Language of the Gods in the World of Men*, 16.

49. Richard Smith, "Trade and Commerce across Afro-Eurasia," in Benjamin Z. Kedar and Merry E. Wiesner-Hanks, eds., *The Cambridge World History*, vol. 5: *Expanding Webs of Exchange and Conflict, 500 CE–1500 CE* (Cambridge: Cambridge University Press, 2015), 239.

50. Our conception overlaps with that of Acri, who thinks of South/Southeast/East Asia as "a single interconnected network." Andrea Acri, "Imagining 'Maritime Asia,' " in Andrea Acri, Kashshaf Ghani, Murari K. Jha, and Sraman Mukherjee, eds., *Imagining Asia(s): Networks, Actors, Sites* (Singapore: ISEAS Yusof Ishak Institute, 2019), 37.

51. Beaujard, *The Worlds of the Indian Ocean*, vol. 2, 467.

52. William C. Wohlforth, Stuart J. Kaufman, and Richard Little, "Introduction: Balance and Hierarchy in International Systems," in Stuart J.

Kaufman, Richard Little, and William C. Wohlforth, eds., *The Balance of Power in World History* (New York: Palgrave, 2007), 16–17.

53. Andrea Acri, Roger Blench, and Alexandra Landman, "Introduction: Reconnecting Histories across the Indo-Pacific," in Andrea Acri, Roger Blench, and Alexandra Landman, eds., *Spirits and Ships: Cultural Transfers in Early Monsoon Asia* (Singapore: ISEAS Yusof Ishak Institute, 2017), 5.

54. Pierre-Yves Manguin, "Trading Ships of the South China Sea: Shipbuilding Techniques and Their Role in the History of the Development of Asian Trade Networks," *Journal of the Economic and Social History of the Orient*, vol. 36, no. 3 (1993): 261–62.

55. Manguin, "Trading Ships of the South China Sea," 262.

56. Beaujard, *The Worlds of the Indian Ocean*, vol. 2, 37.

57. Paul Buell, "Qubilai's Maritime Mongols," *Asian History*, Oxford Research Encyclopedias, July 30, 2020, https://doi.org/10.1093/acrefore/9780190277727.013.472 (accessed 12/5/2022); Tamara Bentley, "Trade in East and South China Seas, 600 CE to 1800 CE," *Asian History*, Oxford Research Encyclopedias, September 26, 2018, https://doi.org/10.1093/acrefore/9780190277727.013.66 (accessed 2/23/2024).

58. Beaujard, *The Worlds of the Indian Ocean*, vol. 1, 289.

59. Wolters, *Early Southeast Asia*, 66.

60. Kenneth R. Hall, "Small Asian Nations in the Shadow of the Large: Early Asian History through the Eyes of Southeast Asia," *Journal of the Economic and Social History of the Orient*, vol. 27, no. 1 (1984): 59.

61. The British were the first-ever maritime rival that China encountered in these waters in the nineteenth century. Martin Stuart-Fox, *A Short History of China and Southeast Asia: Tribute, Trade, and Influence* (Crows Nest: Allen & Unwin, 2003), 21.

62. Hall, "Small Asian Nations in the Shadow of the Large," 64.

63. Wolters, *History, Culture, and Region in Southeast Asian Perspectives*, 37. Wolters made this observation from the perspective of Sinic Dai Viet toward its Indianized neighbors.

64. Wang Gungwu, *China Reconnects: Joining a Deep-Rooted Past to a New World Order* (Singapore: World Scientific, 2019), Kindle Loc. 2596.

65. Angela Schottenhammer, "Imperial Maritime China," *Asian History*, Oxford Research Encyclopedias, May 23, 2019, https://doi.org/10.1093/acrefore/9780190277727.013.209 (accessed 12/5/2022); Geoffrey C. Gunn, *History without Borders: The Making of an Asian World Region, 1000–1800* (Hong Kong: Hong Kong University Press, 2011), 9.

66. Deng, *Chinese Maritime Activities and Socioeconomic Development*, 54.

67. John N. Miksic, *Singapore & the Silk Road of the Sea, 1300–1800* (Singapore: NUS Press, 2013), 98; Schottenhammer, "Imperial Maritime China."

68. Deng, *Chinese Maritime Activities and Socioeconomic Development*, 71.

69. Schottenhammer, "Imperial Maritime China."

70. James A. Anderson, "The Outer Limits of Steppe Power: Mongol Excursions in Southeast Asia," in Timothy May and Michael Hope, eds., *The Mongol World* (New York: Routledge, 2022), 874.

71. Wang Gungwu, "Ming Foreign Relations: Southeast Asia," in Denis Twitchett and John K. Fairbank, eds., *The Cambridge History of China*, vol. 8, part 2 (New York: Cambridge University Press, 1998), 302.

72. Deng, *Chinese Maritime Activities and Socioeconomic Development*, 71.

73. Deng, *Chinese Maritime Activities and Socioeconomic Development*, 55, 57.

74. Wang, *China Reconnects*, Kindle Loc. 2617.

75. Wolters, *Early Southeast Asia*, 67.

76. Charles Holcombe, *The Genesis of East Asia, 221 B.C.–A.D. 907* (Honolulu: University of Hawai'i Press, 2001), 40.

77. Wang Gungwu, *Renewal: The Chinese State and the New Global History* (Hong Kong: The Chinese University Press, 2013), Kindle Loc. 274.

78. Hall, "Small Asian Nations in the Shadow of the Large," 61.

79. Yuri Pines, *The Everlasting Empire: The Political Culture of Ancient China and Its Imperial Legacy* (Princeton: Princeton University Press, 2012), 35.

80. Wang Gungwu, "The Rhetoric of a Lesser Empire: Early Sung Relations with Its Neighbors," in Morris Rossabi, ed., *China Among Equals: The Middle Kingdom and its Neighbors, 10th–14th Centuries* (Berkeley: University of California Press, 1983), 60.

81. Wang, *China Reconnects*, Kindle Loc. 2490.

82. Wang, "Chinese Tribute System," in Ooi Keat Hin, ed., *Southeast Asia: A Historical Encyclopedia from Angkor Wat to East Timor* (Santa Barbara: ABC Clio, 2004), 352.

83. Timothy Brook, *Great State: China and the World* (London: Profile, 2019), 8.

84. On the Mongols' continental exploits, see Ayşe Zarakol, *Before the West: The Rise and Fall of Eastern World Orders* (Cambridge: Cambridge University Press, 2022).

85. Thomas T. Allsen, *The Steppe and the Sea: Pearls in the Mongol Empire* (Philadelphia: University of Pennsylvania Press, 2019), 163.

86. Tansen Sen, "The Formation of Chinese Maritime Networks to Southern Asia, 1200–1450," *Journal of the Economic and Social History of the Orient*, vol. 49, no. 4 (2006): 436.

87. It failed for other reasons, too, including China's attention to the nomadic continental threat from the north.

88. Edward L. Dreyer, *Zheng He: China and the Oceans in Early Ming Dynasty, 1405–1433* (New York: Pearson Longman, 2006), 3.

89. Tansen Sen, "Diplomacy, Trade and the Quest for the Buddha's Tooth: The Yongle Emperor and Ming China's South Asian Frontier," in Craig Clunas, Jessica Harrison-Hall, and Luk Yu-ping, eds., *Ming China: Courts and Contacts 1400–1450* (London: The British Museum, 2016), 26; and Geoff Wade, "The Zheng He Voyages: A Reassessment," *Journal of the Malaysian Branch of the Royal Asiatic Society*, vol. 78, no. 1 (2005): 37–58.

90. Takeshi Hamashita, "The Tribute Trade System and Modern Asia," in A. J. H. Latham and Heita Kawakatsu, eds., *Japanese Industrialization and the Asian Economy* (London: Routledge, 1994), 91–107.

91. Kenneth R. Hall, "Commodity Flows, Diaspora Networking, and Contested Agency in the Eastern Indian Ocean, c. 1000–1500," *TRaNS: Trans-Regional and -National Studies of Southeast Asia*, vol. 4, no. 2 (2016): 406.

92. Robert Finlay, "The Treasure-Ships of Zheng He: Chinese Maritime Imperialism in the Age of Discovery," *Terrae Incognitae*, vol. 23, no. 1 (1991): 8.

93. Jan Wisseman Christie, "State Formation in Early Maritime Southeast Asia: A Consideration of the Theories and Data," *Bijdragen tot de Taal-, Land-en Volkenkunde*, vol. 151, no. 2 (1995): 244.

94. Holcombe, *The Genesis of East Asia*, 101.

95. Holcombe, *The Genesis of East Asia*, 102.

96. Michael Vickery, "Champa Revisited," in Tran Ky Phuong and Bruce M. Lockhart, eds., *The Cham of Vietnam: History, Society and Art* (Singapore: NUS Press, 2011), 378.

97. Vickery, "Champa Revisited," 394–407.

98. G. Coedès, *The Indianized States of Southeast Asia* (Canberra: Australian National University Press, 1975), 136.

99. Barbara Watson Andaya and Leonard Y. Andaya, *A History of Malaysia* (London: Macmillan, 1982), 20.

100. Michael W. Charney, "Warfare in Premodern Southeast Asia," *Asian History*, Oxford Research Encyclopedias, April 26, 2018, https://doi.org/10.1093/acrefore/9780190277727.013.238 (accessed 12/5/2022).

101. Miksic and Goh, *Ancient Southeast Asia*, 233.

102. Wolters, *History, Culture, and Region in Southeast Asian Perspectives*, 28.

103. Anthony Reid, *Southeast Asia in the Age of Commerce, 1450–1680*, vol. 1: *The Lands below the Winds* (New Haven: Yale University Press, 1988), 123. While Reid made this argument for early modern Southeast Asia, it probably holds true for classical Southeast Asia too.

104. There is limited literature on slavery in classical Southeast Asia, although various forms of patron-client relations certainly existed. Miksic and Goh, *Ancient Southeast Asia*, 247.

105. For the excerpt from the Ho-lo-tan ruler's message to China, see O. W. Wolters, *Early Indonesian Commerce: A Study of the Origins of Śrīvijaya* (Ithaca: Cornell University Press, 1967), 151.

106. Anderson, "The Outer Limits of Steppe Power," 882.

107. Reid, *A History of Southeast Asia*, 43.

108. James P. Delgado, *Khubilai Khan's Lost Fleet: In Search of a Legendary Armada* (Vancouver: Douglas & McIntyre, 2008), 166.

109. Paul D. Buell, "Maritime Silk Road: The Mongols and the Indian Ocean," in May and Hope, *The Mongol World*, 460.

110. Hall, "Small Asian Nations in the Shadow of the Large," 63.

111. Miksic, *Singapore & the Silk Road of the Sea*, 66.

112. Miksic, *Singapore & the Silk Road of the Sea*, 112.

113. Miksic and Goh, *Ancient Southeast Asia*, 297.

114. Hermann Kulke, "Śrīvijaya Revisited: Reflections on State Formation of a Southeast Asian Thalassocracy," *Bulletin de l'École française d'Extrême-Orient*, vol. 102 (2016): 45–96.

115. Manguin, "Early States of Insular Southeast Asia"; Paul Pelliot, *Notes on Marco Polo II* (Paris: Imprimerie Nationale, 1963), 839.

116. John N. Miksic, "Śrīvijaya," in Peter Fibiger Bang, C. A. Bayly, and Walter Scheidel, eds., *The Oxford World History of Empire*, vol. 2: *The History of Empires* (New York: Oxford University Press, 2021), 415.

117. Miksic, *Singapore & the Silk Road of the Sea*, 144.

118. Wolters, *History, Culture, and Region in Southeast Asian Perspectives*, 45.

119. Wang Gungwu, "The Nanhai Trade: A Study of the Early History of Chinese Trade in the South China Sea," *Journal of the Malaysian Branch of the Royal Asiatic Society*, vol. 31, part 2, no. 181 (1958): 114.

120. Derek Heng, "Southeast Asian Trade in a Global Perspective, from Antiquity to the Modern Era," *Asian History*, Oxford Research Encyclopedias, June 20, 2022, https://doi.org/10.1093/acrefore/9780190277727.013.540 (accessed 12/4/2022).

121. Jacques Gernet, *A History of Chinese Civilization*, 2nd ed. (New York: Cambridge University Press, 1996), 144.

122. Miksic, *Singapore & the Silk Road of the Sea*, 32.

123. Hamashita, "The Tribute Trade System and Modern Asia," 92.

124. Pines, *The Everlasting Empire*, 35; Miksic, *Singapore & the Silk Road of the Sea*, 32.

125. Schottenhammer, "Imperial Maritime China."

126. Chang Pin-tsun, "The Rise of Chinese Mercantile Power in Maritime Southeast Asia, c. 1400–1700," *Crossroads*, vol. 6 (October 2012): 209.

127. Kenneth R. Hall, *A History of Early Southeast Asia: Maritime Trade and Societal Development, 100–1500* (Lanham: Rowman & Littlefield, 2011), 34.

128. Schottenhammer, "Imperial Maritime China."

129. Tansen Sen, "Early China and the Indian Ocean Networks," in de Souza and Arnaud, *The Sea in History*, 546.

130. Sen, "Early China and the Indian Ocean Networks," 546.

131. S. A. M. Adshead, *China in World History*, 3rd ed. (Basingstoke: Palgrave, 2000), 116.

132. Gang Deng, *The Premodern Chinese Economy: Structural Equilibrium and Capitalist Sterility* (London: Routledge, 1999), 316.

133. Geoff Wade, "Chinese Engagement with the Indian Ocean during the Song, Yuan, and Ming Dynasties (Tenth to Sixteenth Centuries)," in Michael Pearson, ed., *Trade, Circulation, and Flow in the Indian Ocean World* (New York: Palgrave, 2015), 75.

134. Angela Schottenhammer, "China's Emergence as a Maritime Power," in John W. Chaffee and Denis Twitchett, eds., *The Cambridge History of China*, vol. 5, part 2 (Cambridge: Cambridge University Press, 2015), 525.

135. Schottenhammer, "China's Emergence as a Maritime Power," 516–17.

136. Robert S. Wicks, *Money, Markets, and Trade in Early Southeast Asia: The Development of Indigenous Monetary Systems to AD 1400* (Ithaca: Cornell University Southeast Asia Program, 1992), 24.

137. Wicks, *Money, Markets, and Trade in Early Southeast Asia*, 25–26.

138. Timothy Brook, *The Troubled Empire: China in the Yuan and Ming Dynasties* (Cambridge: The Belknap Press, 2010), 219; Stuart-Fox, *A Short History of China and Southeast Asia*, 64; Bentley, "Trade in East and South China Seas."

139. Gakusho Nakajima, "The Naval Power of the Yuan Dynasty," in Michael Balard, ed., *The Sea in History: The Medieval World* (Woodbridge: Boydell Press, 2017), 821.

140. Buell, "Qubilai's Maritime Mongols."

141. Anderson, "The Outer Limits of Steppe Power," 880.

142. Vu Hong Lien, "The Mongol Navy: Kublai Khan's Invasions in Dai Viet and Champa," Working Paper no. 25, Nalanda-Sriwijaya Centre, Institute of Southeast Asian Studies, June 2017, https://www.iseas.edu.sg/wp-content/uploads/pdfs/nscwps25.pdf (accessed 12/6/2022).

143. Beaujard, *The Worlds of the Indian Ocean*, vol. 2, 215.

144. Dreyer, *Zheng He*, 1.

145. Dreyer, *Zheng He*, 1.

146. Angela Schottenhammer, "China's Rise and Retreat as a Maritime Power," in Robert J. Anthony and Angela Schottenhammer, eds., *Beyond the Silk Roads: New Discourses on China's Role in East Asian Maritime History* (Wiesbaden: Harrassowitz Verlag, 2017), 204.

147. Schottenhammer, "China's Emergence as a Maritime Power," 521.

148. Warren I. Cohen, *East Asia at the Center: Four Thousand Years of Engagement with the World* (New York: Columbia University Press, 2000), 164.

149. Tansen Sen, "Maritime Southeast Asia between South Asia and China to the Sixteenth Century," *TRaNS: Trans-Regional and -National Studies of Southeast Asia*, vol. 2, no. 1 (2014): 43.

150. O. W. Wolters, *The Fall of Śrīvijaya in Malay History* (Kuala Lumpur: Oxford University Press, 1970), 176.

151. J. Kathirithamby-Wells, "Introduction: An Overview," in J. Kathirithamby-Wells and John Villiers, eds., *The Southeast Asian Port and Polity: Rise and Demise* (Singapore: Singapore University Press), 2.

152. Anthony Reid, *A History of Southeast Asia: Critical Crossroads* (Chichester: Wiley-Blackwell, 2015), 30.

153. Sen, "Early China and the Indian Ocean Networks," 537.

154. Stephen F. Dale, " "Silk Road, Cotton Road or . . . Indo-Chinese Trade in Pre-European Times," *Modern Asian Studies*, vol. 43, no. 1 (2009): 82.

155. John Guy, *Woven Cargoes: Indian Textiles in the East* (New York: Thames and Hudson, 1998), 55.

156. Dale, "Silk Road, Cotton Road or . . . Indo-Chinese Trade in Pre-European Times," 80.

157. Beaujard, *The Worlds of the Indian Ocean*, vol. 1, 512.

158. For useful reviews of these debates, see Andrea Acri, " 'Local' vs. 'Cosmopolitan' in the Study of Premodern Southeast Asia," *Suvannabhumi: Multi-disciplinary Journal of Southeast Asian Studies*, vol. 9, no. 1 (2017): 7–52; and Pierre-Yves Manguin, "Introduction," in Pierre-Yves Manguin, A. Mani, and Geoff Wade, eds., *Early Interactions between South and Southeast Asia: Reflections on Cross-Cultural Exchange* (Singapore: Institute of Southeast Asian Studies, 2012).

159. Monica L. Smith, " 'Indianization' from the Indian Point of View: Trade and Cultural Contacts with Southeast Asia in the Early First Millennium C.E.," *Journal of the Economic and Social History of the Orient*, vol. 42, no. 1 (1999): 1–26; Susan Bayly, "Imagining 'Greater India': French and Indian Visions of Colonialism in the Indic Mode," *Modern Asian Studies*, vol. 38, no. 3 (2004): 703–44. The Indian advocates of the Greater India Society were also trying to compensate for India's colonial status at that time by envisioning Indian empires in Southeast Asia in the past.

160. J. C. van Leur, "On Early Asian Trade," in J. C. van Leur, ed., *Indonesian Trade and Society: Essays in Asian Social and Economic History* (The Hague: W. van Hoeve Ltd., 1955), 95.

161. Pollock, *The Language of the Gods in the World of Men*, 535.

162. Berenice Bellina, "Beads, Social Change and Interaction between India and South-east Asia," *Antiquity*, vol. 77, no. 296 (June 2003): 285–97; Miksic and Goh, *Ancient Southeast Asia*, 357.

163. However, a recent study supporting this view was based on the study of the genome of just one Southeast Asian individual, who showed considerable Indian admixture. Piya Changmai, Ron Pinhasi, Michael Pietrusewsky, et al., "Ancient DNA from Protohistoric Period Cambodia Indicates that South Asians Admixed with Local Populations as Early as 1st–3rd Centuries CE," *Scientific Reports*, vol. 12, no. 22507 (2022), https://doi.org/10.1038/s41598-022-26799-3 (accessed 1/5/2023).

164. Piya Changmai et al., "Indian Genetic Heritage in Southeast Asian Populations," *PLOS Genetics*, February 17, 2022, https://doi.org/10.1371/journal.pgen.1010036 (accessed 12/7/2022).

165. Stephen A. Murphy and H. Leedom Lefferts, "Globalizing Indian Religions and Southeast Asian Localisms: Incentives for the Adoption of Buddhism and Brahmanism in First Millennium CE Southeast Asia," in Tamar Hodos, ed., *The Routledge Handbook of Archaeology and Globalization* (London: Routledge, 2017), 770, 784.

166. Miksic and Goh, *Ancient Southeast Asia*, 397–401.

167. Wolters, *History, Culture, and Region in Southeast Asian Perspectives*, 54.

168. Lieberman, *Strange Parallels*, vol. 2, 107.

169. Tom Hoogervorst, "Southeast Asia in the Ancient Indian Ocean World: Combining Historical Linguistic and Archaeological Approaches" (D. Phil. diss., University of Oxford, 2012), 47; Bérénice Bellina, "Southeast Asia and the Early Maritime Silk Road," in Guy, *Lost Kingdoms*, 24.

170. John Guy, "Introducing Early Southeast Asia," in John Guy, ed., *Lost Kingdoms: Hindu-Buddhist Sculpture of Early Southeast Asia* (New York: The Metropolitan Museum of Art, 2014), 5.

171. Miksic and Goh, *Ancient Southeast Asia*.

172. Pollock, *The Language of the Gods in the World of Men*, 133.

173. Rush, *Southeast Asia*, https://doi.org/10.1093/actrade/9780190248765.003.0002 (accessed 12/7/2022).

174. Karashima Noboru and Hirosue Masashi, "Coordinator's Report" on the Second International Symposium of Inter-Asia Research Networks (March 8–9, 2014) on "State Formation and Social Integration in Premodern South and Southeast Asia: A Comparative Study of Asian Society," *Modern Asian Studies Review*, vol. 5 (2014): 50, http://www.toyo-bunko.or.jp/research/e-journal/MASR05.pdf (accessed 12/7/2022).

175. Pollock, *The Language of the Gods in the World of Men*, 11, 257.

176. Hermann Kulke, "The Concept of Cultural Convergence Revisited: Reflections on India's Early Influence in Southeast Asia," in Upinder Singh and Parul Pandya Dhar, eds., *Asian Encounters: Exploring Connected Histories* (New Delhi: Oxford University Press, 2014), 10.

177. Pierre Yves-Manguin, "Protohistoric and Early Historic Exchange in the Eastern Indian Ocean: A Re-evaluation of Current Paradigms," in Schottenhammer, *Early Global Interconnectivity across the Indian Ocean World*, vol. 1, 99–120.

178. Acri, " 'Local' vs. 'Cosmopolitan' in the Study of Premodern Southeast Asia," 24.

179. Daud Ali, "The Early Inscriptions of Indonesia and the Problem of the Sanskrit Cosmopolis," in Manguin, Mani, and Wade, *Early Interactions between South and Southeast Asia*, 277–97.

180. Manguin, "Introduction," xvi, xvii.

181. Beaujard, *The Worlds of the Indian Ocean*, vol. 1, 464.

182. Acri, " 'Local' vs. 'Cosmopolitan' in the Study of Premodern Southeast Asia," 20.

183. Ali, "The Early Inscriptions of Indonesia and the Problem of the Sanskrit Cosmopolis," 282.

184. Acharya, *Constructing Global Order*, 42.

185. Kulke, "State Formation and Social Integration in Pre-Islamic South and Southeast Asia," 307.

186. Pollock, *The Language of the Gods in the World of Men*, 234.

187. Pollock, *The Language of the Gods in the World of Men*, 274.

188. Manguin, "Protohistoric and Early Historic Exchange in the Eastern Indian Ocean"; van Leur, "On Early Asian Trade," 98.

189. Johannes Bronkhorst, "The Spread of Sanskrit in Southeast Asia," in Manguin, Mani, and Wade, *Early Interactions between South and Southeast Asia*, 263–75.

190. Johann P. Arnason, "State Formation and Empire Building," in Benjamin Z. Kedar and Merry E. Wiesner-Hanks, eds., *The Cambridge World History*, vol. 5 (Cambridge: Cambridge University Press, 2015), 502.

191. K. T. S. Sarao, *The Decline of Buddhism in India: A Fresh Perspective* (New Delhi: Munshiram Manoharlal, 2012); Miksic and Goh, *Ancient Southeast Asia*, 151.

192. Manguin, "Early States of Insular Southeast Asia."

193. J. G. de Casparis and I. W. Mabbett, "Religion and Popular Beliefs of Southeast Asia before c. 1500," in Nicholas Tarling, ed., *The Cambridge History of Southeast Asia*, vol. 1: *From Early Times to c. 1800* (Cambridge: Cambridge University Press, 1992), 306.

194. Pollock, *The Language of the Gods in the World of Men*, 235.

195. Michael D. Coe, "The Khmer Empire," in Bang, Bayly, and Scheidel, *The Oxford World History of Empire*, vol. 2, 437.

196. Pollock, *The Language of the Gods in the World of Men*, 222.

197. Guy, "Introducing Early Southeast Asia," in Guy, *Lost Kingdoms*, 8.

198. For examples of such politico-literary localizations in eleventh–fourteenth-century Java, see John K. Whitmore, "Kingship, Time, and Space: Historiography in Southeast Asia," in Sarah Foot and Chase F. Robinson, eds., *The Oxford History of Historical Writing, 400–1400*, vol. 2 (Oxford: Oxford University Press, 2012), 107–10.

199. Prior to this, Indic rulers, including the Mauryan emperor Aśoka (~268–232 B.C.E.), had not used Sanskrit to express political power. Pollock, *The Language of the Gods in the World of Men*, 69.

200. Vickery, "Champa Revisited," 366.

201. Richard Salomon, *Indian Epigraphy: A Guide to the Study of Inscriptions in Sanskrit, Prakrit, and Other Indo-Aryan Languages* (New York: Oxford University Press, 1998), 92.

202. Frederick M. Asher, "India Abroad: Evidence for Ancient Indian Maritime Activity," in Matthew Adam Cobb, ed., *The Indian Ocean Trade in Antiquity: Political, Cultural, and Economic Impacts* (New York: Routledge, 2019), 159.

203. Acri, " 'Local' vs. 'Cosmopolitan' in the Study of Premodern Southeast Asia," 17.

204. Murphy and Lefferts, "Globalizing Indian Religions and Southeast Asian Localisms," 782–83.

205. Pollock, *The Language of the Gods in the World of Men*, 273–74. By contrast, the Vietnamese wrote in Chinese characters, even if they were "always pronounced in Vietnamese." See Wolters, *History, Culture, and Region in Southeast Asian Perspectives*, 72.

206. Robert L. Brown, *The Dvāravatī Wheels of Law and the Indianization of South East Asia* (Brill: Leiden, 1996), 75–76, 159–60, 169–74.

207. Kulke and Rothermund, *A History of India*, 160.

208. Andrea Acri, "The Place of Nusantara in Sanskritic Buddhist Cosmopolis," *TRaNS: Trans-Regional and -National Studies of Southeast Asia*, vol. 6, no. 2 (2018): 145, 148.

209. Michael Jacq-Hergoulac'h, *The Malay Peninsula: Crossroads of the Maritime Silk Road*, trans. Victoria Hobson (Brill: Leiden, 2002), 95.

210. Holcombe, *The Genesis of East Asia*, 102.

211. David Henley, "Introduction: Seasons and Civilizations," in David Henley and Nira Wickramasinghe, eds., *Monsoon Asia: A Reader on South and Southeast Asia* (Leiden: Leiden University Press, 2023), 33.

212. Kulke and Rothermund, *A History of India*, 158–61.

213. Peter Sharrock, "Heruka-Mandalas across Maritime Asia," in Andrea Acri and Peter Sharrock, eds., *The Creative South: Buddhist and Hindu Art in Mediaeval Maritime Asia*, vol. 1 (Singapore: ISEAS—Yusof Ishak Institute, 2022), 128.

214. Damian Evans, Christophe Pottier, Roland Fletcher, and Michael Barbetti, "A Comprehensive Archaeological Map of the World's Largest Preindustrial Settlement Complex at Angkor, Cambodia," *Proceedings of the National Academy of Science*, vol. 104, no. 36 (2007): 14277–82.

215. William Dalrymple, "Monumental Angkor Wat and the Lost Ruins of Cambodia," *Financial Times*, August 7, 2022, https://www.ft.com/content/7611e804-6bc6-41d0-bb74-3bf13ecc83c0 (accessed 12/7/2022).

216. Colin Renfrew, "Introduction: Peer Polity Interaction and Socio-political Change," in Colin Renfrew and John F. Cherry, eds., *Peer Polity Interaction and Socio-Political Change* (Cambridge: Cambridge University Press, 1986), 1–18.

217. Rush, *Southeast Asia*, https://doi.org/10.1093/actrade/9780190248765.003.0002 (accessed 12/9/2022).

218. Lockard, *Southeast Asia in World History*, 28.

219. Momoko Shiro, " 'Mandala Champa' Seen from Chinese Sources," in Tran and Lockhart, *The Cham of Vietnam*, 121; Vickery, "Champa Revisited," 372–73.

220. Tran Quoc Vuong, "Viet-Cham Cultural Contacts," in Tran and Lockhart, *The Cham of Vietnam*, 274.

221. Holcombe, *The Genesis of East Asia*, 163.

222. Rush, *Southeast Asia*, https://doi.org/10.1093/actrade/9780190248765.003.0002 (accessed 12/9/2022).

223. Whitmore, "Cultural Accommodation and Competition on the Champa/Viet Coast Over Two Millennia," in Hall, Ghosh, Gangopadhyay, and Mukherjee, *Cross-Cultural Networking in the Eastern Indian Ocean Realm*, 231, 233.

224. Vickery, "Champa Revisited," 376.

225. Whitmore, "Cultural Accommodation and Competition on the Champa/Viet Coast Over Two Millennia," 247–48.
226. Even then, a much-diminished Champa polity continued to exist until 1832.
227. Holcombe, *The Genesis of East Asia*, 102.
228. Miksic and Goh, *Ancient Southeast Asia*, 436.
229. Dreyer, *Zheng He*, 31, 170.
230. Andaya and Andaya, *A History of Malaysia*, 25. Their association with "sea nomads" of Southeast Asia like the Orang Laut was crucial, for such groups were able to protect trade and form navies as well as engage in acts of piracy.
231. Pierre-Yves Manguin, "Trading Ships of the South China Sea," 274.
232. Charles A. Kupchan, "The Normative Foundations of Hegemony and the Coming Challenge to Pax Americana," *Security Studies*, vol. 23, no. 2 (2014): 223.
233. Nicholas Tarling, "Status and Security in Early Southeast Asian State Systems," in Ooi Keat Gin and Hoang Ahn Tuan, eds., *Early Modern Southeast Asia* (New York: Routledge, 2016), 20.

Chapter Four. The Rise of the Indo-Pacific and the Return of Geopolitics

1. Aaron L. Friedberg, "What's at Stake in the Indo-Pacific," *Proceedings* (USNI), Vol. 147/10/1,424 (October 2021), https://www.usni.org/maga zines/proceedings/2021/october/whats-stake-indo-pacific.
2. The White House, "Indo-Pacific Strategy of the United States," February 2022, 4, https://www.whitehouse.gov/wp-content/uploads/2022/02/U.S. -Indo-Pacific-Strategy.pdf (accessed 2/23/2024).
3. Wang Jisi, "China in the Middle," *The American Interest*, February 2, 2015, https://www.the-american-interest.com/2015/02/02/china-in-the -middle/ (accessed 2/23/2024).
4. "Science of Military Strategy (2013)," 18–19 and 309. The full text of this document, which was prepared by China's Academy of Military Sciences, was translated into English and published under the auspices of Project Everest and the China Aerospace Studies Institute on February 8, 2021, https://www.airuniversity.af.edu/CASI/Display/Article/2485204/plas-sci ence-of-military-strategy-2013/ (accessed 2/23/2024).
5. See Graham Allison, *Destined for War: Can America and China Escape Thucydides's Trap?* (Boston: Houghton Mifflin Harcourt, 2017), Kindle Loc. 530. Steve Chan, "China and Thucydides's Trap," in Huiyun Feng and Kai He, eds., *China's Challenges and International Order Transition: Beyond Thucydides's Trap* (Ann Arbor: University of Michigan Press, 2020), 42. Chan's is one of best academic critiques of the Thucydides Trap.

6. The Department of Defense, "Indo-Pacific Strategy Report: Prepared-
   ness, Partnerships, and Promoting a Networked Region," June 1, 2019, 8,
   https://media.defense.gov/2019/Jul/01/2002152311/-1/-1/1/DEPART
   MENT-OF-DEFENSE-INDO-PACIFIC-STRATEGY-RE
   PORT-2019.PDF (accessed 2/23/2024). The phrase "reorder the region"
   is included at the beginning of the document in a message from Patrick
   Shanahan, then acting secretary of defense.

7. Barry Posen, "Command of the Commons: The Military Foundations of
   U.S. Hegemony," *International Security*, vol. 28, no. 1 (2003): 7, 46; Geoffrey Till, "The Changing Dynamics of Seapower and Concepts of Battle," in Jo Inge Bekkevold and Geoffrey Till, eds., *International Order at
   Sea: How It Is Challenged, How It Is Maintained* (London: Palgrave Macmillan, 2016), 184.

8. Phillip Inman, "China Overtakes US in World Trade," *The Guardian*,
   February 11, 2013, https://www.theguardian.com/business/2013/feb/11/
   china-worlds-largest-trading-nation (accessed 2/23/2024).

9. ASEAN, "ASEAN Outlook on the Indo-Pacific," June 23, 2019, https://
   asean.org/speechandstatement/asean-outlook-on-the-indo-pacific/ (accessed 2/23/2024).

10. Evan A. Laksmana, "Whose Centrality? ASEAN and the Quad in the
    Indo-Pacific," *Journal of Indo-Pacific Affairs*, vol. 3, no. 5 (2020): 106–17.

11. See Seng Tan, "Consigned to Hedge: South-east Asia and America's 'Free
    and Open Indo-Pacific' Strategy," *International Affairs*, vol. 96, no. 1
    (2020): 131–48.

12. Amitav Acharya, "The Myth of ASEAN Centrality?," *Contemporary
    Southeast Asia*, vol. 39, no. 2 (2017): 273–79.

13. Amitav Acharya, *ASEAN and Regional Order: Revisiting Security Commu-
    nity in Southeast Asia* (New York: Routledge, 2021), 133.

14. Imperial Japan was perhaps the closest that any Asian power has come to
    achieving maritime regional hegemony. However, this period was fleet-
    ing (1942–1945) and coincided with a global war.

15. Robert Gilpin, *War & Change in World Politics* (New York: Cambridge
    University Press, 1981), 144.

16. Arguably, the inclusion of the United States is itself a manifestation of
    the openness of the regional order in maritime Asia.

17. It was perhaps Panikkar, the Indian scholar-diplomat, who popularized
    this expression. K. M. Panikkar, *Asia and Western Dominance: A Survey of
    the Vasco da Gama Epoch of Asian History, 1498–1945* (London: George
    Allen & Unwin, 1953).

18. Paul Kennedy, *The Rise and Fall of the Great Powers: Economic Change and
    Military Conflict from 1500 to 2000* (London: Unwin Hyman, 1988), 244.

19. Rolf Strootman, "Introduction: Maritime Empires in World History," in
    Rolf Strootman, Floris van den Eijnde, and Roy van Wijk, eds., *Empires of
    the Sea: Maritime Power Networks in World History* (Leiden: Brill, 2020),

17. For a broader critique of Kennedy's Eurocentrism, see Ayşe Zarakol, *Before the West: The Rise and Fall of Eastern World Orders* (Cambridge: Cambridge University Press, 2022), 128–31.

20. Philippe Beaujard, *The Worlds of the Indian Ocean: A Global History*, vol. 2 (Cambridge: Cambridge University Press, 2019), 666; Ronald Findlay and Kevin O'Rourke, *Power and Plenty: Trade, War, and the World Economy in the Second Millennium* (Princeton: Princeton University Press, 2007), 156.

21. Ashin Das Gupta, *Malabar in Asian Trade, 1740–1800* (Cambridge: Cambridge University Press, 1967), 11, 18.

22. Kevin O'Rourke, "Politics and Trade: Lessons from Past Globalisations," Bruegel Essay and Lecture Series, Brussels, 2009, 13, https://www.bruegel.org/2009/01/politics-and-trade-lessons-from-past-globalisations/ (accessed 2/23/2024).

23. James Belich, John Darwin, and Chris Wickham, "Introduction: The Prospect of Global History," in James Belich, John Darwin, Margret Frenz, and Chris Wickham, eds., *The Prospect of Global History* (Oxford: Oxford University Press, 2016), 7–8.

24. Michael Pearson, *The Indian Ocean* (London: Routledge, 2003), 11. Also see Anjana Singh, "Early European Mercantilism and Indian Ocean Trade," in Strootman, van den Eijnde, and van Wijk, *Empires of the Sea*, 252; Andrew Phillips and J. C. Sharman, *International Order in Diversity: War, Trade, and Rule in the Indian Ocean* (Cambridge: Cambridge University Press, 2015); and John M. Hobson, *Multicultural Origins of the Global Economy: Beyond the Western-Centric Frontier* (Cambridge: Cambridge University Press, 2021).

25. Singh, "Early European Mercantilism and Indian Ocean Trade," 252; Phillips and Sharman, *International Order in Diversity*; and Hobson, *Multicultural Origins of the Global Economy*.

26. Barry Buzan and George Lawson, *The Global Transformation: History, Modernity, and the Making of International Relations* (Cambridge: Cambridge University Press, 2015).

27. Michael North, *A World History of the Seas: From Harbour to Horizon* (London: Bloomsbury, 2022), 214.

28. Gerald S. Graham, *The Politics of Naval Supremacy: Studies in British Maritime Ascendancy* (Cambridge: Cambridge University Press, 1965), 44.

29. Derek McDougall, "Regional Organizations and Geopolitics in the Indian Ocean," *Asian History*, Oxford Research Encyclopedias, November 29, 2021, https://doi.org/10.1093/acrefore/9780190277727.013.681.

30. Kenneth Pomeranz and Steven Topik, *The World That Trade Created: Society, Culture, and the World Economy, 1400 to the Present*, 4th ed. (New York: Routledge, 2018), 178.

31. Sugata Bose, *A Hundred Horizons: The Indian Ocean in the Age of Global Empire* (Cambridge: Harvard University Press, 2006), 274.

32. Bose, *A Hundred Horizons*, 27.
33. Patrick O'Brien, "The Myth of Anglophone Succession," *New Left Review*, vol. 24 (November/December 2003), https://newleftreview.org/issues/ii24/articles/patrick-o-brien-the-myth-of-anglophone-succession (accessed 2/23/2024).
34. Kevin Hjortshøj O'Rourke, "Free Trade, Industrialization, and the Global Economy, 1815–1914," in N. A. M. Rodger, ed. (and General Editor: Christian Buchet), *The Sea in History: The Modern World* (Woodbridge: The Boydell Press, 2017), 103–14.
35. Andrew Lambert, "The Pax Britannica and the Advent of Globalization," in Daniel Moran and James A. Russell, eds., *Maritime Strategy and Global Order: Markets, Resources, Security* (Washington, DC: Georgetown University Press, 2016), Kindle Loc. 217.
36. Ian Clark, *Hegemony in International Society* (New York: Oxford University Press, 2011), 104.
37. Lambert, "The Pax Britannica and the Advent of Globalization," Kindle Loc. 222, 271.
38. Clark, *Hegemony in International Society*, 118.
39. Daniel H. Deudney, *Bounding Power: Republican Security Theory from the Polis to the Global Village* (Princeton: Princeton University Press, 2007), 149.
40. O'Brien, "The Myth of Anglophone Succession."
41. For a broader discussion on some of these themes, see Jeanne Moorefield, "Crashing the Cathedral: Historical Reassessments of Twentieth-Century International Relations," *Journal of the History of Ideas*, vol. 81, no. 1 (2020): 131–55.
42. Marc-William Palen, "Empire by Imitation? US Economic Imperialism within a British World System," in Martin Thomas and Andrew Thompson, eds., *The Oxford Handbook of the Ends of Empire* (Oxford: Oxford University Press, 2018), https://doi.org/10.1093/oxfordhb/9780198713197.013.12 (accessed 2/23/2024). Also see Peter J. Hugill, "The American Challenge to British Hegemony, 1861–1947," *Geographical Review*, vol. 99, no. 3 (2009): 403–25.
43. Katherine C. Epstein, "The Sinews of Globalization," in Robert L. Blower and Andrew Preston, eds., *The Cambridge History of America and the World*, vol. 3: *1900–1945* (Cambridge: Cambridge University Press, 2021), 46.
44. William R. Thompson, "The Evolution of a Great Power Rivalry: The Anglo-American Case," in William R. Thompson, ed., *Great Power Rivalries* (Columbia: University of South Carolina Press, 1999), 201–21; Robert S. Ross, "Nationalism, Geopolitics, and Naval Expansionism from the Nineteenth Century to the Rise of China," *Naval War College Review*, vol. 71, no. 4 (2018): 25.
45. Jon Sumida, "New Insights from Old Books: The Case of Alfred Thayer Mahan," *Naval War College Review*, vol. 54, no. 3 (2001): 104.

46. Harold Sprout and Margaret Sprout, *The Rise of American Naval Power, 1776–1918* (Princeton: Princeton University Press, 1967).

47. Andrew Lambert, *Seapower States: Maritime Culture, Continental Empires and the Conflict That Made the Modern World* (New Haven: Yale University Press, 2018), 303, 305.

48. Epstein, "The Sinews of Globalization," 58. Also see Hugill, "The American Challenge to British Hegemony, 1861–1947."

49. O'Brien, "The Myth of Anglophone Succession."

50. Stephen Wertheim, *Tomorrow, the World: The Birth of U.S. Global Supremacy* (Cambridge: Harvard University Press, 2020), 6–7.

51. Christopher T. Sanders, *America's Overseas Garrisons: The Leasehold Empire* (New York: Oxford University Press, 2000), https://doi.org/10.1093/acprof:oso/9780198296874.003.0001 (accessed 2/23/2024).

52. Gretchen Heefner, "Overseas Bases and the Expansion of US Military Presence," in David C. Engerman, Max Paul Friedman, and Melani McAlister, eds., *The Cambridge History of America and the World*, vol. 4: *1945 to the Present* (Cambridge: Cambridge University Press, 2021), 55.

53. Lambert, *Seapower States*, 307.

54. Norman Friedman, *Seapower as Strategy: Navies and National Interests* (Annapolis: Naval Institute Press, 2001), 203.

55. On these and other roles of sea power, see Bruce A. Elleman, *Principles of Maritime Power* (Lanham: Rowman & Littlefield, 2022).

56. Buchet, "General Conclusion," in Rodger, and Buchet, *The Sea in History*, 764.

57. Colin S. Gray, "The Sea and the Soviet Empire," in Rodger and Buchet, *The Sea in History*, 592.

58. Lambert, *Seapower States*, 312.

59. Friedman, *Seapower as Strategy*, 181.

60. James A. Russell, "The Indian Ocean," in Moran and Russell, *Maritime Strategy and Global Order*, Kindle Loc. 4791.

61. Phillip Darby, *British Defence Policy East of Suez, 1947–1968* (London: Oxford University Press, 1973).

62. Russell, "The Indian Ocean," Kindle Loc. 4704.

63. Peter H. Sand, *United States and Britain in Diego Garcia: The Future of a Controversial Base* (New York: Palgrave, 2009); David Vine, *Island of Shame: The Secret History of the U.S. Military Base on Diego Garcia* (Princeton: Princeton University Press, 2011).

64. Friedman, *Seapower as Strategy*, 197.

65. Lambert, *Seapower States*, 329.

66. Jeremy Black, "Looking to the Future," in Rodger and Buchet, *The Sea in History*, 720.

67. Carla Norrlof, *America's Global Advantage: US Hegemony and International Cooperation* (New York: Cambridge University Press, 2010), 17, 180–81 (emphasis added).

68. Steven Haines, "New Navies and Maritime Powers," in Rodger and Buchet, *The Sea in History*, 87.

69. Lambert, *Seapower States*, 328–29.

70. See note 7 above. Also see Barry R. Posen, *Restraint: A New Foundation for U.S. Grand Strategy* (Ithaca: Cornell University Press, 2014), 63–64.

71. Paul Kennedy, "The Eagle Has Landed," *Financial Times*, February 2, 2002, 1.

72. James R. Holmes and Toshi Yoshihara, *Chinese Naval Strategy in the 21st Century: The Turn to Mahan* (New York: Routledge, 2008), 1.

73. Hu Bo, "China in a Multipolar World," in Paul Kennedy and Evan Wilson, eds., *Navies in Multipolar Worlds: From the Age of Sail to the Present* (New York: Routledge, 2021), 223.

74. Tim Winter, *The Silk Road: Connecting Histories and Futures* (New York: Oxford University Press, 2022), 141–83; Nadège Rolland, *China's Eurasian Century: Political and Strategic Implications of the Belt and Road Initiative* (Seattle: The National Bureau of Asian Research, 2017).

75. Mingjiang Li, "Southeast Asia through Chinese Eyes: A Strategic Backyard?," in Donald K. Emmerson, ed., *The Deer and the Dragon: Southeast Asia and China in the 21st Century* (Stanford: Walter H. Shorenstein Asia-Pacific Research Center, 2020), 111.

76. Friedberg, "What's at Stake in the Indo-Pacific."

77. Angela Schottenhammer, "Introductory Remarks: What Is the 'Indo-Pacific'?," *Crossroads: Studies on the History of Exchange Relations in the East Asian World*, October 2017, 89, https://www.ostasien-verlag.de/zeitschriften/crossroads/cr/pdf/CR_16_2017_083-097_Schottenhammer.pdf (accessed 2/23/2024).

78. Lambert, "The Pax Britannica and the Advent of Globalization," 6; Lambert, *Seapower States*, 317.

79. Posen, *Restraint*, 18. On the contribution of Canada and Mexico for America's global position, see Julián Castro-Rea, "Asymmetric Interdependence: North America's Political Economy," in Zak Cope and Immanuel Ness, eds., *The Oxford Handbook of Economic Imperialism* (New York: Oxford University Press, 2022), https://doi.org//10.1093/oxfordhb/9780197527085.013.41 (accessed 2/23/2024).

80. David C. Gompert, *Sea Power and American Interests in the Western Pacific* (Santa Monica: RAND, 2013), 157.

81. Gompert, *Sea Power and American Interests in the Western Pacific*, 68 (emphasis original).

82. William J. Norris, "Geostrategic Implications of China's Twin Economic Challenges," Discussion Paper, Council on Foreign Relations, June 2017; and "China's 'Dual-Circulation' Strategy Means Relying Less on Foreigners," *The Economist*, November 5, 2020.

83. Markus Brunnermeier, Rush Doshi, and Harold James, "Beijing's Bismarckian Ghosts: How Great Powers Compete Economically," *The Washington Quarterly*, vol. 41, no. 3 (2018): 161–76.

84. United States Census Bureau, "Top Trading Partners—May 2022," n.d., https://www.census.gov/foreign-trade/statistics/highlights/toppartners. html (accessed 2/23/2024); and National Bureau of Statistics of China, "China Statistical Yearbook," 2019, https://www.stats.gov.cn/sj/ndsj/ 2019/indexeh.htm (accessed 2/23/2024).

85. William R. Thompson, *American Global Pre-Eminence: The Development and Erosion of Systemic Leadership* (New York: Oxford University Press, 2022).

86. See Yuen Foong Khong, "Power as Prestige in World Politics," *International Affairs*, vol. 95, no. 1 (2019): 119–42. For a general discussion of status in great power rivalries, see T. V. Paul, Deborah Welch Larson, and William C. Wohlforth, eds., *Status in World Politics* (New York: Cambridge University Press, 2014).

87. Wertheim, *Tomorrow, the World*, 7.

88. Fritz Bartel, "The Illusions of the United States' Great Power Politics after the Cold War," in Engerman, Friedman, and McAlister, *The Cambridge History of America and the World*, vol. 4, 537.

89. Ooi Kee Beng, *The Eurasian Core and Its Edges: Dialogue with Wang Gungwu on the History of the World* (Singapore: Institute of Southeast Asian Studies, 2015), 214.

90. Wang Gungwu, "China, ASEAN, and the New Maritime Silk Road," *ThinkChina*, November 16, 2021, https://www.thinkchina.sg/wang -gungwu-china-asean-and-new-maritime-silk-road (accessed 2/23/2024).

91. Ooi Kee Beng, *The Eurasian Core and Its Edges*, 159–67.

92. Graham Allison, Robert D. Blackwill, and Ali Wayne, *Lee Kuan Yew: The Grand Master's Insights on China, the United States, and the World* (Cambridge: The MIT Press, 2013), Kindle Loc. 244.

93. The White House, "U.S. Strategic Framework for the Indo-Pacific," January 5, 2021, https://trumpwhitehouse.archives.gov/wp-content/up loads/2021/01/IPS-Final-Declass.pdf (accessed 2/24/2024).

94. The White House, "Indo-Pacific Strategy of the United States," 5 (emphasis added).

95. "Excerpts from the Pentagon's Plan: 'Prevent the Re-Emergence of a New Rival,' " *New York Times*, March 8, 1992, sec. 1, p. 14 (emphasis added).

96. "Excerpts from the Pentagon's Plan."

97. U.S. Department of Defense, "Quadrennial Defense Review Report," September 30, 2001, 2 (note 1), https://history.defense.gov/Portals/70/ Documents/quadrennial/QDR2001.pdf?ver=AFts7axkH2zWUHncRd8y Ug%3D%3D (accessed 2/23/2024).

98. For an important Australian perspective, see Rory Medcalf, *Contest for the Indo-Pacific: Why China Won't Map the Future* (Carlton: Black Inc., 2020).

99. Manjeet S. Pardesi, "The Indo-Pacific: A 'New' Region or the Return of History?," *Australian Journal of International Affairs*, vol. 74, no. 2 (2020): 124–46.

100. Nina Silove, "The Pivot before the Pivot: U.S. Strategy to Preserve the Power Balance in Asia," *International Security*, vol. 40, no. 4 (2016): 45–88.

101. Posen, "Command of the Commons," 7.

102. Evan Braden Montgomery, "Contested Primacy in the Western Pacific: China's Rise and the Future of U.S. Power Projection," *International Security*, vol. 38, no. 4 (2014): 115–49.

103. Eric Heginbotham et al., *The U.S.-China Military Scorecard: Forces, Geography, and the Evolving Balance of Power, 1996–2017* (Santa Monica: RAND, 2015).

104. Jack S. Levy and William R. Thompson, "Balancing on Land and at Sea: Do States Ally Against the Leading Global Power?," *International Security*, vol. 35, no. 1 (2010): 17. Also see William R. Thompson, "Status Conflict, Hierarchies, and Interpretation Dilemmas," in T. V. Paul, Deborah Welch Larson, and William C. Wohlforth, eds., *Status in World Politics* (New York: Cambridge University Press, 2014), 219–45.

105. Hu Bo, *Chinese Maritime Power in the 21st Century: Strategic Planning, Policy and Predictions*, trans. Zhang Yanpei, ed. Geoffrey Till (New York: Routledge, 2020), 191.

106. You Ji, "The Indian Ocean: A Grand Sino-Indian Game of 'Go,'" in David Brewster, ed., *India and China at Sea: Competition for Naval Dominance in the Indian Ocean* (New Delhi: Oxford University Press, 2018), https://doi.org//10.1093/oso/9780199479337.003.0006 (accessed 2/23/2024).

107. Hailin Ye, "The Strategic Landscape of South Asia and Indian Ocean Region," in Rong Wang and Cuiping Zhu, eds., *Annual Report on the Development of International Relations in the Indian Ocean Region (2014)* (Heidelberg: Springer, 2015), 27–40.

108. Black, "Looking to the Future," 728.

109. Hedley Bull, "Sea Power and Political Influence," *Adelphi Papers*, vol. 16, no. 122 (1976): 9.

110. For details, see Acharya, *ASEAN and Regional Order*.

111. There is a vast literature on America's postwar hub-and-spokes system. See Christopher Hemmer and Peter J. Katzenstein, "Why Is There No NATO in Asia? Collective Identity, Regionalism, and the Origins of Multilateralism," *International Organization*, vol. 56, no. 3 (2002): 575–607; Victor D. Cha, "Powerplay: Origins of the U.S. Alliance System in Asia," *International Security*, vol. 34, no. 3 (2009/2010): 158–96; Amitav Acharya, "Norm Subsidiarity and Regional Orders: Sovereignty, Regionalism, and Rule-Making in the Third World," *International Studies Quarterly*, vol. 55, no. 1 (2011): 95–123; and Yasuhiro Izumikawa, "Network Connections and the Emergence of the Hub-and-Spokes Alliance System in East Asia," *International Security*, vol. 45, no. 2 (2020): 7–50.

112. Matteo Dian and Hugo Meijer, "Networking Hegemony: Alliance Dynamics in East Asia," *International Politics*, vol. 57, no. 2 (2020): 131–49 (this is the lead article in a special issue titled "Networking Hegemony: Alliance Dynamics in East Asia"); Evelyn Goh, "In Response: Alliance

Dynamics, Variables, and the English School for East Asia," *International Politics*, vol. 57, no. 2 (2020): 278–84.

113. Rajesh Rajagopalan, "Evasive Balancing: India's Unviable Indo-Pacific Strategy," *International Affairs*, vol. 96, no. 1 (2020): 75–93.

114. Rajeswari Pillai Rajagopalan, "India's Military Outreach: Military Logistics Agreements," *The Diplomat*, September 9, 2021, https://thediplomat.com/2021/09/indias-military-outreach-military-logistics-agreements/ (accessed 2/24/2024).

115. "Japan, Australia Sign Defence Pact for Closer Cooperation," *Reuters*, January 6, 2022, https://www.reuters.com/world/asia-pacific/japan-australia-sign-defence-cooperation-pact-2022-01-06/ (accessed 2/23/2024).

116. Ketian Zhang, "The Quad and Sino-Indian Relations," *China-India Brief*, vol. 207 (2022): 5–7.

117. Feng Zhang, "China's Curious Nonchalance Towards the Indo-Pacific," *Survival*, vol. 61, no. 3 (2019): 200.

118. Zhang Jie, "The Quadrilateral Security Dialogue and Reconstruction of Asia-Pacific Order," *China International Studies*, vol. 74, no. 55 (January/February 2019), 67.

119. Mallory Shelbourne, "China Has World's Largest Navy with 355 Ships and Counting, Says Pentagon," *USNI News*, November 3, 2021, https://news.usni.org/2021/11/03/china-has-worlds-largest-navy-with-355-ships-and-counting-says-pentagon (accessed 2/24/2024).

120. Nick Childs and Tom Waldwyn, "China's Naval Shipbuilding: Delivering on Its Ambition in a Big Way," Military Balance Blog, May 1, 2018, https://www.iiss.org/blogs/military-balance/2018/05/china-naval-shipbuilding (accessed 2/24/2024).

121. Ian Livingston and Michael E. O'Hanlon, "Why China Isn't Ahead of the US Navy, Even with More Ships," Brookings Blog, September 10, 2018, https://www.brookings.edu/blog/order-from-chaos/2018/09/10/why-china-isnt-ahead-of-the-us-navy-even-with-more-ships/ (accessed 2/23/2024).

122. T. V. Paul, "The Rise of China and the Emerging Order in the Indo-Pacific Region," in Feng and He, *China's Challenges and International Order Transition*, 71–94.

123. The White House, "U.S. Strategic Framework for the Indo-Pacific," 3.

124. The White House, "Indo-Pacific Strategy of the United States," 16.

125. Li Li, "The New Trend of India's Rising as a Great Power," *Contemporary International Relations*, vol. 28, no. 2 (2018): 45.

126. Sumit Ganguly, Manjeet S. Pardesi, and William R. Thompson, *The Sino-Indian Rivalry: Implications for Global Order* (Cambridge: Cambridge University Press, 2023).

127. Gabriel B. Collins and William S. Murray, "No Oil for the Lamps of China?," *Naval War College Review*, vol. 61, no. 2 (2008): 8, 14.

128. Gompert, *Sea Power and American Interests in the Western Pacific*, 168.

129. Cuiping Zhu, "Changes of the International Environment in the Indian Ocean Region and the Strategic Choices for China," in Cuiping Zhu, ed., *Annual Report on the Development of the Indian Ocean Region (2019): Assessments of Indian Ocean International Environment* (Singapore: Springer, 2021), 13.

130. The White House, "Indo-Pacific Strategy of the United States," 10.

131. "Aukus: UK, US and Australia Launch Pact to Counter China," *BBC News*, September 16, 2021, https://www.bbc.com/news/world-58564837 (accessed 2/23/2024).

132. "Japan, U.K. Agree on Defense Pact amid China's Rise in Indo-Pacific," *Kyodo News*, 6 May 2022, https://english.kyodonews.net/news/2022/05/7323f9ef85f8-urgent-japan-britain-agree-on-defense-cooperation-pact.html (accessed 2/23/2024).

133. Srinjoy Chowdhury, "India, Britain Working on Logistics Agreement, Defence Minister May Visit London Next Month," *Times Now*, May 7, 2022, https://www.timesnownews.com/india/india-britain-working-on-logistics-agreement-defence-minister-may-visit-london-next-month-article-91397367 (accessed 2/23/2024).

134. Ralf Emmers, "The Role of the Five Power Defence Arrangements in Southeast Asian Security Architecture," in William Tow and Brendan Taylor, eds., *Bilateralism, Multilateralism and Asia-Pacific Security: Contending Cooperation* (London: Routledge, 2013), https://www.taylorfrancis.com/chapters/edit/10.4324/9780203367087-10/role-five-power-defence-arrangements-southeast-asian-security-architecture-ralf-emmers?context=ubx&refId=793a2e3f-e48b-4d12-b2db-7b0f9a185865 (accessed 2/23/2024).

135. Huma Siddiqui, "India-France Operationalize Their Logistics Support Agreement," *Financial Express*, January 25, 2019, https://www.financialexpress.com/defence/india-france-operationalise-their-logistics-support-agreement/1455043/ (accessed 2/23/2024); Ministry for Europe and Foreign Affairs (France), "France's Indo-Pacific Strategy," n.d., https://www.diplomatie.gouv.fr/IMG/pdf/en_dcp_a4_indopacifique_022022_v1-4_web_cle878143.pdf (accessed 2/23/2024).

136. Frédéric Grare and Jean-Loup Saman, *The Indian Ocean as a New Political and Security Region* (Cham: Palgrave Macmillan, 2022); David Brewster, "The Red Flag Follows Trade: China's Future as an Indian Ocean Power," in Ashley J. Tellis, Alison Szalwinski, and Michael Wills, eds., *Strategic Asia 2019: China's Expanding Strategic Ambitions* (Seattle: National Bureau of Asian Research, 2019), 174–209.

137. Goh, "In Response," 279.

138. Brantly Womack, "Mapping the Multinodal Terrain of the Indo-Pacific," *Settimana News*, February 28, 2018, http://www.settimananews.it/italia-europa-mondo/mapping-multinodal-terrain-indo-pacific/ (accessed 2/23/2024).

139. Rory Medcalf, "Grand Stakes: Australia's Future between China and India," in Ashley J. Tellis, Travis Tanner, and Jessica Keough, eds., *Strategic Asia 2011–12: Asia Responds to Its Rising Powers, China and India* (Seattle: National Bureau of Asian Research, 2011), 200.

140. Hugh White, "Old Friends in the New Asia: New Zealand, Australia, and the Rise of China," in Robert G. Patman, Iati Iati, and Balazs Kiglics, eds., *New Zealand and the World: Past, Present, and Future* (Singapore: World Scientific, 2018), 193.

141. You, "The Indian Ocean."

142. John W. Garver, "Calculus of a Chinese Decision for Local War with India," in Jagannath P. Panda, ed., *India and China in Asia: Between Equilibrium and Equations* (London: Routledge, 2019), 93.

143. Holmes and Yoshihara, *Chinese Naval Strategy*, 27 and 74.

144. Yves-Heng Lim, "China's Rising Naval Ambitions in the Indian Ocean: Aligning Ends, Ways and Means," *Asian Security*, vol. 16, no. 3 (2020): 406.

145. Hu, "China in a Multipolar World," 225.

146. You Ji, *China's Military Transformation: Politics and War Preparation* (Cambridge: Polity, 2016), 137.

147. You, "The Indian Ocean."

148. Hu, *Chinese Maritime* Power, 191.

149. Leah Dreyfuss and Mara Karlin, "All That Xi Wants: China Attempts to Ace Bases Overseas," in Tarun Chhabra, Rush Doshi, Ryan Haas, and Emilie Kimball, eds., *Global China: Assessing China's Growing Role in the World* (Washington, DC: Brookings, 2021), 270.

150. It was America's victory in the Second World War that paved the way for such access; China has only one formal ally, North Korea. China also enjoys what is sometimes referred to as a "quasi-alliance" with Pakistan.

151. Clark, *Hegemony in International Society*, 123.

152. "Ace of Bases," *The Economist*, May 20, 2022, https://www.economist.com/special-report/2022/05/20/ace-of-bases (accessed 2/23/2024).

153. David Boey, "Singapore's Art of the Deal in Defence Diplomacy," *The Straits Times*, October 22, 2019.

154. Ian Storey, "Will China Establish Military Bases in Southeast Asia?," *ISEAS Commentary*, September 28, 2020, https://www.iseas.edu.sg/media/commentaries/will-china-establish-military-bases-in-southeast-asia/ (accessed 2/23/2024).

155. Cynthia Choo, "Singapore, India Conclude Bilateral Naval Pact," *Today*, November 29, 2017, https://www.todayonline.com/singapore/singapore-india-concludes-bilateral-naval-pact (accessed 2/23/2024).

156. Edward Sing Yue Chan, "Beyond Mahanianism: The Evolution of China's Policy Discussion in Sea Power Development," *Asian Security*, vol. 18, no. 1 (2022): 39 and 50. In addition to the Mahanian School, Chan

discusses the Harmonious, Administrative, and Balancing Schools in Chinese naval thought.

157. Lambert, *Seapower States*, 316.

158. Andrea Ghiselli, "The Chinese People's Liberation Army 'Post-modern' Navy," *The International Spectator*, vol. 50, no. 1 (2015): 117–36.

159. Wang Gungwu, "China, ASEAN, and the New Maritime Silk Road," *ThinkChina*, November 16, 2021, https://www.thinkchina.sg/wang -gungwu-china-asean-and-new-maritime-silk-road (accessed 2/23/2024).

160. David I. Steinberg, "China's Myanmar, Myanmar's China: Myths, Illusions, Interactions," in Emmerson, *The Deer and the Dragon*, 366.

161. Christina Larson, "China's Oil Pipeline through Myanmar Brings Both Energy and Resentment," *Bloomberg*, February 5, 2014, https://www. bloomberg.com/news/articles/2014-02-04/chinas-oil-pipeline-through -myanmar-brings-energy-and-resentment (accessed 2/23/2024).

162. Ye, "The Strategic Landscape of South Asia and Indian Ocean Region," 38.

163. Wang, "China in the Middle."

164. Joseph Chinyong Liow, "The Strategic Rationale of China's Belt and Road Initiative," in Joseph Chinyong Liow, Hong Liu, and Gong Xue, eds., *Research Handbook on the Belt and Road Initiative* (Cheltenham: Edward Elgar, 2021), 103 and 109.

165. Hu, *Chinese Maritime Power*, 185.

166. Nguyen Khac Giang, "China Is Making Mekong Friends," *East Asia Forum*, May 19, 2018, https://www.eastasiaforum.org/2018/05/19/china -is-making-mekong-friends/ (accessed 2/23/2024).

167. Xue Gong, "Lancang-Mekong Cooperation: Minilateralism in Institutional Building and Its Implications," in Bhubhinder Singh and Sarah Teo, eds., *Minilateralism in the Indo-Pacific: The Quadrilateral Security Dialogue, Lancang-Mekong Cooperation Mechanism, and ASEAN* (London: Routledge, 2020), 57–73.

168. Edward Wong, "China and Neighbors Begin Joint Mekong River Patrols," *New York Times*, December 10, 2011, https://www.nytimes. com/2011/12/11/world/asia/china-and-neighbors-begin-joint-mekong -river-patrols.html (accessed: 2/23/2024).

169. Lei Jun quoted in Jörn Dosch and Shannon Cui, "China's 21st Century Maritime Silk Road: A Route to Pax Sinica in Southeast Asia?," in Emmerson, *The Deer and the Dragon*, 339.

170. U.S. Department of State, "A Free and Open Indo-Pacific: Advancing a Shared Vision," November 4, 2019, 10, https://www.state.gov/wp-con tent/uploads/2019/11/Free-and-Open-Indo-Pacific-4Nov2019.pdf (accessed 2/23/2024).

171. Shang-su Wu, "Lancang-Mekong Cooperation: The Current State of China's Hydro-Politics," in Singh and Teo, *Minilateralism in the Indo-Pacific*, 80.

172. Kent E. Calder, *Super Continent: The Logic of Eurasian Integration* (Stanford: Stanford University Press, 2019), 133.

173. Murray Hiebert, *Under Beijing's Shadow: Southeast Asia's China Challenge* (Lanham: Rowman & Littlefield, 2020), 337.

174. Wang Gungwu, "Global History: Continental and Maritime," *Asian Review of World Histories*, vol. 3, no. 2 (2015): 217.

175. Acharya, *ASEAN and Regional Order*, 65–99.

176. Amitav Acharya, *Constructing a Security Community in Southeast Asia: ASEAN and the Problem of Regional Order*, 3rd ed. (London: Routledge, 2014), 43–79.

177. Amitav Acharya, *Whose Ideas Matter: Agency and Power in Asian Regionalism* (Ithaca: Cornell University Press, 2009), 145.

178. David Shambaugh, "U.S.–China Rivalry in Southeast Asia: Power Shift or Competitive Coexistence?," *International Security*, vol. 42, no. 4 (2018): 85–127.

179. Tan, "Consigned to Hedge," 131.

180. Joseph Chinyong Liow, *Ambivalent Engagement: The United States and Regional Security in Southeast Asia after the Cold War* (Washington, DC: Brookings, 2017), 16–17; David Shambaugh, *Where Great Powers Meet: America & China in Southeast Asia* (New York: Oxford University Press, 2021), 61.

181. Donald K. Emmerson, "The Deer and the Dragon: Asymmetry versus Autonomy," in Emmerson, *The Deer and the Dragon*, 6, 29.

182. Goh, "In Response," 280.

183. Amitav Acharya, "Why ASEAN's Indo-Pacific Outlook Matters," *East Asia Forum*, August 11, 2019, https://www.eastasiaforum.org/2019/08/11/why-aseans-indo-pacific-outlook-matters/ (accessed 2/23/2024).

184. Dewi Fortuna Anwar, "Indonesia and the ASEAN Outlook on the Indo-Pacific," *International Affairs*, vol. 96, no. 1 (2020): 111–29.

185. Acharya, *ASEAN and Regional Order*, 76–77.

186. Ang Cheng Guan, *Southeast Asia after the Cold War: A Contemporary History* (Singapore: NUS Press, 2019), 191.

187. Martin Stuart-Fox, *A History of China and Southeast Asia: Tribute, Trade, and Influence* (Crows Nest: Allen & Unwin, 2003), 241.

188. See Seng Tan, "ASEAN Defence Ministers' Meeting-Plus: Multilateralism Mimicking Minilateralism?," in Singh and Teo, *Minilateralism in the Indo-Pacific*, 129.

189. ASEAN, "ASEAN Outlook on the Indo-Pacific," June 23, 2019, https://asean.org/speechandstatement/asean-outlook-on-the-indo-pacific/ (accessed 2/23/2024) (emphasis added).

190. Ian Storey, "Southeast Asia's Minilateral Counter-Piracy/Sea-Robbery Initiatives," in John E. Bradford, Jane Chan, Stuart Kaye, Clive Schofield, and Geoffrey Till, eds., *Maritime Cooperation and Security in the Indo-Pacific Region: Essays in Honor of Sam Bateman* (Leiden: Brill, 2023), 309.

191. This paragraph draws from Mark David Chong, "Securitising Piracy and Maritime Terrorism along the Malacca and Singapore Straits: Singapore and the Importance of Facilitating Factors," in Nicholas Tarling and Xin Chen, eds., *Maritime Security in East and Southeast Asia: Political Challenges in Asian Waters* (Singapore: Palgrave, 2017), 43–84.

192. Yinghui Lee, "Singapore's Conceptualization of Maritime Security," CSIS Asia Maritime Transparency Initiative, December 1, 2021, https://amti.csis.org/singapores-conceptualization-of-maritime-security/ (accessed 2/23/2024).

193. John Garofano and Andrea J. Dew, "Conclusion: Access and Security in the Indian Ocean," in John Garofano and Andrea J. Dew, eds., *Deep Currents and Rising Tides: The Indian Ocean and International Security* (Washington, DC: Georgetown University Press, 2013), 302.

194. Hadyu Ikrami, "Sulu-Sulawesi Seas Patrol: Lessons from the Malacca Straits Patrol and Other Similar Cooperative Frameworks," *The International Journal of Maritime and Coastal Law*, vol. 33 (2018): 799–826.

195. Storey, "Southeast Asia's Minilateral Counter-Piracy/Sea-Robbery Initiatives," 308.

196. Ian Storey, "Trilateral Security Cooperation in the Sulu-Celebes Seas: A Work in Progress," *ISEAS Perspectives*, August 27, 2018, https://www.iseas.edu.sg/wp-content/uploads/pdfs/ISEAS_Perspective_2018_48@50.pdf (accessed 2/23/2024).

197. Storey, "Southeast Asia's Minilateral Counter-Piracy/Sea-Robbery Initiatives," 309.

198. Goh Chok Tong, "Keynote Address by Senior Minister Goh Chok Tong at the Official Launch of the Institute of South Asian Studies (ISAS) on Thursday, 27 May 2005, at 8:00 pm at Orchard Hotel," Singapore Government Press Release, https://www.nas.gov.sg/archivesonline/data/pdfdoc/2005012701.htm (accessed 2/23/2024).

199. Prashanth Parameswaran, "India, Myanmar Ink New Naval Patrol Pact," *The Diplomat*, February 23, 2016, https://thediplomat.com/2016/02/india-myanmar-ink-new-naval-pact-on-coordinated-patrols/ (accessed 2/23/2024).

200. Dinakar Peri, "India and Vietnam Sign Mutual Logistics Agreement," *The Hindu*, June 8, 2022, https://www.thehindu.com/news/national/india-vietnam-ink-military-logistics-support-pact-vision-document-to-expand-defence-ties/article65506502.ece (accessed 2/23/2024).

201. Koh Swee Lean Collin, "China-India Rivalry at Sea: Capabilities, Trends and Challenges," *Asian Security*, vol. 15, no. 1 (2019): 5–24. There is some debate as to whether India can play a strategic role to the east of the Strait of Malacca. See Rahul Roy-Chaudhury and Kate Sullivan de Estrada, "India, the Indo-Pacific and the Quad," *Survival*, vol. 60, no. 3 (2018): 181–94.

202. Sam Bateman, "Conclusion: Do Rough Seas Lie Ahead?," in Sam Bateman and Joshua Ho, eds., *Southeast Asia and the Rise of Chinese and Indian Naval Power: Between Rising Powers* (London: Routledge, 2010), 234.

203. "Science of Military Strategy (2013)," 89.

204. Emrys Chew, "Southeast Asia and the Indian Ocean: Maritime Connections across Time and Space," in Sam Bateman, Jane Chan, and Euan Graham, eds., *ASEAN and the Indian Ocean: The Key Maritime Links*, RSIS Policy Paper, 2011, 17.

Conclusion

1. G. John Ikenberry and Charles Kupchan, "Socialization and Hegemonic Power," *International Organization*, vol. 44, no. 3 (1990): 283–315; Amitav Acharya, *Whose Ideas Matter: Agency and Power in Asian Regionalism* (Ithaca: Cornell University Press, 2009); Amitav Acharya, "Norm Subsidiarity and Regional Orders: Sovereignty, Regionalism, and Rule-Making in the Third World," *International Studies Quarterly*, vol. 55, no. 1 (2011): 95–123.

2. Zoltán Biedermann, "(Dis)connected History and Multiple Narratives of Global Early Modernity," *Modern Philology*, vol. 119, no. 1 (2021): 23 (note 31).

3. Jack A. Goldstone and John F. Haldon, "Ancient States, Empires, and Exploitation: Problems and Perspectives," in Ian Morris and Walter Scheidel, eds., *The Dynamics of Ancient Empires: State Power from Assyria to Byzantium* (New York: Oxford University Press, 2009), 12, 14.

4. Fernand Braudel, *Civilization and Capitalism, 15th–18th Century*, vol. 2 (London: Book Club Associates, 1983), 137.

5. Amitav Acharya, *The End of American World Order*, 2nd ed. (Cambridge: Polity, 2018); Barry Buzan and George Lawson, *The Global Transformation: History, Modernity and the Making of International Relations* (Cambridge: Cambridge University Press, 2015).

6. Robert Gilpin, *War & Change in World Politics* (New York: Cambridge University Press, 1981), 37, 138 (note 13).

7. Stephen Jay Gould quoted in Jack A. Goldstone, *Revolution and Rebellion in the Early Modern World*, 25th Anniversary Edition (New York: Routledge, 2016), 60.

8. Evelyn Goh, "US Dominance and American Bias in International Relations Scholarship: A View from the Outside," *Journal of Global Security Studies*, vol. 4, no. 3 (2019): 406.

9. On the various dimensions of power, see Michael Mann, *The Sources of Social Power*, vol. 1 (Cambridge: Cambridge University Press, 1986), 8.

10. D. A. Cohen and J. E. Lendon, "Strong and Weak Regimes: Comparing the Roman Principate and the Medieval Crown of Aragon," in Johann P.

Arnason and Kurt A. Raaflaub, eds., *The Roman Empire in Context: Historical and Comparative Perspectives* (Malden: Wiley-Blackwell, 2011), 100.

11. On the production of power through social relations, see Michael Barnett and Raymond Duvall, "Power in International Politics," *International Organization*, vol. 59, no. 1 (2005): 48.

12. On this dimension of hegemony, see Ian Clark, *Hegemony in International Society* (Oxford: Oxford University Press, 2011).

13. On such elite cooptation, see Ikenberry and Kupchan, "Socialization and Hegemonic Power."

14. Barnett and Duvall, "Power in International Politics," 61.

15. Barnett and Duvall, "Power in International Politics," 45.

16. Buzan and Lawson, *The Global Transformation*, 1.

17. On attraction, see Manjeet S. Pardesi, "Decentering Hegemony and 'Open' Orders: Fifteenth-Century Melaka in a World of Orders," *Global Studies Quarterly*, vol. 2, no. 4 (2022).

18. The Sinic Northeast Asian polities may have historically been attracted to China due to their shared ideology. Feng Zhang, *Chinese Hegemony: Grand Strategy and International Institutions in East Asian History* (Stanford: Stanford University Press, 2015), 7.

19. Hermann Kulke, "State Formation and Social Integration in Pre-Islamic South and Southeast Asia," in Karashima Noboru and Hirosue Masashi, eds., *State Formation and Social Integration in Pre-modern South and Southeast Asia* (Tokyo: The Toyo Bunko, 2017), 315.

20. On the management of diversity in the making of social orders, see Christian Reus-Smit, "Cultural Diversity and International Order," *International Organization*, vol. 71, no. 4 (2017): 851–85.

21. Feng Zhang, "International Societies in Pre-Modern East Asia: a preliminary framework," in Barry Buzan and Yongjin Zhang, eds., *Contesting International Society in East Asia* (Cambridge: Cambridge University Press, 2014), 32.

22. Tansen Sen, "Maritime Southeast Asia between South Asia and China to the Sixteenth Century," *TRaNS: Trans-Regional and -National Studies of Southeast Asia*, vol. 2, no. 1 (2014): 32.

23. Martin Stuart-Fox, *A Short History of China and Southeast Asia: Tribute, Trade, and Influence* (Crows Nest: Allen & Unwin, 2003), 94.

24. Alberto Lucas López and Kaya Lee Berne, "Peaks of Brutality," *National Geographic*, June 2020, https://www.nationalgeographic.com/magazine/graphics/graphic-wwii-and-the-100-deadliest-events-in-history-feature? (accessed 2/23/2024). This list of deadliest events is inclusive of all types of violent deaths.

25. Amitav Acharya's personal notes, January 2011.

26. G. Coedès, *The Indianized States of Southeast Asia* (Canberra: Australian National University Press, 1975), 34.

27. O. W. Wolters, *History, Culture, and Region in Southeast Asian Perspectives*, rev. ed. (Singapore: Institute of Southeast Asian Studies, 1999), 72.

28. Sheldon Pollock, *The Language of the Gods in the World of Men: Sanskrit, Culture, and Power in Premodern India* (Berkeley: University of California Press, 2006), 128.

29. Monica L. Smith, " 'Indianization' from the Indian Point of View: Trade and Cultural Contacts with Southeast Asia in the Early First Millennium C.E.," *Journal of the Economic and Social History of the Orient*, vol. 42, no. 1 (1999): 18.

30. Stuart-Fox, *A Short History of China and Southeast Asia*, 60.

31. Yuri Pines, *The Everlasting Empire: The Political Culture of Ancient China and Its Imperial Legacy* (Princeton: Princeton University Press, 2012), 29.

32. Charles Holcombe, *The Genesis of East Asia, 221 B.C.–A.D. 907* (Honolulu: University of Hawai'i Press, 2001), 57.

33. The large Han fleets that were sent into northern and central Vietnam, as noted in Chapter 3, meant that China certainly had the capabilities to do so.

34. There is the obvious issue of tautology here. The Chinese management of trade through the practices of the tributary system meant that non-tribute-bearing polities that tried to engage in trade with China were branded as pirates. However, there were other forms of regional piracy too, especially in the *mandala* world of Southeast Asia (in intra-Southeast Asian interactions). China did not attempt to "manage" such acts of piracy at the systemic level in maritime Asia. This was hardly a possibility before the twelfth century in the absence of a Chinese navy, and therefore China relied on the tributary system.

35. Pierre-Yves Manguin, "Trading Ships of the South China Sea: Shipbuilding Techniques and Their Role in the History of the Development of Asian Trade Networks," *Journal of the Economic and Social History of the Orient*, vol. 36, no. 3 (1993): 274.

36. Hedley Bull, "Sea Power and Political Influence," *Adelphi Papers*, vol. 16, no. 122 (1976): 1.

37. Takeshi Hamashita, "The Tribute Trade System and Modern Asia," in A. J. H. Latham and Heita Kawakatsu, eds., *Japanese Industrialization and the Asian Economy* (New York: Routledge, 1994), 96.

38. Stuart-Fox, *A Short History of China and Southeast Asia*, 33–34.

39. John N. Miksic, *Singapore & the Silk Road of the Sea, 1300–1800* (Singapore: NUS Press, 2013), 67.

40. Wolters, *History, Culture, and Region in Southeast Asian Perspectives*, 35.

41. Stuart-Fox, *A Short History of China and Southeast Asia*, 32.

42. Miksic, *Singapore & the Silk Road of the Sea*, 94.

43. Miksic, *Singapore & the Silk Road of the Sea*, 94–95.

44. Stuart-Fox, *A Short History of China and Southeast Asia*, 35–36.

45. Gilpin, *War & Change in World Politics*, 145.

46. Paul M. Kennedy, *The Rise and Fall of British Naval Mastery* (London: Allen Lane, 1976), 2; Paul Kennedy, "The Sea and Seapower within the International System," in N. A. M. Rodger and Christian Buchet, eds., *The Sea in History: The Modern World* (Woodbridge: The Boydell Press, 2017), 5.

47. Kennedy, *The Rise and Fall of British Naval Mastery*, 2 (emphasis added).

48. Kennedy, *The Rise and Fall of British Naval Mastery*, 35.

49. Robert Gilpin, "Economic Interdependence and National Security in Historical Perspective," in Klaus Knorr and Frank N. Trager, eds., *Economic Issues and National Security* (Lawrence: University Press of Kansas, 1977), 31; Gilpin, *War & Change in World Politics*, 144; Robert Gilpin, *Global Political Economy: Understanding the International Economic Order* (Princeton: Princeton University Press, 2001), 43–44.

50. Joseph S. Nye, Jr., "Recovering American Leadership," *Survival*, vol. 50, no. 1 (2008): 65.

51. Jonathan Masters, "Sea Power: The U.S. Navy and Foreign Policy," Backgrounder, Council on Foreign Relations, August 19, 2019, https://www.cfr.org/backgrounder/sea-power-us-navy-and-foreign-policy (accessed 2/23/2024).

52. Ken Booth, *Navies and Foreign Policy* (London: Routledge, 2014 [1977]), 248. On the difference between balancing on land and at sea, see Jack S. Levy and William R. Thompson, "Balancing on Land and at Sea: Do States Ally Against the Leading Global Power?," *International Security*, vol. 35, no. 1 (2010): 7–43.

53. Geoffrey F. Gresh, *To Rule Eurasia's Waves: The New Great Power Competition at Sea* (New Haven: Yale University Press, 2020), 175, 272.

54. Geoffrey Till, "The Changing Dynamics of Seapower and Concepts of Battle," in Jo Inge Bekkevold and Geoffrey Till, eds., *International Order at Sea: How It Is Challenged, How It Is Maintained* (London: Palgrave Macmillan, 2016), 178.

55. Till, "The Changing Dynamics of Seapower and Concepts of Battle," 178.

56. Kennedy, *The Rise and Fall of British Naval Mastery*, 3.

57. Andrew Lambert, *Seapower States: Maritime Culture, Continental Empires and the Conflict That Made the Modern World* (New Haven: Yale University Press, 2018), 301.

58. Michael T. Klare, "Mahan Revisited: Globalization, Resource Dependency, and Maritime Security in the Twenty-First Century," in Daniel Moran and James A. Russell, eds., *Maritime Strategy and Global Order: Markets, Resources, Security* (Washington, DC: Georgetown University Press, 2016), Kindle Loc. 6788.

59. Michael Mastanduno, "Order and Change in World Politics: The Financial Crisis and the Breakdown of the US–China Grand Bargain," in G. John Ikenberry, ed., *Power, Order, and Change in World Politics* (Cambridge: Cambridge University Press, 2014), 167.

60. Michael Mandelbaum, *The Case for Goliath: How America Acts as the World's Government in the Twenty-First Century* (New York: Public Affairs, 2005), 92.

61. David Shambaugh, *Where Great Powers Meet: America & China in Southeast Asia* (New York: Oxford University Press, 2021), 87.

62. See Graham Allison, *Destined for War: Can America and China Escape Thucydides's Trap?* (Boston: Houghton Mifflin Harcourt, 2017), Kindle Loc. 2718.

63. Bruce D. Jones, *To Rule the Waves: How Control of the World's Oceans Shapes the Fate of the Superpowers* (New York: Scribner, 2021), 155, 305.

64. Jones, *To Rule the Waves*, 305.

65. Michael Pearson, *The Indian Ocean* (London: Routledge, 2003), 3.

66. Angela Schottenhammer, "Introduction," in Angela Schottenhammer, ed., *Early Global Interconnectivity Across the Indian Ocean World*, vol. 1: *Commercial Structures and Exchanges* (Cham: Springer, 2019), 1; Philippe Beaujard, *The Worlds of the Indian Ocean: A Global History*, vol. 2 (Cambridge: Cambridge University Press, 2019), 660.

67. Ronald Findlay and Kevin O'Rourke, *Power and Plenty: Trade, War, and the World Economy in the Second Millennium* (Princeton: Princeton University Press, 2007), 151.

68. Sebastian R. Prange, "The Contested Sea: Regimes of Maritime Violence in the Pre-Modern Indian Ocean," *Journal of Early Modern History*, vol. 17, no. 1 (2013): 9–33.

69. Tom Hoogervorst, "Commercial Networks Connecting Southeast Asia with the Indian Ocean," *Asian History*, Oxford Research Encyclopedias, December 22, 2021, https://doi.org/10.1093/acrefore/9780190277727. 013.541 (accessed 2/23/2024).

70. Amitav Acharya, "Power Shift or Paradigm Shift? China's Rise and Asia's Emerging Security Order," *International Studies Quarterly*, vol. 58, no. 1 (2014): 158–73.

71. Gresh, *To Rule Eurasia's Waves*, 287.

72. Mandelbaum, *The Case for Goliath*, 224.

73. Kevin O'Rourke, "Politics and Trade: Lessons from Past Globalisations," Bruegel Essay and Lecture Series, Brussels, 2009, 28–29, https://www.bruegel.org/2009/01/politics-and-trade-lessons-from-past-globalisations/ (accessed 2/23/2024).

74. Stephen G. Brooks, G. John Ikenberry, and William C. Wohlforth, "Don't Come Home, America: The Case Against Retrenchment," *International Security*, vol. 37, no. 3 (2012/2013): 41. On bipartisan support for sustaining liberal hegemony in the United States, see Carla Norrlof, "The Waning of Pax Americana?," *Great Discussions* (2018): 19.

75. For a discussion of China's trust deficit in Southeast Asia, see Amitav Acharya, *ASEAN and Regional Order: Revisiting Security Community in Southeast Asia* (London: Routledge, 2021).

76. For the related but different argument that the United States is in fact the last superpower, see Barry Buzan, "The Inaugural Kenneth N. Waltz Annual Lecture, A World without Superpowers: Decentered Globalism," *International Relations*, vol. 25, no. 1 (2011): 3–25; and Acharya, *The End of American World Order*.

Index

Page numbers followed by the letter "f" indicate a figure.